THE SECRET ANNIE OAKLEY

MARCY HEIDISH is the author of the highly acclaimed novel, *A Woman Called Moses*, made into the popular TV film starring Cicely Tyson. Her other novels include *Witnesses* and most recently *Miracles: A Novel About Mother Seton*.

THE SECRET ANNIE OAKLEY

BY

MARCY HEIDISH

A PLUME BOOK

NEW AMERICAN LIBRARY

NEW YORK AND SCARBOROUGH, ONTARIO

Cover painting, "Mount Hayes" (detail), by Sanford R. Gifford.
Cover photo by Herbert Vose. Courtesy of Vose Galleries of Boston

 PLUME TRADEMARK REG. U.S. PAT. OFF. AND FOREIGN COUNTRIES
REGISTERED TRADEMARK—MARCA REGISTRADA
HECHO EN HARRISONBURG, VA., U.S.A.

SIGNET, SIGNET CLASSIC, MENTOR, PLUME, MERIDIAN and
NAL BOOKS are published *in the United States* by New American
Library, 1633 Broadway, New York, New York 10019,
in Canada by The New American Library of Canada Limited,
81 Mack Avenue, Scarborough, Ontario M1L 1M8

Library of Congress Cataloging in Publication Data

Heidish, Marcy.
    The secret Annie Oakley.

    1. Oakley, Annie, 1860–1926—Fiction. I. Title.
PS3558.E4514S4   1983   813'.54   82-22498
ISBN 0-453-00437-7
ISBN 0-452-25514-7 (pbk.)

First Plume Printing, April, 1984

1 2 3 4 5 6 7 8 9

PRINTED IN THE UNITED STATES OF AMERICA

In Memory
of
Eva French

There was a child went
Forth every day;
And the first object he
looked upon, that object
he became.
And that object became
part of him for the day,
or a certain part of the
day, or for many years,
or stretching cycles of
years. . . .

—Walt Whitman

One need not be a chamber
To be haunted—
One need not be a house;
The brain has corridors
Surpassing material place.

—Emily Dickinson

Fancy sometimes helps us out in this
big round world.

—Annie Oakley

PART ONE

NEWARK, NEW JERSEY

JULY 14, 1905

"*And so. I decided. I decided, and I'm telling you this so you'll understand, I wouldn't let anyone find out. I would be free of it once and for all. I would not let this mark me anymore—not me, not my family, not anything I might have. I made the changes, made them where changes last. In the Bible records, in the graveyard, on the stone. And had done with it—I thought.*

"*No one knew. I was careful, I made sure. I realized no one would understand. And now, if they turn it up, if they bring it out after all this time—I just couldn't bear it is all.*

"*Over the years, mostly, it got to seeming farther away. As if it had to do with someone else, not me. Off and on, of course, I've been afraid someone would find out. But no one did, and we were busy—and then this Chicago business happened.*"

THIS Chicago business—damn it to hell for all it's done and all it's caused, damn it double for refusing to end.

The detectives were here, I saw them. They sifted our trash, talked to the tradesmen, God knows who else, and moved on. They've been to Cincinnati, worse, they've been to Greenville, asking their questions, creasing their dollars, tilting their hatbrims over their notes. Even when we can't see them, she thinks of them. I know it; I know her. They're always in her mind, going down the old roads, opening the old doors. She sees them in her sleeps, and in her water glass, and in the mirror as she pins her hair; sees them lighting cigarettes, showing cards like one the bellman saw—*Pinkerton Agency/Day or Night/We Never Sleep*. They've not yet found what they're looking for, what they can use. Not exactly, not yet. Until they do they'll keep on looking and until this is settled the lawyers say we can't think or work.

Look at us—Christ, if this isn't one sweet shame. Sitting here. Just sitting. Sitting here with the trunks and the guns, in the suite on the third floor of the Continental Hotel in Newark, going nowhere. Look at this—costumes all over the bed, the skirt with the fringe, the blouse with the rose, the hat with the star; laid out for mending, not wearing. She's doing what she's always done between seasons, between engagements: tightening seams, trimming embroidery. Between engagements—as if that's what this is.

It's what I tell myself. Sometimes I believe it. Like this afternoon, for a minute I forgot. It was the light, the way the dusk gathered in, fading the pattern in the wallpaper, tenting the room around me till it seemed this was another of a thousand late afternoons we've known, that soft slow slack time before an evening show, all as usual, us as usual: me at the desk with my chair tipped back, she with her head tipped back in the bath.

I can see her through the door, cupped in the porcelain tub. Behind her head, a square of towel. Her hair up with combs. Her face moist and shining, eyes closed. Eyes puffy from tears. Her breasts, round and full, float on the water. As always I am stirred by the sight of her. But she lies so still for so long, I feel uneasy. I'm not used to seeing her that still, even off-season, off-hours. Even in our rooms, tents, trains—all those places where we'd mark off the floor and walk through the act, the turns, the jumps, the stunts, swinging with the guns empty-chambered till it was sharp, it was right. And that done, if there were no shells to load, nothing to hem, darn, press, well by God she'd move the furniture around. All she's moved here are our photographs, swept them into a box. Said they made her feel worse. All those pictures of us with the Wild West, Cody, Sitting Bull, at World's Fairs and Earl's Court and Madison Square Garden, all those pictures of her lifting guns, looping shots—I know what she means. Now: this quiet, I hate it. Not working feels like illness. Not working leaves too much time to think. Too long idle, too long stock-still; not our habit, not our way. Worst of all, this fear, hers. We've shared feelings so long now, passing them back and forth through the air, I can't help but breathe in this one too.

No wonder in that, it's always been that way. Or so I'd like to believe. I'm her husband these twenty-eight years, her manager twenty-four, I've never liked to think there's been secrets between us for long. And now she's speaking of parts of her life I never knew before. All these years, these tight warm wedded years, she never told. Even me; even me. It aches me to know that, aches and angers me both.

So I say damn them, damn them all. Damn the detectives, damn the lawyers, damn William Randolph Hearst. Damn the Chicago papers and the whole Chicago business for starting this and making her remember, and for making me realize, after all this time, how much of her I've never known at all.

I am supposed to be setting this down in some sort of order so I'd best begin where the whole of it does: Last August, '03, when that woman was arrested in Chicago for stealing to buy dope, morphine—that wanderer who gave her name as Annie Oakley. There was supposed to be a resemblance. Her autograph was good, her certainty magnetic. A reporter rushed up a story, passed it through a night editor, put it out on the wires to the entire Hearst chain and beyond. It made deadline all over the country, we saw it next morning over the coffee and bacon: the headline, FAMED LADY SHOT STEALS TO PROCURE DRUGS, the "life story," all of it. You bet we sued, fifty thousand dollars worth, fifty papers in all. We were advised against it: dangerous to take on the big chains, dangerous to take on Himself. Hearst is talking about countersuits now, looking for anything—everything—to smear us with, discredit her, keep us out of court. The detectives are Hearst's, the ones we've seen, the ones in Greenville, everywhere else. I guess he wanted to scare her. I guess he has.

I wish I knew why. Why this much. Afraid as she is of what the detectives could find, she's almost as afraid to talk about it, telling me little by little, in pieces at night, facing away from me in the dark. We'll be having more of these talks; the ones that end in weeping, the ones that scatter wide of the mark in reminiscing. I'll be passing more hours at this desk, piecing together what I know and what I've never known till now. I must stick here and write this counterstory, a story we will hold in reserve, in case: in case our suits don't get to court, in case they do and things get dirty, in case Hearst turns things up to hurt her. Then I'll release it, and only then, for the record, to clear her name. I hope it doesn't get to that, though it's true enough if you lie down with dogs you get up with fleas. Sad work it is, this writing, not work I'd ever choose. A comeback story, that's what I'm longing to write now, MISS OAKLEY EMERGES TRIUMPHANT FROM RETIREMENT . . . if I ever do get to write it, that's the dear thing. After all my years in the show business, for the first time I'm turning pessimist.

* * *

The show business runs in my family: there's my brother Michael with his blackface act, song-and-dance; I booked him with the Primrose & West Minstrels where he put over his big song "Shortnin' Bread." There's my sister-in-law in traveling operettas too, and back in Dublin my people have appeared at both the Gaiety and the Garth. Myself, I've been in the business most of my grown life, sharpshooting acts mostly, though I did spend eight months trying to learn a decent trade, glassblowing, and I was christened for St. Francis in the hopes I'd become a respectable horse doctor. I was born and raised in County Kildaire near the shrine of St. Bridget and the Sign of the Times pub, but I'm an American now, thanks be to God, naturalized back in '77. I came over from Ireland alone at thirteen and from my childhood have little remaining of brogue or religion, but an abiding love of verse, words, ballads. From my life on the road I've a deep mistrust of staying rooted too long in one place and a tendency to pin paper money inside my clothes; when I first kissed Annie she drew back at the crackling. From both Ireland and the show business I've certain dislikes, what some call superstitions: hats on the bed, birds in the window, gloves on the floor, cats, salt, hunchbacks, and I'm careful how I look at the new moon. I write poetry and contracts, the poems tender and the contracts tight, and publicity for the papers, a good hand I am at it too. I believe in luck and I've mostly had it till now, kicking around and finding work, finding the talents within myself as marksman, showman, best of all as manager. And husband. That's a gift as well. It was the first two leading me to the last two, to Annie.

I watch her now, shifting lower in her bath, the waterline pulled to her chin like bedclothes. For an instant, feeling my gaze, her eyes open, those gray eyes of hers, so clear they seem to have their own weather. She looks me a question as a child might, awakened in the night. A child when I met her, married her, a child she still looks to me sometimes now. *Oh mouth of honey.* So much I wish to say, to ask, none of it I do. *Put your darling black head my heart above.*

8

I shrug. Her eyes close. She'll stay in the bath till the water goes flat cold, till I finish at my desk. It's been mine for years, this desk, traveling with us; even the green-shaded lamp is mine, casting a familiar lime-shaped wedge of light on my shirtsleeve. Everything is here that tells me this is home, trunks and targets and table-lace, the gun rack and the sewing basket, the shotshell loader and the new Singer, her gloves on the table, the warbonnet on the wall. Home as we've mostly ever been, but still not quite home now. Not till I understand, not till then.

I need to make sense of this, of what she's told me and what she'll be telling me more. I need to set it against what I've always known of her, of us, and make it fit somehow. We need to have this counterstory, even the lawyers advise it, to hold in case. But more than that I need to piece it together for myself. I need to feel I know her again, need to feel once more that I know who she is. And that this part of her she's held away, hidden, is not between us. I write what I remember, trying to make it square with what she says, and even after we've put out the light it all rackets about in my mind. Always before she was the one who couldn't sleep. So many nights I've felt her leave the bed, heard her steps across the floor, seen her in the corner in the lamplight with her embroidery hoop at four in the morning. And now I'm the one awake in the nights, I'm the one sitting here in the light in the suite on the third floor of the Continental Hotel while she lies back, spent, in the bath.

FIRST time I noticed something wrong, something I couldn't quite explain or understand, it was in Lima, Ohio, and we were starting out and on the road and playing a dump called the Key. I remember the Key, it had been a barn before they put in the seats and put up the letters VARIETY THEATER; the place still smelled faintly of cows. I remember the Key, and I remember that smell, and I clearly remember the cabbage.

We added the cabbage in Lima.

And the eggs, the potatoes too.

I remember her standing in Koenig's Grocery on Main Street, holding in her hand a perfect head of cabbage and being embarrassed by the attentions of the grandfatherly clerk. She looked so girlish then, younger than twenty, hair down loose, that smocked yellow dress—the clerk mistook her for a bride buying fixings for her first home-cooked meal. Some lucky gent would have some fine supper, you betcha, the clerk said, winking at me as I leaned on the counter, watching her. She looked down, flushing, even shyer than usual, which only made the clerk's grin broaden. She glanced over at her purchases. Just a few extras to make it extra-extry special? the clerk asked. She fumbled with her money, slowly uncreasing a dollar bill. She didn't know how to tell this man that she wasn't taking these groceries home to a kitchen, wasn't planning to boil this cabbage, fry these eggs, bake these potatoes. She didn't know how to tell him that she planned instead to take them down the street and shoot them to pieces in front of five or six hundred people.

The clerk asked if she was maybe making a nice pot roast.

Cole slaw, she told him finally.

It was our last night at the Key, the night we always tried out new stunts. We were on after a midget number, I remember; the groceries made a mess onstage but a grand show in the air and ordinarily she would have wondered if the clerk from Koenig's had seen his produce slawed, scrambled, and hashed. Ordinarily she would have asked if I'd seen him out in the house, if she hadn't suddenly realized someone else she knew was in the house, sitting right over the footlights.

All I noticed at the time was that she seemed to freeze for an instant, just after we put some .22s through a spread of cards, aces, and tossed them into the audience as souvenirs. That was when she first saw him, but thought she was imagining; put it from her mind and went on through the setups, the shots, the candle flame and the dime and the glass balls, the wrap-up and the last turn. It wasn't until we were coming downstage for our bows that she seemed to freeze again. Her hand tightened on mine as it did sometimes when she was stirred by the applause. For a moment there was an odd look on her face, a kind of wince, as if she'd just stepped on something sharp. And then it seemed to pass. Whatever I may have sensed, I never really knew till now what she saw.

Someone she knew. Someone she used to know.

Someone she had known once.

She put it different ways, as if trying to get close to some truth she couldn't bring herself to speak. Even now, after she's told me what happened that night, she's still unable to tell me his name.

She had leaned forward, curtsying into the applause, into the light, and she had looked over the lights for the grocery clerk and seen someone else: someone she knew, used to know, knew once. He was there, just across the footlights, front row left. His face was lifted toward her. It seemed suddenly to float above his collar. Just as suddenly she stopped seeing the tables and chairs and waiters, the people standing in the back, the programs stacked in the aisles. For an instant all she saw was a swell of faces pointing at her like fists. Then the curtain was closing, the lights dimming out. She didn't remember coming offstage, didn't remember me saying I was getting our supper, could she bring down the shells. She didn't remember the shifters pushing past her in the wings, the next act going on. She edged close to the place where the stage manager stood to count the house; not caring who saw her, she squinted through the gap between the proscenium and the curtain. Maybe she'd seen wrong after all. She had to know. She had to know if he would be asking for her after the show, if he would be waiting at the stage door. From where she stood she could see his seat, the shadow of a profile, but she still couldn't be absolutely certain who it was.

She turned away and left the wings, going out into the hall that ran the length of the theater. Instead of turning right toward the stairs leading to the dressing rooms, she turned left and walked to a door that opened on the house a yard or so beyond the footlights. Here the floor sloped sharply upward and the wall angled around the jut of the stage on its other side; here she stood, watching the crack beneath the door, waiting for the house lights to come up after the next act finished. With the lights up it wouldn't be so noticeable when she opened the door. With the lights up she would be able to see him plainly, once and for all. She could hear the laughter on the other side of the wall. She could hear the music come up louder, flaring into a finale. The music ended; there was the first pattering of applause. The crack under the door brightened. She took a breath and, just wide enough to let her see, she opened the door.

He was there. He was the one. She knew it then.

Someone she knew, used to know, someone she'd known once.

Someone she'd hoped never to see again.

She knew the slope of the shoulders, the slant of the neck, the ruddy clean-shaven cheeks, that aging cherub's face. A feeling came over her like the dampness in cellars. Standing there in the doorway to the theater she felt herself falling away from herself and the air was green and charged and there was the smell of spring medicine boiling over, the green air was making her sick. For a moment she was unable to move, even as he turned, even as he looked toward the door and saw her. She caught the recognition in his eyes. He rose from his seat and still she was unable to move, rooted there as if he still had power over her. He started edging down the row, coming toward her, saying her name, the old name. She saw it forming on his mouth, she heard it, and she broke away from the door and she turned and she ran.

She ran past the door to the wings, past scaffolding and ropes and stacked chairs, her footsteps clattering after her in the hall. Somewhere behind her she heard a door slam but she didn't turn, didn't stop.

She ran down the first flight of stairs, rounded the landing, ran down the rest, the dim hall snaking out ahead of her. She passed doors and doors and one more door and then she was pushing one open, she was pitching through the doorway of her own dressing room.

Only then did she turn, look back.

No one was there.

The dressing room was empty and very still, very bright. Her breathing rasped in the silence. The trunk was there. The gun rack was there, our names stamped on the glass. She stared at the words, stared at her reflection above them. Her face, wild-eyed, startled her. A woman's face. Clean. Whole. Untainted. A woman's face, with makeup and a hat, above the shooting medals pinned to her blouse.

When I came in a few minutes later she was still there, trembling as if from a chill, so white it scared me. Her hands were so cold. She always wore her wedding ring on a chain around her neck onstage to keep it from catching in the guns; she had both ring and chain clamped so hard in her fist they'd made a deep mark in her palm.

I don't know what I thought. I held her, talked to her; her teeth chattered against my shirt. She didn't stop shaking till we left the theater, leaving at her insistence long after everyone else had gone, just before the doors were locked.

After that when we played towns north of, say, Dayton, and south of Lima, just about anywhere between Bellefontaine, Ohio, and Muncie, Indiana, she would awaken before it was light and look ill before performances; it always passed as soon as she went on. Sometimes she would look through the curtain during the first number, scanning the audience; sometimes she avoided the stage door. It was only in these places, a small segment of our route, and she was so at ease elsewhere, so remarkably free of stage fright, it wasn't hard to overlook. She told me that she was afraid because these places were close to home and she'd realized she might upset her family. Someone who knew her mother could see her, it would humiliate her mother to hear of it; her mother didn't approve, I knew that, it was the Quaker in her after all.

So she told me, the first year of our act, on the road.

So she has always told me all these years.

I don't think she set out to deceive me. I don't think she

figured she was doing that at all. It was, of course, partly true. I think she tried to believe it herself, all of it, because of the shame, because of the pain. I think she tried to believe it whenever the fear came, starting right then in vaudeville, in those early years when she was first wearing her new name.

Our names, mine and hers, were on the programs whenever there were programs, otherwise they were on those A-frame signs in front of the theaters and on the mirror of the local drug store, written in soap. First time we saw our billing it was on the mirror of a People's Lunch where we sat with our elbows on the counter, staring through the pie platters and the phosphate beakers, admiring the curlicued white letters like cake frosting there on the glass: BUTLER & OAKLEY.

It was Butler & Oakley on the breadbasket route through Ohio and Iowa and Indiana and Illinois, through towns called Cross Roads and Delight and Don't Blink, towns I'm not sure are still there. It was Butler & Oakley in the small theaters of the big cities, Chicago, Cincinnati, and in the big theaters of the small towns, every town had one—those drafty made-over barns and stables and granaries, big enough to hold a camp of lumberjacks on a Saturday night and mostly called the Apex or the Palace or the Jewel. Sure, we played the dives and slabs, but we never played the Dime Museums with the freaks and we never played honky-tonks. Of course the places we did play weren't too respectable either back then, early eighties, with vaudeville still moving out of the stag halls and into the family houses; I remember those damn dress patterns they used to give out to prove the show was clean enough for the ladies: *rustle-rustle*, Jesus, I remember.

It was Butler & Oakley, mostly number three on the bill in the wake-'em-up slot, mostly on before a singer and after a comic, six days a week, four and five and often six times a day, Thursday through Wednesday, with one night on the train for the jump between the Ideal and the Imperial Boarding House, between the Royal and the Right and even the

White House, all for actors only, special rates, three meals and a bluff, animals allowed. Small-time boarding houses, small-time bookings, moving up maybe to medium-time but never big-time; detouring into the circus, touring for a season with the melodrama *Slocum's Oath*, doing our turn while they changed the scenes, us and a dancing bear named Jenny.

It was Butler & Oakley, on the breadbasket route, in the number three slot as usual, the night—I'll never forget it—she wore that red dress.

Those first few months of our act she wore her own dresses onstage, dresses she'd made from *Godey's Lady's Book* patterns; girlish styles with puffed sleeves and ruffles and smocking, material in the soft colors of soda creams and nougat candies. She looked so very young in them with her hair loose down her back, and she looked so small in them, next to the long guns, the comics backstage used to say to her, "Well, baby, you up past your bedtime?" and it wasn't long before she didn't like it.

Whatever theater we played, she'd stand in the wings watching sidewise the women, the singers and strutters who'd played the honky-tonks: their dresses, the way they piled their hair on their heads, the way they did their makeup, put on perfume. They looked hard-faced to me, those cookies, those dolls, but she studied them with a hushed longing, as if to nibble the edges of the aura they cast and so become like them. I remember how her face lit up that evening when one of those women sidled over to her backstage: Faye Clio—so she styled herself—half of a sister act called Kiss 'N Tell; they played squeeze boxes and sang "Good Night, Irene." She was wearing a gown of acid-green satin, tight, cut low over a pair of pendulous breasts wired up into a jutting shelf; her lips were painted into a red pout like some monstrous strawberry and her hair was caught up with a large waxen rose on a comb. I could find nothing in the least charming about her but the way Annie gazed, I knew she found Faye Clio exquisite. I can still hear the *click-click* of those long oval nails on the barrel of Annie's Winchester, back there in the wings.

"Well," said Faye Clio, throaty-voiced, sharp, "aren't you

the little honeybunch. Innocence is your number, hmm? Innocence and guns. Like striptease with a child. Real small-time." *Click-click*.

Annie ducked her head, stung, and moved off with me to the dressing rooms. For the rest of that evening she was quiet, something working in her mind, and for the rest of that week she stayed up sewing at night after I was asleep. When we opened at another theater five days later, she had another costume—I'll never forget how she looked, walking out of that dressing room just before our call, no time to change, in that new red gown.

Here was Annie, swathed, sheathed, tubed in satin the color of beets, the color of blood, swaying down the hall with the stature of a queen, the slink of a whore, her shoulders and the curve of her breasts and the soft crevice between, milky, shining, bared to the light. Here she came, her hair swept up on her head as if under a crown, as if into a cap, her rouged cheeks sitting bright on her face, her rouged lips smiling, smearing; Annie posing, preening, pirouetting before me, one hand on her hip, one hand on her rifle.

For a moment she must have thought I'd been struck dumb by this siren, this vamp she'd revealed in herself. An instant later she saw the horror in my eyes. Finally I started to laugh, unable to help myself, and her eyes glared out at me from that powdered unfamiliar face.

"I *like* it," she hissed at me.

"They'll hate it," I whispered back, and then we were on.

At first they whistled, those men who always sat in the first few rows; then they went silent. She made shot after shot but they were just sitting on their hands, the air in the house chilled, suspicious. The silence held whenever she took a shot, but we alternated every pair and whenever it came my turn the men cheered raucously for me: "Git her, beat her, whup her good, git her before she shoots your balls off, mister." It started to spoil her concentration, that jeering, and she took one miss, then another; then she had a shot lying back over a chair to hit a disk I tossed into the air. The way she looked draped over that chair in that gown —I have to admit, it dented my own concentration and inspired from the house such renewed catcalls she missed that shot as well. Under the rouge her face had changed, her lips a straight red slash; as soon as the act was over she stalked off into the wings, not looking around, not saying a word, and just kept walking.

I found her out in the theater alley, her face wiped clean, a shawl pulled over her shoulders, that gown bright as spilled wine against the barrel she'd perched on. She looked up, her eyes angry but not, I saw, at me: at the house, at the gown, at herself.

"Said I wouldn't ever take it too light, let you down, now look," she said, her eyes filling. "Bet I got us canceled, got us shut."

The theater manager appeared in the doorway, a burly German named Schiller with brick-dust hair and a nose like a spoon, shaking his head at us.

"You said you vas *sharp*shooters?"

"The crowd threw her."

"Naa naa, she threw the crowd."

"We can change that."

"One more chance but nix on the costume." He turned to her. "Sweeties, you can't outshoot the fellers and give 'em the hots same time, it won't play."

"But I don't want to look like a kid anymore," she said with something like a wail in her voice.

"*Liebchen.*" Schiller looked at her. "I'll say it plain, with boobies like that, you don't look like a kid," he said, and dropped his cigar in the sandbucket by the door and went back inside.

She stood there amazed for an instant; then we both burst out laughing. That week she started making new dresses, slim-sleeved and stripped of ruffles, but somehow after all that she still couldn't throw out that red gown.

Now and then I'd sense in her something troubled, something hidden, withheld; certain weeping dreams and withdrawn times, certain things she'd never discuss. Not often; nothing really, and it was little I heeded it. Not quite sixteen when she married me, what could she have to hide, what had she time to regret, to secrete? She seemed such a small snippet of a girl sitting across from me on all those trains, her dark head leaned up against an endlessly sliding spread of flat fields and red barns, her shoes scarcely skimming the floor. Just five feet tall, she was light as a child to swing down on the platform, with a child's glad shriek of laughter. Her head never quite reached my shoulder; I could always see the whole of the part in her hair.

It seemed to me that I was the one, ten years older, who'd been out in the world committing the sins, me and my pals, my partners—Baughman & Butler, Butler & Graham, and what fine men of the world we thought ourselves too. As a bride she had come on the road with me and Baughman, then with me and Johnny Graham, putting up with his high talk and, toward her, his courteous suspicion. It annoyed him that he couldn't dazzle her: a leggy steed of a man, God bless him, he oiled his hair and pinked his cheeks and was always aflash with rhinestone stickpins. She'd roll her eyes whenever we were billed as look-alikes, a gimmick dear to theater managers who presented us as "Paired Shots Trading Paired Shots." Actually we looked a pair only from the last row, just two tall men with dark hair and mustaches and matching jackets was all.

Graham thought her odd, I know, this girl who liked guns more than he did, shooting with me in the clubs and galleries wherever we went; she never explained. Quiet, contained, she watched the act from the wings and tried to finish her schooling betweentimes. I remember her reading in the dressing room under a sign for BEST BEER & CIGARS, her back to a wall of peeling yellow paint, her long hair screening her in with a McGuffey *Reader*. She was studying like that the day Graham collapsed with typhoid before the first show at the Crystal Hall in Springfield, Ohio. I remember the somberness of her face—and the light in her eyes. She couldn't hide it, not quite. She knew, even as she wrung out cold towels and I called a doctor, she knew she was going on.

She sat in the back of the empty theater while I fixed it with the manager, an hour till showtime, the house dark, the curtain raised. Beyond, the stage was a dim tangle of ropes and props and scrims, the red draping on the arch like a shabby window valance. Before it the piano player sat in shadow, picking out the tune to "My Darling Clementine," amber light on his sheet music and gartered shirtsleeves. Around him the place still felt hushed, churchlike, not yet smelling of ale and smoke, only of paint and dust.

I slid into the seat next to her. She was hunched there, knees drawn to chin, fingers like ice. I was used to her pulling in sometimes, when things were new, and we sat together without speaking, her hand pressing a tense little rhythm, timed to the song, into mine. After a while there was a sputter from the balcony as the spotlight was lit, that sound of the lime cracking under the gas flame in the lantern, and the stage lifted out of the shadows. The advertising curtain dropped down into place, its squares leaping out at us in the light: RELIEF FOR PILES! TRUSTWORTHY TRUSSES! CHEAPEST FUNERALS HEREABOUTS! The piano player stepped his tune up into quarter-time, humming along now, and a stagehand came out with a long torch like an acolyte's to light the first of the borders and foots. Behind us someone began opening the theater doors. We looked back, looked at each other. It was time to go load the guns.

Standing back in the wings a half hour later, she didn't seem to hear the opening swell of music, the creak of the gasboard, the call "Houselights to half." She didn't seem to see the first act going on. Her lips moved, though not in prayer: she was going over the act in her mind, step by step, the way she'd seen it so many times. I leaned closer. "Left turn left," she was whispering, "turn cross right." She stood dead still in the shadowed back curtains while Gronk the Man-Fish played a trombone in a tank of water and Lacy & Ryan followed with their Irish number. She stood dead still through their harp-and-limerick routine and she stood dead still through their earsplitting rendition of "Drill Ye Tarriers Drill" and the *thunk-thunk* of their wrap-up clog dance. I was next to her as they clumped back in after their bows and then we were being announced: *Butler & Graham —Those Daring Far West Boys . . . with little Annie Butler standing in for Mr. Graham. . . .*

There was a loud groan from the house, a pelting of boos.

"Amateur night!" someone yelled. "Not on my money."

She flashed me a look of sudden desperation. What could we say? There was no more time, they were pushing us on. In the end we said nothing at all, only squeezed hands tight back there, and then she was following me out into that thin bright silence.

It was so quiet, my first two shots, I could hear the spent shells hitting the stage. Then it was her turn. I'll always remember how she looked, stepping forward in her green-sprigged summer dress, a Winchester .22 in her hand. In the light I could see the damp shine of her face, the gleam of the buttons on her bodice. I could see the small silver drops at her ears leaping like sparks. Her hair, waist-long then, streamed over her sleeves. She jerked her head, tossing it back over her shoulder, and walked to her mark.

She was near but not too near. Not so near it would be easy. She cocked the rifle, hands steady, eyes level on me. Her face was serious, studious, as if still poised above a book. She watched me and she waited. And there: like a magician I made the dime appear between my fingers, and as my hand rose her arm rose, the rifle snug in her shoulder, and higher steeper angling right: glint-aim-*pull*—and a sweet *ping*: in the air a glittering arc, dropping into the darkness, rolling off into the well of clapping hands. Before the clapping stopped she had turned, crossed, taken the shotgun. More difficult now, more danger. She kept her back to them, the seam down her spine to them, and walkwalkwalk and wait and wait and now: spin, turn. I was her conjurer, I had set dancing on the air five glass balls, globes of light circling my head. And she was moving with them, the gun was her shoulder was her arm, and she could see the line it cast into the center of each spinning crystal, and she was spinning with them and they with her and *now*-and-*now*-and-*three*-now-*five* she reached them, touched them, turned them into sea spray floating off into the lights, turned them into her laughter and mine, turned them into the explosion of applause from the stomping cheering dark.

Faster then, she had them, it was coming, it was cracking,

it was right, and we put over five shows like that with only one miss apiece, and then the curtain was jerking shut. We stood there stage center, the both of us breathless and grinning and wringing wet, and the audience brought us back three times; the fourth time I sent her out alone. As soon as she got offstage I lost my dignity and picked her up and she kissed me full on the mouth, all of this against theater rules, but the stagehands just smiled and asked us to let the tenor through and the theater manager just pounded us on the back and said, "Kids, kids! No spooning in public, keep everything like it is, you killed 'em." Graham's brother had come to take him home, off the road for good, and it seemed what we'd talked about as happening some day was happening all at once. After five shows and no supper and hot coffee we were nowhere near to calming down. We stayed up most of that night in the Imperial Boarding House.

I can still remember that room we had. The wallpaper— little clocks in a repeating pattern all over it. Rattling iron bedstead. Wobbly pine bureau, old programs lining the drawers, stained night pot below. I can't think now what made it seem so fine, all these years, in my mind. I suppose it was like so many rooms we'd had with dirty white curtains and moth-eaten blankets and patches of mildew on the rug. I suppose it only had a glory to it because of that night, because of us. We were sitting up with beer and sandwiches at three in the morning and we kept talking at once; we were walking through new stunts, I could see so many grand things to try out with her now. Jesus, she'd surprised me: even shooting with her in the galleries, the clubs, I hadn't any idea how she'd be on a stage. Neither had she.

There she was, sitting next to me on the bed, sitting cross-legged in her chemise and drawers, her hair up in a knot on her head and a sandwich in her hand, an orange streak of makeup still on her jaw. There she was, my wife, my girl, face flushed, soul afire that night, pointing with a bottle of beer and telling me how it felt, being out there.

Out there. *Out there.*

The way she said that. The feeling she put into those two words. She said them in just that way only when she was talking about two places: out on stage or out in the fields.

"Oh you know, so many times," she said, "before I ever saw a theater, and the circus but once, I used to sit on this one fence out there. Out in the fields. Just longing to see something different. Something fine, big. And this one time, I remember, a flock of wild pigeons came over—birds wing to wing, maybe a mile across, they went on like that for hours. Just around sunset their feathers got to looking like they'd turned gold. And rose, and purple. Like some magical creatures in a story. And I just sat there and watched, wanting them to go on and on and never stop. I sat there till after dark. And I knew they were still up there, I could hear their wings. . . . And out there tonight, you know, I thought of that, it just came into my mind maybe halfway through . . . but this time, this time, I thought, I wasn't just sitting, watching . . ."

She drained her beer, her face moist, shining.

"Just for a second there, when we first came out, I froze . . . I mean, here it was"—she spread her palms as if handing me the stage. "And I kept saying to myself, just think of the hunting. Just think of the fields, the birds. And then it was all right, it was fine, it was—I don't know, out there in the fields, hunting alone, I used to feel so . . . tall over everything, you know, everything so flat. And the grasses, they'd go on and on. And I'd wade into them like water, up to my knees, my waist . . . and sometimes, sometimes I'd get to feeling I could touch just anything with the rifle, anything, reach up, let the air out of a cloud . . . And that feeling, you know, it came with me, out there onstage. Well, I didn't expect it, not like that . . . not exactly, can't explain it, never talked this way, crazy, it is."

The things we talked about that night. The things we decided, the plans we made. We drew stage blocking on laundry paper, we scanned maps and circled towns and time-tables; I was reading her advertisements from the papers, *Wanted/boy-girl team/novelty act/fast pace*, and she was laying out her dress patterns, thinking of costumes, this one but shorter, that one but looser, this one or this one and what did I think. The bed came to be afloat with paper, a nest of maps and newsprint and schedules, the whole of the quilt sweetly crackling.

She held a pattern up to her shoulders, standing on the mattress and posing there for me a moment; then her face sobered, her eyes a deeper gray.

"Jimmie," she said, her name for me sounding clear and grave in the quiet room, "I keep remembering. There we are—shooting at each other. Some people, they'd say we're fools. Well, I know . . . I know the danger. I've seen the gents with the missing fingers. And worse." Absently, firmly, she straightened a picture over the bed. "I've seen—I know. I've thought about it so many times, watching you. Wanting to be out there with you. Just the two of us." She took my hand. "Never said how bad I wanted it, for fear you'd say no. And now it's happened, I promise you, Jimmie, I won't take it too light. I won't let you down like Graham, going on late, joking around . . . and I'll take care of you, I swear, each shot." Her face brightened again, and then she was swaying down the bed, half-step, half-step-turn. "Tonight, you know, out there—it was like we were mind readers. I want it to be that way always. I don't ever want you to be sorry you let me try."

I touched her cheek. "I won't be," I said. "And you know I keep promising you someday I'll buy you a house, a grand big—"

"No," she cut in sharp. "Told you I don't want that. Let's don't talk about it. Let's don't wind up in some house somewhere, standing still, not going anyplace anymore. Don't you see I *like* the moving, the different places, never one week the same? Houses—they don't always bring good." Her voice had shifted, her face turned away. "Houses—I know how they can be sometimes. Sometimes when they've stopped. Stopped like a clock, something gone wrong inside. Houses like that, there's a smell to them. A look to them. Houses—I used to believe in houses. Not anymore." For an instant a space rose between us like a patch of damp air. Her eyes, clouded, looked out beyond my shoulder, at the room but not at the room, at nothing I could see. Then they came back to the bed, to the crisp litter of all our plans, and to me, and her eyes cleared. She shrugged off whatever it was that had clouded them, and I shrugged it off with her, paying it no more heed.

Maybe I shouldn't have done. Now I wonder. But at the time, how I could have done else I don't know. Not that night, not with that tang of triumph to our beginnings. Not with her face lifting into that wide quick smile of hers, her fingers tracing down my shoulders, and the two of us looking at each other and sweeping all that paper off the bed. Not that night with my hands sliding under the lace of her chemise, and her thighs hard and firm as a boy's, clasping me like a rider on a horse, and her breasts pouring sweet into my mouth, her hair clinging in strands to my face. Not that night, not for many nights to come.

We played out the summer as Butler & Butler, and I arranged by letter for us to play Cincinnati that fall, booked into a string of variety houses there: a great streak of luck, that was, and the only hitch at all was our billing. Two of the theater managers wired that they had too many husband-and-wife teams double-billed and didn't want another; we were on if she could find herself a new name. She brooded over this more deeply than ever I could have expected, that last week on the road before Cincinnati. I could see her pondering it as she pressed my shirts and rinsed her stockings and fried our eggs over the gas jet in the room, and I could see it keeping her awake on that last overnight jump we had, coming into Cincinnati on the train.

It was chilly that night, cold for September; we'd filled the hot water bottle for the first time that season. Our car was empty, a threadbare car so overheated the air within it seemed to swim; under the yellow lamplight the floor spread around us like an old platter, chipped and scarred, passing us over the dark mesh of the rails. I woke on that train before it was light, missing her head on my shoulder, and saw her stretched out on the seat opposite, her head propped against her mending bag. She lay gingerly, having by that time picked up my habit of pinning money into linings. Besides that, I knew, her pockets held several square cloth sacks filled with an orderly arrangement of combs, pencils, handkerchiefs, pins, tubes of lip balm, rings of keys; everything in its own bag, nothing mixed: I imagined her pleated with even rows of small belongings. There were certain words she used to say to herself, nights on trains, to put herself to sleep, words she was memorizing from her books . . . *epoch, iambic, Druid*, I could hear her murmuring to herself, but she couldn't seem to keep her eyes closed. Her lids fluttered, and her hands. Strung around her neck was the grouchbag, the cloth purse where we kept our weekly earnings. She fingered it, tucked it back inside her cloak, reached for it again, as if to check it—as if to calm it. Then she shifted her weight, half sitting, and took out one of the small notebooks she mostly carried with her. I could tell by the sweep of her hand on the page, the same sweep over and over, that she wasn't noting some new word, some remembered expense. She was writing and rewriting, as she'd done all week, her maiden name, the only name she'd thought of for her billing; writing it over and over, as if in the process it would gain the shine, the shape of how she wanted it to be. *Annie Mozee, Annie Mozee.* It only comes to me now, in hindsight, how tight her face was, how grim; how her knuckles stood out gripping the pencil. At the time, drowsing, I only thought she looked restless and I drifted back to sleep.

When I awoke it was getting light and she was gone. I sat up. Her mending bag was there on the seat opposite, and her gloves, but I couldn't see her in any of the seats in the car. It wasn't till I'd walked up the aisle that I spotted her, crouched over the stove down at the far end. I saw her before she saw me; saw such a look of rage on her face I stopped, startled. I'd never seen her look quite that way before, deliberate and fierce and white-lipped, feeding her notebook, page by page, into the belly of the stove. She knelt there, her cloak pooling around her, watching as the words on the pages curled and burned: pages filled in her open-stitch hand with that name, her old name. Intent and unaware of me, she stayed coiled like that till every page was gone, and then she hurled the stove's door shut so hard it set the chimney to clanking. Still she crouched there, and all at once she put her head down on her knees and cried as if her heart was broken on her. I came nearer, feeling like an intruder, and she looked up at me, eyes streaming, saying nothing, only shaking her head. Her face had gone red and blotchy; her hand, as I took it, was sticky with tears. I pulled her to her feet and she swiped at her eyes with her sleeve, standing there as if about to speak, while the car switched and swayed around us. After a minute she followed me to our seat and leaned against it, shaking her head once more. She was just tired, I explained it away, just jittery. Just tired, just jittery, she agreed, and she closed her eyes until we got in and we said no more about it.

We had a week in Cincinnati before we opened at Wood's Theatre and we used the time to work up some new stunts, trying them out in a spread of fields just beyond the city. We were there early every day, shaping what became the act we've had all these years, and out there the mood on her seemed to lift somehow. The work went well, and even with the endless repetition, the stunts seemed to snap along as they hadn't quite before. If she had been jittery, she wasn't out there, holding sticks of chalk between her fingers, her hand stiff as a policeman's, while I shot the sticks into white bursts like clouds on the sky behind her. If she had been tired, out there she was sharp, shooting an apple off our poodle's head; turning her back with the rifle over her shoulder, sighting in her hand mirror—I remember her face in the glass, eyes narrowed and pensive like a woman inspecting the straightness of her part.

I watched her there, pacing back and forth in her brown workdress, skirts pinned up to the knee; the rifle, then the shotgun, then the pistol in her hand. Unable to quit till she had it, unable to quit even after she had it, each stunt done again and again, then again, she kept up a soft mutter to herself till her finger slid to the trigger, "C'mon Annie walk now watchit watchit c'mon." Mostly unsuperstitious, she wore a lucky charm pinned to her hat even so, a thin silver star I'd bought her for her last birthday. The star glinted in the sunlight with the guns: the Winchester, the Parker Brothers, the Smith & Wesson—again, again, big smile, again. She snapped through the stunts, dead on; she spun, she turned, she sailed through a jump over the low gun table. I had taught her almost all I could, now she was starting to teach me. And in her eyes I saw some of the gaiety returning, her love of the work starting to take over again.

It was one of those autumn afternoons when the light, long and low, lies like a benediction across the earth's face, and the birds seem to hang charmed in the air, and there is everywhere a scent of apples and the promise of a hearthside. She felt it and turned a sudden cartwheel through it, her skirts windmilling over her head, her petticoats frothing up like cream. When she came level, laughing, she put her arms out to me and I swung her up on the wagon, letting the horse wander into the nearby village, its church spire and clustered houses polished by the late sun. We had thought to buy more powder, we had thought to find some lemonade; we just sat there on the wagon seat. Maybe it was the sun, the day, the work—maybe it was that sampler of a village that held us. I looked at Annie, her face dewy with sweat, her eyes transfixed by something over my shoulder. I followed her gaze. There was a small signboard neatly painted with the name of the village. "Oakley," I read out, and even as I did she was reaching for a notebook. She wrote the name out carefully, studying it. She said it aloud, there and that evening, over and over: "Annie Oakley, Annie Oakley." It was right, we both knew it.

It went on the program at Wood's that week and on every program after that, on the trunks and on the gunrack, on everything she's ever owned or signed since. The name seemed to belong to her so soon and so surely, we fast forgot it had ever belonged to that cluster of houses on the outskirts of Cincinnati.

Phoebe Ann Mozee.

Annie Butler, Mrs. Frank E.

Annie Oakley.

Names for her were talismanic, transforming, more than I ever realized then; each transformation a change, each change putting bad times farther away. Oakley: a name that meant *out there*, both ways. A name, I see now, that also meant she was at one more remove from the past. A name that had no familiar ring, that came not from a person but a place. A name that would never make her remember anything she didn't want to summon back.

27

During our first year as a team in vaudeville, her name was a charm, her old fears slept enchanted. It was not till the next year when we played Lima that the charm's power lessened somewhat.

Somewhat. No more than that. It was still a name that fit her, suited her, a name that looked fine on the programs and sounded smart on the announcers' tongues. It was still a name that reminded her of who she was, not where she had been. She knew that. She knew it was still a good name; her good name. But after Lima she knew too that it could never keep her completely safe.

She knew this; not me. It strikes me now how much I didn't know. How little I knew of her thoughts then, and when I met her, married her, and how little it seemed to matter at the time.

I met my wife in a shooting match, Thanksgiving Day, 1875.

It made good copy later—that "major match" as her "first major appearance" in a "major arena" at the tender if not major age of fifteen. In truth the arena was a run-down rented shooting park and the match, which drew scant notice, was arranged half as a bet, half as a joke, in a Cincinnati saloon.

She had been in town three months by then, down from Greenville and in from the fields, staying with her sister and brother-in-law. As a market-hunter, for two years twice a week she'd sent her quail in on the train to the Highland House on Mount Adams but she'd never before been to Cincinnati herself. I like to think of her roaming about, new to it, seeing it for the first time at night: at night with the gaslights and boatlights and oil lamps set out front of every

28

seventh house, the way the city spilled, shimmering, over its hills and river. It looked enchanted to her, that summer at night, as enchanted as she'd hoped of the Queen City of the West. No other city ever looked quite that way to her again; no other city was the first one she had ever seen, and seen for the first time on her fifteenth birthday.

I've often wondered if I passed her on the street in those months, or in a shop, or walking by the river. She liked to watch the river, the way it changed; sleek as feathers, rough as fur, the color of plums and grapes and asters in the quayside markets. She confessed to crossing back and forth on the Suspension Bridge just to look out, leaning over to see the stoves and hams and kegs of beer on the packets sliding beneath her. In August when she came the river was down and the low-water boats were out; in autumn the river was higher and the steamboats were back and she could hear their whistles, high and clear, all the way up to the porch of her sister's house in Fairmount.

As I walked from my lodgings on Elm Street to my bookings on Vine, she was riding the horsecar down Walnut, going with her sister to the crowded Public Landing, just to look, caught up in the swirl of people and vendors and hawkers, stepping back from the herds of pigs driven toward the slaughterhouses at Mill Creek. I could have seen her a dozen times, a girl with a white straw bonnet and a pink gingham dress, gazing up at the columns of Pike's Opera House, turning her face to the spray from the bronze hands of the statue in Fountain Square. I might have brushed by her on the Mount Adams incline or at a counter in Shillito's emporium, but in fact the nearest contact we had that summer was a month before she arrived, when I dined alone one evening at the Highland House and ordered quail—quail she had shot and drawn and gutted up in Darke County, wrapped in swamp grass, and shipped in on the train for ten cents a bird.

I didn't see her that summer or early that fall, even where it was most likely of all. Starting that July I played Cincinnati houses for the better part of a year, the Loewen Garten and other beer halls a couple of blocks past the Vine Street Bridge, across the canal in the section called Over-the-Rhine.

It always did seem farther away than it really was; maybe it was the narrow streets, maybe the brick houses that put me in mind a bit of Dublin. I liked roving there under the chiming clocks and the signs for GUTES ESSEN & GEMÜTLICHKEIT, listening to the thick chuckle of the language and lingering in the buttery air by the bakeries, watching the men in their big aprons rolling out strudel dough. There was always music coming from somewhere, from the beer gardens and the *sangerfests* and the church spires, and spattering through the Bach chorales was often the sound of gunfire from the galleries and *schützen* clubs all around. Now and then, that fall, I heard about some kid going from gallery to gallery, winning free games for an older brother, brother-in-law; some kid from upcountry somewhere. I didn't think much of it, there were always stories like that. I didn't meet this reputed *wunderkind* anywhere, not at Stuttelburg's gallery, not at Grünewald's, and I certainly didn't know that's who I was looking at, that evening in November when I saw her through the blue air of Weilert's saloon.

Weilert's was a place you could hear outside from the street, a thrum like that of a meadow in midsummer, rising steadily as you pushed in through the frosted swing doors. It was always full, people cramming in at the bar and the long tables, and the waiters were always running. I never saw a Weilert's waiter walk. They would speed through the crush, aprons flapping, steins by the fistful held over their heads. Occasionally there were spectacular collisions; no one seemed to mind, that was Weilert's. Everything there was the color of beer and cigars and sausages, brown in the checks of the tablecloths, in the stripes of the waiters' aprons, and a blonde smell rose from the sawdust on the floor. A haze of smoke always hung over the length of the room between the picture of Beethoven at one end and the picture of Mendelssohn at the other, the band in between, and it was under the Beethoven, one night after my show, that I first saw her: a fine-boned girl in a lavender dress, its sleeves puffed, her long dark hair streaming over those sleeves. She was sitting with a small pretty woman who looked to be her sister, and a shaggy collie-faced man who looked to be thoroughly, merrily drunk. I would like to say I noticed only because of the girl but that wouldn't be quite true. I noticed mostly because of her but also because of the drunk—he was yodeling—and also because of the portrait above them which seemed to be staring, with some disapproval, at me.

I was at a table halfway across the room, drinking with some pals and gallery owners, all of us members of the same shooting club and looking toward the Thanksgiving matches we were holding next day. One of the men there was a hotel-keeper, name of John Frost; an Englishman, he was, a handy one with his tongue, and he and I had a joking feud between us on account of our birthplaces. He looked even more the dandified Britisher than usual that night with his brilliantined hair and waxed mustaches, his pince-nez and his preference for whiskey rather than beer. I remember how he drew from his case a ready-rolled cigarette and pointed it, unlit, at me.

"Francis, I'm going to get you," he said, "mark my words."

I shifted my eyes away from the table under the Beethoven.

"My hotel is turned lunatic asylum," Frost went on, tapping his forehead with the cigarette. "Your fault. Actors all over it. Singers, comics. Let one in, they all follow. One goes about in a beard, talks like President Grant. Show folk. Spare us all." Frost looked around our table. "Know what this crazy mick did to me last night?"

"Don't believe him," I put in. "He'd say anything but his prayers."

"He asked me to reserve the bridal suite," Frost went on. "Friends of his coming in for their wedding night. Very famous, very elegant couple, he says, a credit to my hotel. Very well, I do as he asks. And who registers in their name but a pair of midgets—this high, upon my word. Teeny Ted. And his Little Lizbet. And their troupe of performing dogs. Hounds, gentlemen. On my sofas. God knows, in my beds. My lobby looked like a circus. Champagne. Midgets. Hounds on their hind legs. Dancing. Francis, you've got one coming to you, and soon."

And there was laughter all around the table. Another round was called for, and the *Wienerwurst* man came by with

31

his tray and his boy with the bread and salt, and the accordion swung into a polka as I glanced across the room again. The girl in lavender was watching the dancers, her chin on her hand, and the collie-faced yodeler was silent, watching us. Frost followed my gaze and snorted, laughing. He leaned forward, lifting his glass in a mute toast to their table, and across the room the drunk raised his stein to Frost.

"It's all arranged," Frost said, "your comeuppance, Francis. I intend to be there tomorrow when you meet your challenger."

"You better hope he sobers up in time," I said, and our entire table was off in a fit of knowing laughter.

"You wait." Frost had a wicked gleam in his eye. "Francis, you'll get yours."

And so I did.

I did, that Thanksgiving Day, up at Schuetzenbuckle, Shooter's Hill. It was windless and warm, unseasonable, crowded; there must have been a hundred matches on the slate. The balding hilltop hefted the park into the air, sunning it with its constant clamor, its awning of smoke, its smell of strudel and onions and gunpowder. Shots cracked; beer kegs rolled. The grass bloomed with cigar butts and dead pigeons, and the boys rushed by with fresh birds, stuffing them into tin traps like church footwarmers. Pretzel men and cigar men and herring men circled the crowd, singing, calling, rattling the coins in their aprons, and men in shooting coats flowed between the tables and ranges like guests at a wake, drinking and jostling at one end, standing in silent scrutiny at the other, returning, joking, to drink again.

Through the smoke and the noise and the shoulders I glimpsed the collie-faced man from Weilert's, the man I'd come to think of as Frost's ringer. He looked stone sober that afternoon, sporting a green hat and carrying an old muzzle-loading rifle; I figured he had to be pretty fair if he was matching that against a shotgun. At his side, in a gray bonnet, was the woman with him the night before, and next to her was the girl; bareheaded, her hair held back with a white ribbon, her dress pink and her cape over her arm. I found my eyes staying on her as she glanced about, her gaze coming to rest on the brick building behind me, our rented clubhouse: a prim grandmotherly building laced into a corset of white trim and wide verandas. She looked at it longingly, as if she'd give anything to go inside; as if inside there would be rocking chairs and braided rugs and clocks ticking and a dozen other things that had nothing to do with all these jostling, ogling men. Myself included. She must have felt me looking and she looked back at me, her eyes lingering on the medals pinned to my jacket. Then she turned abruptly, following the green hat and gray bonnet, and I watched her dress wafering through the crowd. I wasn't far behind when the three of them reached the target line.

The groundsmen were drawing the line fresh, I remember, and they were still raking dead birds off the field. The girl was holding the muzzle-loader then, I thought for the ringer, while he laid the gear out on the table: shot pouch and powder flask, cap box, wads, ramrods. I could see her eyes ticking over them, mostly avoiding mine, glancing at me sidewise now and again. In that dress, next to the long rifle, she looked at once like a grave-faced child and a full-breasted woman. I brought my eyes back to the man beside her as Frost swooped down upon me. I can still see him leaning on his cane, his gloves caught up like a bunch of flowers in one hand, eyeing her, eyeing me, waiting.

"Who's the gent?" I asked him.

"Name's Joe Stein, I thought you'd met by now."

"And the girl, by the way?"

"Girl? What girl?" Frost looked innocent. "Oh, that girl—you must mean his sister-in-law. That little girl, Francis, is your opponent. Your challenger. Your comeuppance, that's right—behold." And then he couldn't contain himself any longer, he broke into a laugh and looked at Stein and Stein was laughing too. My face, I know, was all they'd hoped.

I saw her turn away, wincing at the laughter, frowning down at her pink skirt as if she wanted to escape from it; so pink, so full, there amidst all that corduroy and leather. The sight of it billowing out around her seemed to make her feel worse, as if she were trapped in a piece of marzipan. Her hand smoothed at it, eyes averted, till the referee called "Time" and rattled out the rules, two traps, twenty yards, twenty-five birds each, gun below the elbow till the call of "Pull." The crowd was hooting before he'd finished; she was white-faced as I won the toss and grassed my first bird.

"Dead," sang the referee.

I stepped back as she walked to the line. She capped her rifle. She cocked her rifle. All she had to do was call "Pull," but she just stood there, her hands shaking, her dress trembling all around her. Her back had stiffened into the posture of a child called suddenly to recite in class. Sweat slowly beaded her forehead as she raised the rifle, then lowered it again, looking down at her hands. I could hear her breathing, fast and shallow; I could hear the edgy murmur from the sidelines. And still she stood there shaking, slightly off-balance, like someone standing up on a moving train, and still she could not seem to make that call. I felt sorry for her, sorry about the whole thing; I shouldn't have allowed it. I stepped toward her and she looked at me, seeing the pity in my face. Something seemed to shift in her eyes. They stared at me, startled at first; then defiant. She turned back to the line. She took a breath and she wiped her hands on her pink skirt and she called "Pull."

There was the clang of the trap springing open behind the mound and the pigeon was streaking into the air. Her rifle swung up, her eye snapping onto the bird and staying with it, and she got some lead and pulled out ahead and dropped the pigeon on the rise, well within the boundary line. She lifted a little up off her heels to watch it, and she bounced on them an extra second, smiling suddenly but just to herself, forgetting me till we turned toward the loading tables together. Not bad, I thought, not bad.

I couldn't help watching her at the tables—there was little enough I had to do, just break open my shotgun, pop out one shell and drop in the next, and there she was with her muzzle-loader, cleaning, measuring, ramming, and my eyes straying to her and hers to me the whole time till we were back at the line.

Those birds, that day, they ran pretty swift, and we kept grassing them, staying even, and then the referee was calling ten and ten. By that time she didn't look scared in the least, she had caught the rhythm of it, and I glanced at her sharper each time she brought down another bird. After that first ten she threw me a smile each time the referee called "Dead," enjoying my surprise; each time I surprised myself by smiling back.

And it was twelve and twelve, and fifteen and fifteen, and I missed my sixteenth and she missed her nineteenth and we were even again when it was twenty down and then twenty-four; that last shot sneaked up so soon, the referee calling in his high nasal voice, "Match point, ladies and gents, your complete silence." There was a hush as I walked to the line and drew my last bird, a real twister, quartering right—I just grazed it through the tail, spraying feathers in the air as the bird flew on and away. There was a murmur from the side: "Miss," called the referee. I stepped back, startled and yet not displeased, watching her move to the line. I remember how she looked there, her dress blazing pink in the sun, that wide sweep of pigeon-littered grass before her, the hushed blur of faces alongside—and that swing of dark hair, tossed over her shoulder as she called "Pull." The trap clashed and her bird was spinning high, another twister, and just at the last it darted forward, but she had the swing, caught the dart, and, oddly elated, I felt that hit even as she squeezed: *Dead!* called the referee.

Then they were shouting out our names and scores and the Steins and Frost were around her, and the purse was in her hands: fifty dollars in a little bag she held out before her, palms up, as if it were a bowl of broth. All of a sudden, once it was over, she looked shaky again, her face flushed. She gave the purse to her sister, going to gather up her gear, and I was right by the table, waiting for her. I put out my hand to her and she took it, raising her eyes to me.

"Sharp shooting, Missie," I said, "no joke."

"Thanks, you too, Jimmie," she said, so flustered she'd forgotten my name and said the first one into her head, flushing even deeper then.

That evening I left a note for her in Joe Stein's mailbox and after a while there were a lot of notes like that, and I remember them, they run together in my mind like one long letter, all those notes with the names we first used that day.

Dear Missie, may I have the honor of calling on you and congratulating you again in person and . . . my dear Missie, thank you for the grand afternoon and thank your sister for her fine ginger pie and . . . my dear Missie, may I send you more tickets to my show, I so look forward to seeing you again and . . . Missie, dear, if a fellow could have danced till sunup it was me, with you, at Weilert's, I'm still thinking of . . . my sweet Missie, meet me if you can at Eden Park behind the boathouse where we were before, I'll be waiting for . . . my Missie, Eden Park again —noon—sending all my love to . . . my darling Missie, I'd wed you without herds/Without money or rich array/ And I'd wed you on a dewy morning at day-dawn gray . . .

Your Loving & Hopeful,

Jimmie

W HO was she, where had she come from, before Schuetzenbuckle, before Cincinnati, this girl I was taken with so fast?

I remember going up the hill in Fairmount to Lydia Stein's house and sitting through Sunday dinner at the big walnut table, politely conversing and praising the pie, my eyes all the while on her, wondering that.

I remember sitting with her on the slippery horsehair sofa in the parlor, not talking much, listening to the clock tick and watching her pleat her skirt between her fingers, and her watching me watch. Her eyes, sidelong on me, were eager and wary, as if I shed light, cast ripples I couldn't see. The afternoon sun lay on the arms of the sofa like lace; around us the house creaked and forked like a tree, holding us there on that bough, and didn't we sway a little, and didn't we look down, and didn't we wonder how to move closer without losing our perch.

I remember walking with her Over-the-Rhine and talking more, and dancing with her at Weilert's and talking all evening, and sitting in a flat-bottomed boat in Eden Park and kissing her, and how she held her hat on with both hands, and then with one hand, and then let her hat slide into the stern, her two hands holding me. I remember us back on the horsehair sofa, not talking much again, just pressing close.

All I can recall her telling me about herself then, about where she'd come from, was that she'd grown up near Greenville two counties north, and lived there with her mother and brother and sisters and a stepfather or two. She had hunted for the Cincinnati hotels to bring in money, to help pay the mortgage, and that done she'd come down to stay with her sister and finish her schooling on her own. She mentioned she'd earned money sewing too, but mostly when she talked of times before the match she talked of market-hunting.

I remember I came to call one afternoon and found her at her sister's old Singer, and I said don't get up, and she said have a chair, and over the machine's light clatter she talked of slow fire and trigger work and length of pull, her feet on the treadle and her hands guiding the hem of a flowered lawn dress.

"Three drams powder, one ounce number eight shot, that was my load," she said, her eye on the needle. "I cut my own wads from cardboard boxes, thought I had the best gun and load on earth, well don't laugh."

"Ah, sorry—that muzzle-loader?"

"Shoots a real even pattern, handles perfect."

"I do seem to remember noticing that."

"Out there, hunting with it, if you'd seen me—"

"Wish I had done."

"—you'd have laughed then, for sure. No flowered lawn there." She smoothed the cloth and shook her head. "Woolen skirt, big hat, long johns in winter. All my gear hanging off me. Rattling like all get-out! And winter, summer, pulled down over everything, a burlap sack—kept my clothes from getting all ripped on jaggers." Her mouth lifted in a sudden smile; her nose, faintly freckled, crinkled at the bridge. "Those sacks . . . they'd smell of whatever'd been in them. I'd be going down a corn row, you know, kicking up quail—

and all the time I'd be inside this big smell of coffee, flour—oats." Her eyes darted to me, sidelong. "Me in my sack—wonder what you'd really think, seeing me like that, reeking all over of coffee?"

My face must have clearly shown what I'd think. She smiled again, winding more thread around the bobbin. A filigree of shadows fell through the wheel across her smooth blue lap, her thighs moving against her skirt as she went on sewing. Did she miss it much, the hunting, I asked, half afraid of the answer, did she want to go back?

"Nooo . . . don't want to go back." Her feet paused on the treadle; for a moment her hands were still. "Sometimes I miss it though . . . August, September, wild blackberries, I'd fill my hat with them. Berries all warm from the sun. And those seedpods from milkweed, you know, floating by like little umbrellas. And the quail all around, going *putt-putt* out there, feeding. I remember how Maryjane, my sister, she used to come out and sit with me sometimes, she'd always—" She broke off, a tremor in her voice, her head bent lower. After a moment the machine resumed its clatter under her voice. "*Quail*, I was telling you about the quail—there were maybe twenty coveys I kept track of, I'd be out after them at dawn. . . . I'd hear other hunters, but I kept to myself, liked it that way. Couldn't shoot then if I thought anyone was watching me." She gave the wheel a spin, glancing up then with laughter in her eyes. "Then that match. Lord, all those people watching me at once. And—don't ask me why—I figured I'd be shooting against someone from Over-the-Rhine. Someone fat. And short. And bald . . . And there you were." She looked at me sidewise and kept sewing, a faint rosy mist spreading up over her skin. "I sure noticed you. I noticed all those ladies gazing at you too. I noticed everything about you. . . . Your medals. That hat with the feather in the brim. No gloves, long hands like a piano player's. Blue coat, blue eyes. And how you kept looking at me. Just the way you're looking at me now . . . just like that. What are you smiling at—Jimmie, I have to finish this—what are you doing?"

I was lifting her hair in my hands, kissing her down the nape of her neck, and the machine stopped its clatter, and that dress got hemmed another day. What did I care then where she came from, or she about me for that matter. We didn't seem to take much interest in anything that had happened before that match, in things that didn't have to do with us together, and we were off and going all the time: out to suppers, theaters, to my show, but mainly to the shooting clubs and galleries that let her in. I guess it was an odd way to conduct a courtship, so much of it on one target line or another, but neither of us seemed to care. There was a sheen to us, a fine gloried glaze that was hard to frown at, hard to crack. I see it now as I didn't then, looking back at myself, at her.

Look at her, how grand she was in her dresses, stepping across those big mown outdoor ranges, lining up with all those gents in their peaked caps and patch-elbowed coats, her skirts slicing out among the trouser legs, her face prim and shut against the stares. Look at her, how fine she was in those shooting galleries, the tiny silver drops bobbing at her ears as she laid her cheek on the rifle's comb, gaslight on her hair and black powder on her hands, all those jerking rows of yellow metal ducks behind her. And her face with that sheen; I'd look at her and wonder if it was me that put it there, me or this orgy of shooting. I'd look at her in delight, almost disbelief—never had I thought to find a shooting pal, a comrade-in-arms who would step to the mark in a foam of petticoats. For her part, she had always thought a suitor would laugh at her shooting, make her stop or drop her flat, and she marveled that it wasn't so.

A scent of DuPont Eagle powder hung over us, effervesced from us that spring out in the fields, the two of us with our guns rambling farther alone, having worn out our chaperone Joe Stein. Us, drenched in sun. Her, out ahead, her face damp, ashine. Her voice calling, her skirts skimming the weeds, and me back in a long-ago day in Ireland, running with my girl cousins through the pasture after we'd all made First Communion. Holy and proper the whole morning long, we had burst from the house, my cousins' white dresses blowing like love letters across the grass, their laughter coasting back to me, "Fran-cis, Fran-cis," their voices so bright . . . bright still, even far off, the memory floating within me mellow as wine, floating me back to this field, this girl, to Missie.

We sat together, leaning back on our elbows, watching the tides of the wind through the field, watching each other. There was a faint beaded mist on her upper lip, there was a weed in her hair. She plucked it off, her eyes flickering toward me modest, earnest, abashed. I leaned closer, my arm around her, her lips salty on mine, the gingham of her dress crisp with starch and warm from the sun, her breast soft within its crispness, under my hand.

"You must have a lot of callers like me, coming round." She shook her head.

"Now that I can't believe."

"I . . . never had a fella before," she said low, as if in shameful confession, then looked up at me through her tumbled hair. "But I've wondered . . ."

"Mmm?"

"Wondered what it might be like."

"And?" I kissed her again. "What's it like then?"

"Oh like . . . August, wild blackberries, maybe like that."

"Only that?"

"And . . . taffeta. Like . . . lime-green taffeta."

"That sounds pretty fine."

"I used to wonder . . . sitting out in the fields, sometimes, hearing those things clinking in my pocket. I'd carry them around with me, in a little bag—a thimble, and a moon-shaped stone. This one button like a ruby. And that favor I got at my sister's wedding, a tiny thing made of tin. All the girls got one—different charms, the one you got meant something about your beau. Clover for luck, cup for joy, ring for marriage. I got a cup. And I remember my sister, how she said, 'A fine beau for Annie.' Well, I'd keep those things in my pocket, and after a while I'd forget about them. And then I'd hear them ringing in there. I'd take them out, look at them again. And they'd shine in my hand, *Annie, fine beau.* And I'd wonder, what would I say to him, this beau, when I met him. Finally, in a book, I found the word I knew I'd want to say . . . if I could . . . if I could say it out loud."

"Tell me."

"Well, it was . . . *adore* . . . such a beautiful word, I thought."

"It is, no one's ever said that to me before."

"No one?"

"Never. You . . . you are saying it, aren't you?"

"Yes . . ." She looked at me. "I'm saying it . . . to you."

We planned to marry when she turned sixteen that summer but by June we couldn't wait any longer. Joe and Lydia Stein witnessed for us at the Cincinnati courthouse, on three hours' notice, bless them. We worried they'd try to stop us; in fact they seemed relieved. There were only a few minutes that weren't smooth and they went by out of my sight, over my head, upstairs in the Steins' house; just a brief sound of raised voices when she asked Lydia to tell her mother for us. I know she feared what her mother would say and small wonder: she so young, me ten years older, and in the show business, and Irish, and not yet a citizen, a lapsed Catholic to top it off, and more I couldn't say. But whatever happened upstairs was soon over, Lydia consenting, and whatever happened in Greenville I didn't hear, and anyway that's not what I think of when I think of us marrying. What I always think of is the Fourth of July that year: the pops and sparks during that fortnight of the big Centennial of '76, a holiday time that took in our marriage, swept it up, and seemed to celebrate it with us.

That's how it seemed the evening of the Fourth when we went up on the incline to the top of Price Hill and looked out over the city. We wandered past the bandshell and danced in the pavilion. We held hands in public and bought red-white-and-blue cotton sugar and cold chicken. We watched the light fade on the huge lithographs of George Washington on the Suspension Bridge and an hour before sunset we watched hundreds of hot-air balloons drift into the air, people waving from their baskets, blue balloons, red ones, globe-shaped, pear-shaped, one marked *The Cincinnati Enquirer*, one wafting down at Price Street near the brow of our hill. As it got darker we watched the pinwheels, the red lights, the blue and the white blooming over the city, and the tails of the rockets, the wheeling fire of the Roman candles. Everywhere there was light, sound, the smell of sulfur, and not for an instant did it stop. The city blushed and blazed for us, paled and blazed again; the roar from the fireworks sank and swelled for hours, long after we were back in our room at the Bevis House, watching at the window, listening still. But the sound I remember best came at midnight and was not the fireworks, not the cannon fire, not the musket fire, but the sound of churchbells, clear and sweet, and everywhere, it seemed, for us.

Whenever we've passed the Bevis House since, I've always thought of that time, that first room. We lived there two months and if she ever felt strange in that room, that night or any other, she never let on. If she ever felt a wrench of homesickness, I never saw the signs. It was years after that she told me how she'd felt the morning of our wedding day, going up the stairs to the room I'd taken for us; going up alone, while I was out, to put her things away.

"To put them away. And to look," she said. "And how long those stairs seemed, going up there. How loud that key clicked in the door. I waited a minute before pushing it open, before going in. I stood in the middle of that room a long time, my dresses all bunched in my arms. It was so quiet inside. It seemed so empty. And all of a sudden I wondered what on earth I was doing there. I looked around at the curtains blowing in, those blue curtains. I looked at that white chenille spread on the bed. That little lamp over it in the shape of a tulip. And your razor on the washstand, some pocket change you'd left on the dresser. And I got this sinking feeling. It was such a nice room, and I didn't see how I could ever live in it, ever feel that was home. I put my clothes in the wardrobe. I put my hairbrush on the washstand next to your razor, my sewing basket on the windowsill. I looked around again—and I still had that sinking feeling. Just before I locked the door I looked back. And I thought, people probably don't get carried over the threshold in hotel rooms. I could feel tears coming into my eyes, tears, I didn't want to be crying on the day of my wedding.

"Well, of course it turned out people did get carried over thresholds in hotels after all, and the room seemed different to me, that second time through the door—that big bunch of flowers you'd set on the dresser—peonies, all those peonies, the room smelled of them. And best of all that wonder of a sound, that clock ticking, you thought it would make the room seem homier, that clock, and it did, it did, all night and especially in the early mornings.

"I'd wake in that room very early and I'd watch it get light. I'd listen to the sounds of the market down there in Court Street, the wagons rumbling in, unloading, and the cook from the Bevis House going out to get fresh eggs. I'd see your shirt over the back of the rocker, my shoes underneath it. Your hat with the feather, there on the dresser. And you, sleeping there in my arms, your hair down over your eyes. And I'd think, How did I come to be here? How was I ever so lucky, who blessed me? Did you ever know what I was thinking then? Did you ever see me smiling, trembling too, a little, in that high old bed? There I was, not sixteen yet, and I was lying there in that room, in those sheets with you, with this man who seemed so wonderful to me. And no one had ever said that would happen. And no one had ever promised me that. And it had happened even so, in just half a year, it was real.

"I'd see my nightgown in a heap on the floor. And I'd shiver and think of getting up to put it on. And I wouldn't move. I'd just stay there, watching you. Your head against my shoulder. Your hand, in my hair. You seemed to love me so much, and what did you even know about me? So many things you didn't know, so many things I didn't tell you. Old things, from before, things I was afraid you'd find out somehow. And stop loving me. Sometimes, very early, when the room was still shadows, I'd think of telling you. And then it would get lighter. And I'd be able to see more, see you shifting in your sleep. Your face against my breasts. Your lips opening on my skin. And I wouldn't wake you. I wouldn't want to tell you anything then. Not then, not ever. Could you really know me? Did it matter? I'd tell myself no. And I'd tell myself, this is where I live, in this room with you. This is where I live now. And all the rest is gone."

SECRETS. I had my own.

There were things I hadn't said, never found a way to mention during that spin of a courtship; things that had nothing to do with me anymore, that I never thought I'd have to speak of again. In the way of such things they'd faded, turning faint in the spot where they hung in my mind, and it was seldom I glanced at them after a while. And then I had to look at them once more. Now as I watch her struggle to speak of old things, I know her pain, thinking back on mine then.

I had to tell her, another summer, out on the road, one morning after I got the mail. How angry I was, I remember, going up the stairs to the room, angry it had happened, angry I'd been trapped into telling. It never occurred to me she might know how it was. It never occurred to me, even then, she might have anything behind her that ached. I must have thought I alone had the age and wit for regrets, and so it never occurred to me to do else but slam into that room, spoiling for a quarrel, deciding if we quarreled I wouldn't have to tell her then, maybe not at all.

She smiled at me and winced at the slam, standing there in her nightgown, cooking breakfast over the gas ring. The frying pan in her hand held a shuddering mass of yellow, and the air seemed larded with the smell of eggs and coffee. Fine smells to me mostly. Foul then, foul as spoiled fish. The scrape of her fork on the pan irked me. The hang of her nightgown, crisp and white, irked me. The tidy array of her clothes laid out on the bed irked me, and when I spied her hat there among them, I swept it onto the floor.

"I told you, how many times, never do that."

"Do what?" She turned from the pan.

"Hat on the bed, never, how many times."

She looked at me, appraising, likely figuring how long I'd been awake, questioning not the superstition but the tone of voice. I heard her fork scrape the pan again, turning the eggs in that neat circular way she has, and I glared at the bed.

"Why is it we always get a room with one of these blankets, look at this. Holes. Moths. Thin as a shroud. You could read the paper through that blanket, you could sight targets through that blanket, why do we always get blankets like that, every damn room."

She looked at me again. "I'll ask for another, I'll tell them."

"Watch it, that's burning."

"It's not, it's fine, what's wrong?"

"What's wrong is this room, why here, burnt eggs, bum's blanket, why does it have to be here? Why do I have to tell you in this dump—tell you we have to get married again."

She turned off the gas, the low ring of flame going out with a small gasp, and for a moment she stared at me, the pan still in her hand, the smell of coffee hovering about us like an anxious hostess trying to put things to rights.

"We have to get married again," I repeated, my voice thinner. "Because of me. Because it wasn't right, I didn't know it, in Cincinnati."

Her eyes were still fixed on me, the fork lifted like some strange signal in her left hand.

"It wasn't right," I went doggedly on. "Because there was another time. Because I was married before."

"Don't tell me this," she said suddenly, her voice high and clear. Very carefully, very precisely, she wiped her hands on a towel, and folded the towel, once, then twice, and laid it down on the bureau. On its very center she placed the frying pan, and then she just stood there, still gripping the handle. Apart from the shock of it, of learning what she had, all of her own secrets must have been jarred, jostling through her like a crowd of stumbling sleepers, jolted half awake by the sound of confession.

I stood by the bed, shuffling in my hand the half dozen scraps of paper I kept in my pocket, names of theater managers, high hands in poker, recipes for dog food, good stage jokes. I remembered myself standing in the schoolyard after class, telling everybody the one about the two tinkers, making them all laugh, laughing away the sting of a switching I'd just had inside.

Finally she spoke, her eyes big, her hands clasping her elbows as if she was cold.

"Why didn't you tell me?"

"I was afraid you wouldn't have me."

"I would have."

There was a silence. I could see the sun on the mirror, the rug, on her face.

"I would have, Jimmie," she said, softer.

"I thought of it so many times. Couldn't find the right one, afraid to spoil any, you can't know how that is."

"Yes," she said swiftly, "I do know."

Her eyes scanned my face as if rapidly trying to read a page of fine print. There was something in her eyes, sympathy, tenderness, and something else; some wish to speak, to add something more. I ignored it, rushing past it toward my own acquittal.

"It was long ago. I'd just gone eighteen, it was done, it was bad." I took a breath. The distance across the room seemed vast, a gaping space, a sea. "Two babies . . . that was the worst part, they've a stepfather now. It was all of it finished before I ever met you. I had the divorce papers, thought it was settled—and now I'm reading it's only just final after all these years. Something to do with immigration, paperwork lost, postponed. Missie, I wish you never had to know. I never wanted this in our lives, but I'll tell you, tell you it all if you want, the sorrow's mostly gone from it, she was—"

"Jimmie, don't," she said. "Don't, it doesn't matter now."

She came to me and put her hands on my shoulders. I felt her fingers, strong and firm. Her lips parted, as if to speak. Her eyes, a deepened gray, seemed to weigh something again, something undecided, in the balance. She drew a sharp breath and again I misread her, that sound, those eyes.

"I wish it could be like it never happened," I blurted out. "Wish I could make it that way, for you, for us both."

She spread her fingers like a pianist reaching an octave, striking the notes, and something shifted in her eyes; no questions there then, only resolution.

"It can be." Her hands came up to touch my face. "We won't talk about it. We don't need to, we won't. We won't let anything from before ever touch us, not ever, tell me we won't, promise me."

I promised, grateful, lightened, amazed. I'd thought I'd have to beg her forgiveness, be penanced for years, and here she'd absolved me; swiftly, completely, forever. I didn't realize then that her adamance had anything to do with her own fears, with her own renewed will to keep the past away. Now, knowing her as I do, I know she would have pardoned me anyway. But I wonder, were it not for her own inner reasons, if she could have let it go without a question, one searching word. And I wonder, had I started softer, listened more, if she might have told me then what she kept clasped to her, curtained, instead.

But that morning I wondered little. I was only relieved, and once it was over, shaken, slightly dazed. It was she who moved smoothly out into that day for us both, like a canoe with a tired passenger; it was she who made the inquiries, found the minister, set the time, and before noon we were standing at his door. Just before it opened she slid off her wedding ring, and in the sight of the rose walls and the fringed shades and the carpet the color of dried beef, we made our promises again, and I slid the ring back on her finger. I looked down at her, her profile taut as a smell of boiling cabbage rose over our vows, as the minister's wife sang in a whiskey voice "Amazing Grace." We signed the certificate, Annie after me, turning away, handing it quickly back: it was done. We were again man and wife, and within minutes we were again at the theater, linked to the familiar rhythm of the day. That rhythm led us along, rising and falling over the course of the five shows, and leaving us that evening at a gathering in someone's room; the sort of gathering that happened at least twice a week on the road, and yet that time seemed different.

We stood in the hall of that boarding house like travelers in a cold station and that room was our train, stopping there

47

for us, steaming, glowing, warming the night. It took us up, moved us on, lifting us in with people we knew well, people we knew slight, into that misting of smoke, that soft shuffling of shoes and cards, the sound of beer and ice sloshing in a laundry tub on the floor. It brought us back to where we'd been before, gave us a seat; offering, like trays, towels stamped *Best Room & Board*, spread with cheese and pears and sardines. It spoke to us in phrases we knew, voices talking good houses, bad food, hot numbers, and welcoming the guests of honor who had just come through the door—a pair of creatures in white tights and white tutus and snug white plush suits, a sister act with saxophones called the Musical Swans.

"We were the Singing Swans," said one.

"Then we were the Dancing Swans," said the other.

"And how they'd pelt us, Lord what we've been through together," the first one said. "We finally hit it right tonight."

Across the room, past the sisters' fleecy torsos, Annie looked over at me.

"Thought we'd split up, then we got the horns," said the second swan. "That's what changed it, now we're cooking."

Through the laughter, the pattering of applause, Annie's skirts rustled as she edged toward me.

"We lived through it, now we're on our way."

We won't let anything from before touch us.

"The horn, that's the ticket."

We won't, promise me.

"To you both," someone said, raising a beer to the swans, and Annie's fingers pressed mine.

S HE took to the show business life right away, the traveling and the rooms and the trains, and if you happened to be at the depot as we descended from our car, and if you saw our little procession, me with the threadbare carpetbag, she with the dented hatbox, the porters with the battered gun trunk and the clothes trunk and the cage for the poodle, you would have seen her smiling; and if you lived there, you wouldn't have smiled back, for if you looked at us once you'd know what we were—not gaudy, no sequins, but none-theless showfolk, strollers, stage scum, Gypsy types, and you'd pay to come see us but you'd lock up your silver, your sister as well, and no tipped hat, no touch of gold or token of grace could ever make us quite respectable.

We *are* respectable, she'd insist, and to her we were, so was the life; respectable, rare, new as the morning, and for all the sitting and waiting there was to it, she never seemed bored.

Her lap almost always held sewing or schoolbooks and after a while she wore the grouchbag, handled the money; she had the best head for it. In the late evenings while I cleaned the guns, she'd bend over the wobbly writing tables in those boarding-house rooms, counting the coins, listing expenses in her ledger, *5¢ beer, 90¢ brass shells, 30¢ curl-papers*, or she would write carefully in her copybooks, her texts spread open before her, *the siege of Atlanta . . . the rivers of Ohio . . . my love is like a red red rose.* I'd watch her sitting there, frowning, intent, in a room strung with clothesline and hung with damp shirts and stockings patter-ing onto the rug in a faint drizzle. She'd sit with one foot tucked up under her, her hair shining in the lamplight, look-ing at once like a schoolgirl and a schoolmarm, glaring sternly at the pages, her papers and notebooks piled precisely around her, edges flush, as if to pass some unmentioned military inspection.

She would study on the trains and in the theaters but mostly in the boarding houses, the dog by her chair, con-centrating as if by a fierce act of will amidst all that noise around her; especially in summer, all the doors open on the sopranos singing to their ceilings, the comics joking to their mirrors, and the acrobats leapfrogging down the halls. Sometimes she'd sit outside in a nearby field, under a tree, against a fence; sometimes, if we were flush, she'd take a book and sit in a drugstore, drinking a lime phosphate while she ran her finger down the words in her speller. I thought she'd be one place or the other, that day I came back to our lodgings and couldn't find her.

I'd been to send a telegram that morning, arranging our next booking before the week was out, and I'd come looking for her afterward in all the usual places: up in the room, down in the front parlor, out in the swing on the porch. She wasn't anywhere, but her hat and her copybooks were gone, and it was a fine day, warm and hazy, late September; I remember the goldenrod was out in front of that sagging sign for IDEAL LODGINGS: ACTORS WELCOME. I started down the road again, toward the drugstore, looking for her along the way; it was a small backwater town in Indiana, the kind where meadows lapped the edges of the street every few lots. A short ways down, an old cemetery fringed the road, the kind kids whistle passing, its wooden fence rotting and half fallen down, its narrow gate cut like the lid on a coffin and overhung with an iron crown of thorns. The land inside looked dry as skin, shadowed by spindly elms, and beneath them the gray stones slanted askew, as if hurled there by some harsh and hasty hand. So it looked to me, though I'll admit I don't like cemeteries, always feel some superstitious dread near them; I walked on quicker to get by this one. Some movement beyond the gate caught my eye, turned my head toward it again: the flutter of a dress in the breeze. A girl was roaming there, her blue skirts wavering between the tombstones, her straw bonnet tilted down and away. She walked slowly, mournfully, I thought at first; then it seemed more like a window-shopper in a town, walking and pausing and wandering on a few steps before pausing again. There was something about her that alarmed me, something about the span of her waist, the set to her hat, the length of her hair. From the back and at that distance she looked like Annie. She walked like Annie. Unable to help myself I called to her. She turned, saw me, seemed to jump; it was Annie indeed. I must have looked as startled as I felt; so did she, hesitating a moment, then coming to the gate with her copybooks in her arms. She was just having a look around, she said, having a walk between the history and the grammar, and wasn't I silly to look so pale. I supposed I was.

Off and on I'd see her other times, other towns, sitting in some sunny old graveyard, her back against a stone, an apple in her hand, scribbling away in her copybook. I came to admire her matter-of-factness about such places, the library-like stillness she'd found for herself in them—especially since I knew I couldn't enter one without muttering "Bless us and save us" out of long habit. I admired her, that is, until I found the book.

One morning while she rustled behind the dressing screen in our room, I riffled through the neatly piled papers on the writing table. I was looking for the address of a theater in Akron when I came upon a notebook I hadn't seen before, under the others. I picked it up. A sheet of paper came out in my hand. A skeleton's head grinned out from it at me, a skull surrounded by the branches of a weeping willow: the design on the top of a tomb. I opened the book, turned the pages. It was filled entirely with drawings of gravestones. Fascinated, chilled, I went through them. She had sketched them clearly in pencil: gravestones crowned with cherubs' heads and cherubs' wings, with praying hands and grazing sheep, with Reapers and Saviors. She had copied down the inscriptions in exact print, so they stood out on the page in script and boldface and fancy lettering, *Called Home* . . . *Awaiting Glory* . . . *Just at Rest*, and over and over in every style of printing imaginable, *Here Lies, Here Lies*. She had sketched them from all angles, with the precision of a sewing pattern; the fierce gaze she'd caught in the eyes of an angel stopped me short. I thought of all those bright afternoons I'd seen her in the cemeteries, scrawling what I'd supposed were sentence diagrams, the stanzas of a sonnet. I turned to the front of the book, then to the back, looking for something that might explain it, and saw an envelope neatly fixed to the cover with common pins, an empty envelope addressed to *Edwin Nickol Monuments, Versailles, Ohio*. This I was holding in my hand as she stepped forward into the room, saw what I had, and with one quick sweep snatched it from me, lips tight, eyes afire.

"What is this, what are you doing?" I stared at her.

"What are *you* doing, in my things, my books, just as you please?"

"I needed an address—what's this about, what's wrong?"

"What's wrong is you prying," she threw back at me. "You should have asked me, could have, I was here, right *here*."

"Did something happen, someone die? Christ, that gave me a hell of a turn."

"Then you deserve it, poking like that, no one died. I was sketching, just sketching, what's the matter with that?"

"And that?" I pointed to the envelope in her hand.

"My uncle," she said after a pause, a pause just a bit too long. "My uncle in Versailles. Runs that business, so what, I was writing to him, so what."

"Uncle, I didn't know about an uncle."

"I can't remember to tell you about every relation everywhere—what's it matter, why should you care?"

"I care about you is why." My voice was rising. "It scared me is why, still does, makes no sense."

"To you, maybe. Makes perfect sense to me, why shouldn't it?" Her eyes narrowed on me, her fingers crimping the envelope they held. "I know what I'm doing, know what I'm about, it's nothing to do with you, nothing."

"If something's wrong you better tell me, damn it, Missie, just—"

"Nothing's wrong, in fact everything's right, just right, you stop hollering at me, you've got no cause, no cause at all."

"Missie, I am *asking* you *what this is about*. Jesus sakes, what are you holding back on me for, you tell me that."

"I'm not—why are you at me and at me like this, you stop drilling me like I'm committing some kind of, some kind of crime, I'm not. You've no right to know, not everything. Not every single thought in my mind, do I press *you*? Do I have to know everything, do I drill you? Have I ever made you tell what's yours to keep—don't you touch me—have I?"

Her voice had sharpened, turning harsh and rough. Her face, reddening, had gone blotchy, and her fists gripped the sides of her skirt as if for steadiness. I'd held my hand out to her but she'd jerked away. After a moment she crossed the room and shoved her book into her trunk, slamming the lid and clicking the locks; an unnecessary precaution and one sure to wound. And then she just stood there, leaning on the trunk, her fists clenched on the lid. I watched her, infuriated by her turned back, her secrets, her questions. The ridge of her spine was taut beneath the green cloth of her dress, her hair falling forward to hide even the faintest curve of her face. I heard her take a breath, a sharp one, as if she meant to speak, but she went on standing there stiff and still, her fists like twin white knobs on the dusty trunk. I waited a moment more, then grabbed up my hat and slammed out.

That was the first time, I think, that we'd ever stopped speaking, not touching or talking for the rest of that day, except when the act forced us to it; when we met that noon at the long dinner table in the boarding house, the silence between us seemed to clang like cold metal.

I never did see that particular notebook again. I never saw her sitting with her books on the sunny slopes of cemeteries again either, and I felt bad about it often, watching her trying to study amidst the boarding-house noise, the dressing-room hustle. From time to time, among the letters we mailed, I'd notice one addressed to Versailles; not often, just now and then. The last time I saw one slide into a mailbox, we were at a train station and we were on our way to Louisville, Kentucky, to try out for a troupe that had just changed its name from *The Rocky Mountain & Prairie Exhibition* to *Buffalo Bill's Wild West*.

I never brought any of it up again. I sensed I had, that day, come near to something that mattered to her as much as I did; and in the end, I suppose, I didn't care to know more. What I didn't realize was how very near I'd come to all that was hidden within her, all she held shaded away. Now I think of things that happened, things she said in those years, and they strike me differently. Now I hear the shadows in her voice I didn't hear then, and the strength. I see the depth and age in her eyes I didn't see before. I didn't see the face within her face; didn't see it, didn't try. She never said what was wrong. Aside from that one time, I never asked.

She was my little girl, I wanted nothing to be wrong with her. Nothing with her, nothing with us. She was my little

one, a *ghrádh*, my love, and she had come along when I
thought there'd be no more brides for me, when I thought
certain times were gone for always. I couldn't bear to think
of anything about her blighted, harmed, hurt, and I realize
now how often when I saw the trouble in her I turned from
it. What did I know of her then, in those early days? I knew
what she told me; what she wanted to tell. I knew what I
saw; what I wanted to see.

PART TWO

NEWARK, NEW JERSEY
OCTOBER 10, 1905

THEY were here again today. This morning; a detective in the lobby. I saw him when I went to buy a paper. He was slouching under the Continental Hotel Bar sign, he saw me all right. He wanted me to see him too, I'm sure. Up in our suite I said nothing of it. She knows somehow, all the same.

She sews; I pace. She has learned not to pass the window, I pass it continuously. She avoids asking what I see. I avoid mentioning the man by the lamp post, watching me watch her. I look him murder. She snips out new fringe—fringe for the costumes on her lap, those short Western skirts, and lace-holes for the leggings; skirts for Little Sure Shot, leggings for the Maid of the Western Plains.

With the mood on me tonight it's easier thinking of finishes, not starts. Just now I'm unable to call back quickly the first day I saw her in that costume, the day we started our life with the Wild West. What comes back clear as air instead is the way it finished for us in that train wreck three years ago.

Last time we saw the Wild West it was scattered all over some godforsaken railroad embankment somewhere between the last and next-to-last stand of the '01 season, somewhere in the middle of North Carolina and the middle of the night. Ninety-two horses were killed in that wreck, horses we'd ridden and slipped bits of supper to for years; some of them crushed in the corral cars, some of them sprawled on the ground, speared on shafts of wood, guts spilling onto the tracks, eyes wild, screaming and screaming into the darkness till the cowboys shot them. I can hear it still.

I can see it still: us shivering there with the rest of the company, blankets over our shoulders, glass under our feet.

Everyone squinting in that cold white glare from the engine's headlamp, the headlamp of the freight train that hit us. Everyone suddenly seamed and old in that light, Bill Cody in his purple dressing gown, gray hair rumpled, leaning over the crushed ribs of his big white horse. All around us wagons pulling in, lanterns swinging, and a rising rush of voices: people coming in from the town nearby and men shouting "Clear the tracks" and the advance man saying what about the fifty dozen eggs and the hundred-five gallons of milk he'd arranged for. Someone reporting the buffalo safe and someone closing a deal to haul away the horses for the price of their hoofs and hides; two boys making off with the twisted gilt letters ripped down off a car: BUFFALO BILL'S WILD WEST. And then Annie wavering on her feet, sagging against me. That evening, what would have been the last evening of our last season, she was in the hospital, her back bruised and her hair gone white at the roots. Now I think of that night, that wreck, that finish as I watched her head bend over her sewing, her hair grown in the color of the sheets on the bed behind her.

I thought I'd gotten over the shock of it, her hair. She has, though she wept helplessly into mirrors for months. She only wears the wigs onstage now; at Pastor's, in matches, she looks the same as ever to the crowds. We were coming back so strong on our own, damn it, when this Chicago business stopped us; stopped us and set us to looking closer at each other, I suppose, and I'm stunned all over again by her hair.

It's not what I should be noticing about her, my wife with her young girl's body, her still-young face; not her ashen hair. It's not what I should be remembering about the Wild West either, the wreck. As if that's all that ever happened to us there—our family, our home, hometown all those years.

The good old days.

Well, and so they were.

We were so happy there, mostly, there where she became who she is, there with that big clan ringing us round, putting the old fears at a greater distance. She stopped looking for faces in the audience there; the arena was too big, she said, too hard to see. I know there were still those times, the troubled ones, and I know I didn't see them often enough, not for what they were. But there were less of them there, I think; or maybe that's how I want to remember it.

I want to remember it right. But those good years, they're a part of this story too—those spans of tranquil time when the Wild West carried us within it like one of those enchanted cities from my childhood tales: the kind that reappears now and again, here, there, perhaps everywhere, and then vanishes in the night, somehow beyond the rules and regular hours of the world it visits.

O UR second summer with the Wild West a woman traveled two days in an old spring wagon to see the show play Staten Island. She had brought with her several of her children; one, an ailing baby, died on her lap during the afternoon performance. The woman carried the baby outside, laid it down in her wagon, and went back in to watch the rest of the show. A canvasman noticed this and, believing the woman to be in shock, told us about it directly after the performance. With her costume still on and a ten dollar bill in her hand, my wife went out on the lot and found the woman sitting on the tongue of her wagon, surrounded by four or five ragged children. Annie asked about her plans for the burial; the woman looked up matter-of-factly and said she didn't have any. She planned to see the Indian tepees and the bronco corrals. She planned to see the evening performance. She could bury the baby anytime, she said, but she might never in her whole life have another chance to see Buffalo Bill's Wild West.

That stays in my mind now as I think back on our time with the Wild West, how it was. Of course when we joined up the show wasn't famous yet, wasn't yet what it became;

just shinnying up its third season, sixty thousand in debt, hoping to lure more crowds from the circus. And this was no circus, sir, thundered its press agent John Burke, in a bar where we'd met on the road. *Circus*: he didn't much favor that word, this was different, this was educational, this was *history*—picture it, Mr. Butler, a visit West in three hours, part rodeo, part theater, can't you see it now—riding, roping, rip-roaring dee-splays of Western skills; rootin'-tootin' dramas of Western life, raids, rescues, right-over-wrong, starring the great cavalry scout Bill Cody himself—may I call you Frank, it's a surefire showcase for a sharpshooter, have a cigar, think it over.

I immediately spotted John Burke as another Irishman with the gift of blarney, and I had my doubts about his outfit, we both did: this ragtag show, begun as some July Fourth "Blow-Out off in Nebraska"; this scout turned actor by some Eastern entrepreneur; this troupe of cowboys and "critters"—doubts we had indeed, that spring of '85, when we came to give it a try.

I remember that ball park in Louisville, Kentucky, where the show was set up the day we arrived. The ground was mushy from April rains, slurping at our shoes as we ran through some stunts for John Burke and Nate Salsbury, Cody's partner and manager. Everyone else was out at the parade that noontide so they sat alone in the stands, Burke big and untidy, his belly doming his vest, his face the color of rare roast beef; Salsbury small and trim beside him in that top hat and cutaway he liked to sport—us in front of the blood-and-biscuit-colored buttes painted on the backdrop, both wearing new Western-style costumes Annie had made us. I'd sold the act for the first time as a "single," her doing all the shooting, me doing all the managing and throwing the targets; a stroke of genius, I'd thought, but her heart wasn't in the act that way and it showed. Even though her shooting was dead on, there was something so hesitant, so subdued about it that Nate just sat there afterwards, spinning his hat on his finger, his thin face thoughtful, his fingers in his beard. He conferred softly with Burke who finally strode down to us, tucking in his shirt, and the first word he said to us was "Pictures." It was a question and he repeated it,

"Pictures, pictures, show me, nonono not those, tintypes, place downtown, tell 'em we want her in costume, we want her with the rifle, we want her with a genuine dead rabbit in her hand. Genuine, understand. Ever hear of P. T. Barnum? Forget him. He likes humbug, we like genuine. We got genuine Sioux, we got genuine Wichita, we got genuine cowboys from North Platte, we want a picture of a genuine girl sharpshooter with a genuine dead rabbit, see if the crowds pop for it, three-day tryout, we like you by then, you like us, we'll talk, good, fine, supper's at five."

We were back at the ball park by sunset with a sheaf of tintypes: Annie in her fringed skirt set against the peeling sylvan backdrop of the photography parlor, the doubt in her eyes as genuine as the rifle on her arm, the rabbit in her hand. We paused at the gates an instant, some sense of strangeness overtaking me too as we stood there, looking again at the Wild West's show lot.

It spread before us like a village, the peaks of its tents slanting into the long evening light, peach-colored light sliding down steep-pitched canvas, pooling in the crisscross of paths below. The Indian tepees clustered together like an assortment of bright paper hats, tents and tepees all overhung with a smell of hemp and horses, wood fires and steak chops and poster ink. We passed the ammunition wagon, its glass target balls set out to cool like muffins in dozen-cup molds, and we passed some Indians still costumed and painted from the arena, eating Cracker Jack and swinging in a pair of red hammocks. From the corral we could hear the lowing of steer and then, as we drew near the cook wagon, the *nick-nick-nick* of maybe fifty loaves of bread being sliced. I remember the smell of carrots, all those carrots, all those onions simmering over an open fire in a kettle the size of a bathtub, and a basket of coffee grounds deep enough to pot an orange tree in. Serving boys were weaving back and forth between the cook wagon and the mess tent behind it, the tent with its flaps rolled up and a haze of smoke hanging over its red-and-white tablecloths.

We hesitated on the edge, trying to pick out the faces of Burke and Salsbury, and the rumble of voices stopped abruptly. Annie's hand tightened on mine. The eyes of fifty

Indians, fifty cowboys, twenty Mexicans, and eighty crewmen were suddenly upon us, and then there was a slow shuffling as they all rose to their feet in the presence of a lady. Directing this rise was a man whose face had gazed out at us from glossy posters and dime novel covers: the dark hair long to the shoulders, the trim goatee, the eyes that said *look here*. He had a way with him, Bill Cody, coming toward us at a leisurely lope, fringe swaying on his jacket, a diamond pin winking from the knot of his red neckerchief; except for that diamond, he still looked more like the scout and buffalo-hunter he'd been, less like the actor he'd become. Every move drawled out of him loose and easy, bending over her hand, gripping mine, and then there was that rich rippling baritone introducing us to all. He touched the air as if to sign it; his company formed a double line, and he motioned us to follow him down its length, shaking every hand: rough hands cuffed in plaid flannel, calloused hard hands, bronze hands ringed with bear teeth, hands reaching out from under blankets and serapes, and after the last hand was shaken the eyes were still on us. We sat in silence through the soup and the steak, hearing the clink of every fork. I could see spots of color on Annie's cheeks, the tip of her nose; myself, I had the worst case of fidgets since I'd left the Church. We were relieved when the meal ended and we were shown to our tent, and that first night on the lot we sat up talking cross-legged on our cots, still half wondering what we were doing there, wondering if we'd stay.

"Doesn't feel like the circus," I said, "bless God."

"Sure doesn't feel like vaudeville," she said, and sighed.

"We don't have to stay."

"We may not get asked, you think? Salsbury, you saw his face."

"Just playing it tight, waiting to talk terms, I'd say."

"I don't know. . . . Jimmie, we ever see any of those dramas Cody did when he came East . . . *Scouts of the Plains, Scouts of the Prairie*, names like that?"

"Buntline's stuff—not one, why?"

"Salsbury asked me if we had, I sure wish I'd said yes."

"Me too, I told him we saw every one twice. Well, it won't matter, the act will."

"It's down, I know it." She pushed her hair back and sighed again. "It's me—just feels all wrong as a 'single.' "

"It's just new."

"Don't you miss it?" she said after a long moment.

"Right there with you."

"I mean . . . Butler & Oakley."

"We've been through this, darlin, the act's sharper this way, who else has a girl marksman? Believe me—I'm better at the managing, you're the better shot."

"No," she flared up. "No, I'm not, I won't be, not if it means it'll change, like those other teams—one gets the billing, next thing you hear they've split up."

"That's not us." I shook my head. "Those teams, they both of them want the lights. I'll always be happier writing the deals in the back, don't you know that?"

"It's just . . ." She looked at her hands, at the glint of her ring in the light. "It's always been the two of us."

"It's still the two of us. Always."

We were quiet a minute, watching the tent breathe around us in the night air like some great gray genie squatting over our heads. We'd sat up late talking in hundreds of boarding house rooms hundreds of nights, but this was the first time we'd ever whispered, trailing off, listening, and listening again. There was no sound from the town beyond; only the whicker of a pony, then a bleat from the corral, the breeze fingering ropes and canvas, and from the lot's edge the sound of a guitar. We joked that it was the press agent but knew it was a cowboy, their tent lay that way. We knew too that in spite of ourselves the spirit of the place was starting to reach us there, our roof sloping sharp over our heads, the grass stretching away under our cots, and that sense of a camp pitched all around us, as it happened that night, under a skyful of stars.

Annie was more covered up than usual, well aware she was the only woman on the premises; that sweetened the sight of her to me all the more. She had engulfed herself in a voluminous blue wrapper she seldom wore, but the wrapper had come open as we talked, showing the curve of her thigh and that small mark like a tiny raspberry inside it, and I drew her against me, her mouth warm on mine, her arms slipping off the silk, and handfuls of her hips I pulled down on me, our cot creaking loud in the stillness, till all at once we heard whistling on the other side of the canvas. It sounded as if it was right above our heads. I felt her breath catch against my neck, felt her stifled laughter. The whistling moved off a few feet and turned into humming, then soft singing in the unmistakable baritone of Bill Cody, *tenting tonight, tenting tonight, tenting on the old camp grounds.* The singing and shambling of his boots grew fainter then, but even after we were drifting toward sleep we heard it like a bright thread on the darkness, and whenever the breeze brought it back I'd feel her smiling into my shoulder. We heard him often throughout the years, walking his camp, keeping watch over all, but we never did know if he heard us that night.

I can't say what one thing broke the strangeness for us. Maybe it had something to do with that night, that whistling somehow. Maybe it had to do with being a part of the Wild West as it moved the next day; it worked like a road show, it looked like a roundup, and it traveled like an army.

It traveled, that next afternoon and overnight, with ammunitioners, hostlers, blacksmiths, veterinarians, pin-drivers, canvasmen, confectioners, butchers, and cooks; it traveled with the fanciest stoves and the foremost stabling and the finest portable fifteen-seat privy on the road. It traveled, with its cowboys and Indians and buffalo, on a passenger train it boarded, invaded like a band of pirates, taking over five cars and hanging out the windows, and as the train pulled out there were girls running alongside, waving, blowing kisses, hollering "Tommy-Johnny-Willy, you come back, you write," the cowboys waving their hats, tossing kisses back, and behind the girls on the platform stood men in longjohns and suspenders, staring wistful-eyed at the cars lurching by. The train stooped over us, seating us, settling us, squeezing us in two by two as if into some unruly ark; in with the smell of leather and urine and plush, in with the swearing and guffawing and the shuffle of cards, with the smoke and the speech we were starting to know, Cody talking slow and Burke talking big and Nate talking fast: Nate strolling up the aisle in his velvet-collared coat, with that patent-leather voice and the eyes of a priest, a kindly pastor, ministering to the men and the boys and the baggage; elegant, amused, gently advising, "Gentlemen, do avail yourself of some soap, next stand, the excellent *savon* we display for your use in the bath tent, and if, gentlemen, during the next stand, you seek a bit of *divertissement*, do refrain from urging her to follow you to the train, to hurl herself, as it were, after you down the tracks, the general idea is to appear wholesome as pie for the people, need I elucidate further?"

It was Nate who first detached himself from that staring tobacco-spitting army and came to crouch beside us, showing Annie pictures of his wife, every female relative he could find, and telling of his years as a song-and-dance man in vaudeville. It was Nate who waved over Johnny Baker, a gray-eyed kid who'd run off with the outfit and who sat by Annie in a cheap shiny suit too short in the sleeves, glancing up at her with the shy expectancy of a boy about to pass a note in school. Both of them were with us when the conductor came through, spotted Annie apparently stranded in the midst of that raucous crew, and hurried over, aghast.

"You're in the wrong car, ma'am, this bunch here, they just took it over, sorry, very sorry, a lady like you trapped with these circus types." He dropped his voice. "Sitting right next to one."

"That one," said Annie, "is my husband."

For an instant the conductor's face swung above her like a lantern; then, assuming she'd made a joke, he emitted a short little laugh and urged her again from her seat.

"These men," she said, "I'm with them, really." The conductor's eyes changed, taking on the slick darkness of raw liver.

"You can't tell me, madam, that they're *all* your husbands."

"No," Annie said, hearing the sudden silence around her. "No," she said, a new gleam in her own eyes. "Brothers."

And so it seemed, as the conductor scuttled away through the whistling, stomping "Heyheyheys" of the car. More and more of the men came to squat in the aisle by us, talking, teasing, offering smokes, and that night as we leaned our seats back into that snoring brotherhood, we felt more at ease than we had, bolt upright, in the mess tent. At dawn the train pulled into Toledo, Ohio, and we rode into town packed all together in the wagons, stealing in like raiders about to take the city; moving through the slim lilac light past the silent courthouse, the shuttered grocery, trailed by milkmen and paperboys and dogs, torches marking our way to the lot. And once on the lot Nate and Johnny shepherded us again as we walked around and watched the show pitch, putting up with the precision of a seventeen-jewel watch.

Within thirty-five minutes the cook wagon's stoves were lit and its three sides let down and it was serving breakfast, its coffee urn catching the first of the sun.

Within forty-five minutes they were liming the privy and haying the horses, and the tents were spread flat on the grass like folded dinner napkins, awaiting their ropes and pegs.

Within an hour and fifteen minutes the tenting was almost up and noon dinner was started, the smell of soup floating through the *tunk-thunk* of the pin-drivers and the *whup* and crack of canvas shaken out like sheets on a bed.

Within an hour after the street parade noon dinner was served in the mess tent and Annie was again ill at ease, not because of the men or the meal, but because within another hour the show would start and she'd be on. Nate said she'd be on first, right after the Grand Entry; she was to start with light charges and slowly increase them, readying the animals and audience for the rapid-fire blanks to follow. More than that, we knew, she was opening the show; it was up to her to hook the house right off.

"I'll always remember that—me all nerved up, walking back behind the backdrop that day, first show," she said. "I think of it now when I can't sleep, just play it over and over in my mind. And I can see it, I'm moving, I'm out there, out there on horseback, all of us out for the Grand Entry—the bugles, lights, and faster, once around, I can feel the hair jumping off my neck, I see Bill Sweeney turning from the band to throw me a wink, and I can hear the cheers from the crowd, the faces blurred, unrolling like wallpaper. And there's Frank Richmond, so tall, taller with his top hat, megaphone coming up and—I know this in my sleep too—'Ladies and Gentlemen—The Romantic West Brought East In Reality—History Itself In Living Lessons'—and there go the cowboys out ahead, red shirts, white hats, ponies half wild, and there, the Indians screaming in after them, all those feathers—red, green, yellow, flying down their backs like kites, the crowd whooping at them, and then, the applause louder, I can see him from the tail of my eye behind us, 'Ladies and Gentlemen, the Honorable William F. Cody Presents the Wild West'—him on his big white horse, diamond flashing, horse down on one knee to the stands—up again, hat high, and the crowd cheering us all off. Next thing, I hear it, my name—'the Little Maid of the Western Plains,' and we're out there, just us, and it's quiet, I'm cold, we start. Everything seems so slowed down, like we're under water, like it's a dream. The dime just drifts into the air from your hand, the wheel of candles turns so soft and lazy like an old spinning wheel. And then the cheers, and then it's faster, the guns feeling good, fitting me tight. Letting me reach. And I see the target over my shoulder in the mirror, glass shines—target breaks, I can feel each hit, feel them in my hands, my back teeth, and now the guns are louder, hotter in my hands, clay disks breaking up piece by piece— faster still, faster, more smoke, and I'm ducking down under the smoke to see, and I'm throwing my hair back and swinging and turning, loving it now, wanting more targets, more rounds, more shots—wanting to stay out there forever. And you're juggling the glass balls, glass starting to shower, cheers, glass breaking like balloons up there over my head, more cheers, it's over too soon, *walk-walk-bow*, I want more, and *kick-step-off*—back behind the backdrop into that mass of feathers, and all those Indians going thumbs up for me, *me*.

"After that it goes so fast, fast and loud, and the Indians are whooping out there around the settlers' cabin, arrows slanting, and Cody's chasing them, the crowd yelling 'Git em, git em,' the blanks cracking, people falling down, and then the Indians are back behind the flaps and the cowboys are charging out, out on the wildest buckers, on Suicide, on Dynamite, and then the buffalo are trooping in behind the backdrop with us, big shaggy smelly dears, there they go— stamping out with the Indians through one flap, cowboys charging back in through the other, and now they're wheel-

ing out the Deadwood Stage Coach, and Cody's yelling
'Water down that dust'—he's riding out to rescue the
wagon train, and back there behind the flaps everything's
smelling of horses, warpaint, gunpowder, and before I know
it we're out there again for the Grand Finale. And suddenly
it looks so beautiful to me, our procession there, red shirts,
painted backs, feathers blowing, all of it in that halo of dust,
dust glowing, and Cody's hat high to the stands, to us all,
and the band going into 'God Bless America,' the crowd
cheering, standing, yelling for more—and back behind the
drop again, whole company crowding in, mounting down,
rolling out smokes, loosening up, and there's Cody, still on
his horse, riding up and down, hollering at us, hollering out
his notes:

" 'Goddamn, when that Indian shoots you, kid, fall *down*,
Chrissake, not *five* seconds later, not *one* second later, *when*
he fires. . . . Chief White Eagle, gotta move your warriors in
on that wagon train faster, and *hey* you John Nelson, next
time you let reporters ride in the Deadwood Stage you make
'em empty their pockets first, there was nickels and dimes
shootin' outta that rig whole way around. . . . Hey allya,
listen up, next time the cavalry gets ambushed I don't wanna
see no dead soldiers on their feet before it's over, understand? . . . And *you*, you groundsmen, get that horseshit
outta those aisles double quick, you want some gent in a
white suit to send us a bill? . . . Grand Entry drooped, I
know all those cheering faces make a man a laughing hyena
with happiness, that's still no excuse. . . . It's damn good but
it ain't perfect and that's how I want it, you know that,
specially since one a these days this outfit's bound to play
New York City, that's right. One fine day we mean to take
on those so*phis*ticates, those *city* men, and knock 'em back
on their custom-tailored *asses* . . . meantime y'all best live up
to this lady's example here, that's right, she's with us now
on, her and her gent, if she don't mind my language . . .
that's right, we got a lady shot here gives us all plenty to live
up to in the arena, you seen her work, you know what I
mean. If not . . . *watch* her.' And he lifts his hat to me.

" 'Welcome to the family,' he says.

" 'They'll want that in writing,' Nate says.

" 'Pictures,' says John Burke. 'More pictures.' "

"It got to feeling like family so soon, Jimmie, and it got so I didn't want anything to touch it, turn it, spoil it for me. And so, when they started coming on the lot I cringed inside, I wished they'd go away, all of them, I shrank from them and tried to avoid their eyes.

"But I couldn't. Not for long. They'd be outside our tent, they'd be outside the trains. They'd be waiting, watching close, knowing who to come to. Who to touch. Who'd turn them away. I'd see them peering around the edges of the canvas. Slipping past the fences, under the gates. So dirty, so thin. And they'd stare, they'd stare with those big smart eyes. And I'd find myself staring back. They'd always pick me out. They'd always find me, those straggling children, those smudgy-faced beggars who came on the lot. Selling papers, shining shoes. Offering to take in washing and have it back before we moved on.

"I'd always find something for them, something to launder, I know you never understood. I know it was a nuisance sometimes, the times with the sharp-fingered ones, the ones who'd steal. The kind I shouldn't have trusted but I did. I knew them, thought I did. I forgave them, forgave them all. Even that girl who came, shabby, small, her face in the shape of a thin little heart. I watched her. How she'd learned to move quick. Getting warm at the fires, snatching scraps from the cook wagon. I knew she'd find her way to me. She had a mother, she said. A mother who did laundry, an ailing mother, so little money. I should have known better. I did know better. What was I thinking when I looked at her, what did I tell myself? Who did I see when I looked at her—I wouldn't ask myself that then. Wouldn't let myself think it, think anything like it. I knew my chest got tight, watching her, watching them. I knew it stopped when I gave them something. I gave that girl nightgowns to wash, hand-smocked, I'd embroidered them myself. I hadn't meant to tempt her—they were too fine for her, of course, I should have known. By the next evening I knew they were gone. Still, I looked for her face all the while we were packing up. Even at the depot I looked, I believed. I wanted to believe she was good, wanted to believe they all were—it happened again. Each time, I never told. Each time, I thought, they just need a chance, a start. And if I give it, they'll know it. And I'll know it. And everything will be all right.

"I didn't think anyone noticed. I didn't want anyone to. But of course John Burke, he was everywhere. It was right after that time with the girl, he invited that first orphanage, free, to the show in my name. Waif's Day: good copy, he said. He didn't know what it meant to me, I know. I couldn't talk about anything to do with it, not to anyone. Not even to myself. And surely not that night we were sitting around the mess tent, all of us, trading those stories.

"Remember? Everyone there, nine, ten o'clock, crowds all cleared off for the night, where were we, Des Moines? Everything quiet around us, July, warm, fireflies out there in the dark. The tent with its sides rolled up, catching the breeze. Just the roof and us in that big square of light. Seemed so safe, sitting there, everyone feeling good, fooling around— the hostlers had put a buffalo in the bath tent with some of the cowboys, they were still laughing about it, I've an idea you had something to do with that too.

"And then it started with someone, was it Nate, saying he was so poor when he was little he never had a bath till he was three or four, his mother just held him under the pump. And then one of the cowboys, it was Buck, saying that was nothing, *he* was so poor when *he* was a kid he didn't have a bath till he started to school and the teacher dunked him in a pond. And then Cody saying, hell, that was nothing at all, when *he* was a kid *he* was so poor *he* didn't have a bath till he was twelve, not only that, he had to earn money *giving* baths on Saturday nights to cowhands in the barbershop. And then they just kept going around the tables, everyone telling hard-luck stories about growing up, the stories turning sad as they went along. I remember you talking about coming over alone from Ireland, and Cody pouring a whiskey and telling how his father was knifed out in Kansas. And then it came around to me. And I heard my voice coming out fast and high saying, 'I don't remember anything like that. We always had enough. Always, even after my father died. We were clean, we were decent, we were a real family. We stayed together, always. My mother used to sing hymns with us, my mother said prayers with us every night, we were decent, we were clean, we were always together, no matter what.' And there was just a little silence. And then someone else was talking, and it was over with.

"Well, what did it matter what any of us really were in the past? We were all of us different now from what we'd been. Buck Taylor there, legs up on the table, he'd been so bashful when he'd worked on Cody's ranch he couldn't even say good morning, and now he was King of the Cowboys, wherever he went ladies were calling 'We want Buck.' And Dave Payne, next to me, rolling cigarettes, he'd just been a squatter out in the territories, now he was the Oklahoma Raider, the Cimarron Scout. And John Nelson, just a guide for a wagon train, and Blue Hall, Mustang Jack, all like that. The Indians—enemies, some of them, before, Noble Rock and Rain-in-the-Face with wounds from Little Big Horn. Even Cody was different, not that poor kid he'd been, not anymore. And what did it really matter? What did anyone care what we'd been before? What mattered was all of us together, like we were. We were there, we were good. We were all together and we were a family, and that seemed even stronger after Sitting Bull came."

Sitting Bull joined the show our first season, just a few weeks after us. He was there only the one summer; it seems much longer than that now. He came to us a villain, the slayer of Custer; came to us from Little Big Horn by way of the prison at Fort Randall and the reservation at Fort Yates and the Eden Museé waxworks palace where he'd spent time the year before. He left us as a friend; most everyone felt that way. I was one of the few who didn't, but Annie was closer to him than anyone.

When I think of him now, I think of him with her. I think of them riding their horses together in the sunrise, it still gives me a twinge. I think of him pounding in tent-pins as he liked to do with the drivers, her watching him with sewing on her lap. I think of him as he looked on the show lot, not in the arena: that short strong frame of his, ox-broad shoulders straining the cloth of a denim workshirt, the shirt tucked into striped railroad trousers; graying braids swinging to his waist with the rhythm of his mallet, his crucifix bobbing at his neck and his face, pitted from smallpox and shining with sweat, the color of a good saddle. "The Chief," everyone on the lot called him with a kind of cheery respect, even the roustabouts, even the Indians who weren't Sioux, but out in the arena that first time, the audience called him "you bastard."

We were in our tent dressing for the show when he arrived on the lot, escorted from his reservation by John Burke, and we didn't see him till we'd come through the flaps behind the backdrop after the Grand Entry. He was there in the Enclosure, standing up in a small buggy styled like a Roman chariot, his costume of fringed cream doeskin and his warbonnet of white eagle feathers floating out behind him to the ground. He looked imperious as a cardinal, as the medicine man he was, chief of the powerful Hunkpapa Sioux, glaring straight ahead with the expression my father used to silence us in church. He was glaring still as John Burke climbed into the buggy beside him and slowly drove it out to circle the arena. We pressed forward, all of us at the flaps, watching that column of feathers beside Burke's fleshy Irish profile, and almost directly we heard the audience start to hiss. The sound rose like steam from a kettle, then like steam from an engine. There were thousands in the stands that day in Buffalo and by the time the buggy trundled into its second circle the hisses were jeers, the jeers were a wall, "*Murderer, bastard, red coon.*" We caught a glimpse of Burke's face, red and moist, and Sitting Bull's, expressionless, rigid, save for the eyes which so clearly showed hurt I was surprised.

The buggy sped back in behind the drop and before it could stop the Chief had sprung down, brushing off Cody and Nate, stalking to the far corner of the Enclosure. He was there when we went on and we thought he'd be there when we finished, but when we came back in after the act he was right at the flaps, his eyes on Annie. He watched her in the Enclosure all through the show, and as soon as it was over he was following us to our tent with his interpreter Bill Halsey, Sitting Bull speaking all the while rapidly, gutturally, in Sioux.

He had a daughter, a daughter her age, his only girl, he said, standing there amidst the ordinary things of our tent, looking like an exotic bird in his feathers, drawing on the air with big calloused hands. Annie watched him, wary, intrigued, drawn to him already, I could see.

"The hissing," she said, "that cursing, sorry, they don't mostly do that at all."

He motioned as if to say it was nothing but his face was softer than the snap of his hand.

"I'm sure it'll stop if you stay."

He smiled. "I chose to come, stay," he said through the interpreter, Halsey's voice blending with the fresh rush of words. "Like the museum last year, the money was pretty." He smiled again and her laugh came out surprised, charmed. "One place I didn't choose, St. Paul city, they brought me there when they finished the railroad. Flags. Music. Crowds. They wanted an Indian chief to make a talk, two soldiers brought me from Fort Yates. One talked for me, no one else knew Sioux. I came out there on the platform before them and I said in my language, 'I hate you. I hate all white people. You are thieves and liars. You have taken our land and made us outcasts. So I hate you.' The soldier looked at me. Then he read out from the speech in his hand, 'I welcome you on behalf of my people to the West.' " Sitting Bull broke off, grinning at Halsey; then his laugh filled the tent like a hearty aroma, mingling with Annie's.

"I don't hate so much now," he added in his own halting English. He looked around the tent, hesitating then. "I break in," he said and moved toward the flaps.

"No no, not at all, what can I . . . tea, would you drink some tea?" she asked. He bent his head as if honored, sitting straight and still on the grass by a trunk while she brewed the tea over the spirit lamp. She served it, sitting cross-legged with him and Halsey, in her excitement forgetting my cup; I looked on, leaning up against the tent-pole. Sitting Bull cradled his cup in his large square hand as if it were an egg he might smash, watching Annie all the while.

"My daughter," he said again, "my daughter, your age. She had an eye, my daughter, your eye. She came with me when I hunted, this grown." He held his hand a child's height above the floor. "This grown, my daughter, just small, my girl gone."

He stared at the canvas across from him, lips set, eyes suddenly bright, and Annie's eyes were fixed on his face. I remember that look now, and their dark heads bent over the guns she showed him, and the sound of her voice stitching through his, like thread through leather.

After that he was at our tent every day.

He sat there as we moved east through Boston, where he was hissed again, and he was there as we moved north through Canada, where he was cheered. He liked to sit on a trunk and watch her sew, putting a finger on a knot for her; he liked to sit out front while she napped in her hammock before each show, warning people away and hushing anyone near—including me, to my annoyance. She watched him, in her turn, when he'd shamble around the show lot, whistling, quickly at home among the tents and horses, and when he'd squat by his tepee, selling his photograph, and especially whenever he'd move among the bootblacks and newsboys and beggars on the lot, handing out Cracker Jack and coins.

She watched him with Cody, smoking and speaking in Sioux; they'd known each other in the Dakotas during Cody's time as scout and guide. "*Pahaska*," the Chief called him with respect, Long Hair, but it was Nate Salsbury that Sitting Bull adopted into his tribe as a son, it was Annie he adopted as a daughter, and after that they were always together. The four of them would sit up late at night in the empty mess tent, clustered around a table, and I'd see them as if through a lit window, their happiness reflecting back at me. The Chief would be at the table's head, arms folded, beaming like a big papa; he and Cody would tell stories of the frontier, Nate and Annie sitting rapt as two children listening to parents talk of times before they were born.

"—riding that fast—"

Cody's hands long, fluid, sweeping the air, swimming through it to show a breadth of prairie, a depth of water.

"—river so deep, *Pahaska* charge—"

Sitting Bull's hands short, sharp, cutting the air as if slicing a loaf, then patting it together.

"—now Chief, I think you're exaggeratin' there—"

And the sound of their laughter; her laughter on the dark with the fireflies that summer, her hands fitting him for a coat like Nate's: swallow-tailed, velvet-collared, grand. "Like little white chief's," he'd say, and she would hold the material up to Sitting Bull, glancing from him to Nate, pinning up the goods, snatches of talk floating out all the while.

"Chief—watch the pins."

"Ah-ah."

"Velvet, look, just came."

"Fine as Nate's?"

"Oh, finer."

"Better tailor than Nate."

His hand on her hair a moment, light, quick. Pins in her mouth, catching the light, her face lifted toward him a moment, smiling.

"Turn, Chief."

"... beautiful ..."

"Turn."

"... everything so ..."

"Pins!"

"Ah."

"There."

Across his back, chalk marks; his head bent, voice tender. "Why so good to me, little one?"

Her on her knees before him, the cloth in her hands.

"Why so good?"

Her chin lifting, that shine on her face in the light. That shine and a quick breath, a shake of her head: her feelings too strong to speak.

When we slept on the lot that summer I'd hear the rustle of her clothes, the snap of her hairbrush as she hurried to meet Sitting Bull before the camp waked, to ride with him un-watched in the dawn. He was teaching her, she said, showing her stunts and slides to use in her act, the opening part on horseback. She would return in time for breakfast, her voice bright as fountain water, the words foaming from her; she'd look as if she'd sipped wine, been dancing, her face luminous and her eyes lit. It was from the riding, I'd think, but knew it was not. She looked that way when they hadn't been riding. I followed her one morning, ashamed of myself, unable to stop, skulking through the sleeping camp after she'd left the bed for the arena.

Most of its vast open space had already carved itself from the dimness, the tenting around its sides still shadowed. Light buttered the ground, lifting it into my sight, and across it I saw them, the dark shapes of their horses rising beneath them. Over and over they trotted, then galloped, then trotted again, the pale sun picking out his braids and crucifix, her flying hair. Over and over she leaned out, sliding fast down the horse's flank, aiming to snatch up a gun from the ground, and I could hear him calling to her, the sounds repeating, her voice touching his. The light grew and they came past again so I could see their faces: his, massive and flat, the flesh starting to slide off the bones with age; hers, smooth, small, taut with effort, and on both the same vividness, a sense of shared speechless joy wrapping them round like a shawl.

Something hot crouched in my chest. I turned and walked back alone without signing to them, without interrupting. As if I could, I thought, smashing a stone with my boot; as if I could. She had never shared the act with anyone else before. She had never looked so happy with anyone but me. I knew I couldn't get used to it, wouldn't try, and when he announced her adoption I ignored it. I never understood it, didn't care to, not till now with her telling me about it again.

". . . 'Hushabye,' he used to say to me, Jimmie, I'll always remember that. It was a word he'd picked up from some lullaby he'd heard somewhere, I guess he liked the sound of it. 'Hushabye, little one,' he'd say for hello when I'd meet him in the mornings, in the arena to ride, 'well, well, hushabye.' I still hear it, the way he'd say it . . . brisk, gentle. Glad to see me. It amazed me so, how glad he always was. Amazed me—mattered so much to me. Like the name he gave me. It mattered so much, what it meant . . . to him, to me . . . I never could talk about it.

"I remember how it was after the Chief adopted me, named me. John Burke went rushing out to tell the reporters, get it up on the posters. And there it was, all over everything, *Wantanya Cecilia*, Little Sure Shot. And I know, it couldn't have been better if John Burke had named me himself. But that wasn't what mattered to me. What mattered to me, so much, so much, was who I was named for.

"One of those mornings, early, out at the arena, he met me and he said, 'It's time.' I didn't know what he meant, but I followed him, watched him make a fire in the sunrise. He prayed to the sunrise, he prayed over the fire, chanting in Sioux. I can still see it, how it was. The sun coming up. And that fire snapping. Him swaying there, eyes shut, wrapped in that fine purple blanket. His hands spread, first over the fire, then over me. I'd forgotten till then he was a medicine man, not only a chief. And I understood, you know, what power he had, just looking at him there. I understood something sacred was happening. He lit his pipe from the fire, he passed his pipe to me. After he drew on it, he knocked the ashes out onto a rock, prayed again. And then he motioned for me to hold out my hands. He marked my hands with the ashes, a circle on each palm. And he laid in my hands a quiver of arrows, that plain leather quiver. His face was so sober. And he told me who had owned those arrows before me. Some of them were tipped with purple feathers, some white. The purple ones were his. The white ones had been his daughter's. The one who could shoot like me. The one who had died at my age. That was when he said her name for the first time. He said her name and he gave it to me. And for a minute I couldn't say anything. I looked down so he wouldn't see the tears in my eyes. And when I looked up, I saw the tears in his.

"I wish I'd told you that, Jimmie, wish I'd told you then. I held it inside, so dear—it was like that first can of top-grade powder I ever had, I couldn't make myself break the seal on it. I just kept it. Took it out into the fields with me, took it back in at night. I never thought I'd have another can of powder so fine. So many things, I've held like that. And shouldn't have. But with Sitting Bull, I know, you always wondered what was it so fine. What did it come to, really. How much could he give me, just a summer like that. He gave me a quiver of arrows. A warbonnet. A name. And something else, Jimmie, I don't think I realized then. Then I just thought, This is a friend I must have, no matter what. But now I think, somehow, he gave me a little piece of time I lost. Time I missed with my father. Time I wanted so bad.

"I never talked to him about my father. I never talked to you about him. I've never been able to. Never been able to think of my father without the bad times coming back . . . times that started when he died . . . that never would have happened if he hadn't. Times I never wanted to think about, talk about again. And how often I wanted to scream, Why did you go, why Papa why? And how often I wanted to say, Look at me Papa, look at me now. Look how I can shoot, Papa, look who I grew up to be, oh Papa Papa can you see. And that summer I felt how it could have been. That summer I had it. I had it with Sitting Bull.

"Was it wrong, him making me his daughter, seeing in me a girl who was dead? Was it wrong, how I saw him? Maybe it was, maybe it was foolishness, I don't know. But what pleasure it gave him, teaching me that slide, how patient he was. And how it made me feel, seeing him so proud. I'd ride with him and think of sitting up on the wagon with Papa, that great treat, going with Papa to town. I thought of it that summer and for the first time it didn't hurt. For the Chief, just for an instant, maybe he was teaching his daughter to ride fancy. And for me, just that one summer, it was as if the bad times had never come, never touched me at all.

"I never said good-bye to Sitting Bull. The day he left to go back on the reservation, that last day of the season, he talked about the weather. The sky. The rain. He saw a hard winter coming. And he talked about death. His, he could see it, he said. I wouldn't listen. I didn't want to believe what he saw. I always thought I'd be with him again. I always thought he'd come East. Or we'd be playing out West, and I'd see him in the audience, him sitting there so proud. 'That's my daughter,' he'd say, 'my daughter.'

"And why not? Cody said we were started, we were going places—said we were on a roll, a sweep. We'd travel the country north, south, west, but first we'd take on the big time, first we'd take on New York. And that's what we ended up talking about, that last day. 'After New York, Chief,' I said, 'see you then.' He just stood there in his railroad trousers and his fine new coat, touching that velvet on the collar, tents coming down all around us. I saw how his eyes filled. He shook his head. So I said it again, firm, for both of us, 'Chief, after New York.' But all he did was touch my cheek and say 'Hushabye.' "

T HE day she almost died near the start of the next season was the day Buffalo Bill's Wild West opened for the summer to play New York.

All around us on Staten Island were reporters and photographers and all through the company there was the feel of conquest, and in our tent there was darkness, the flaps down. Outside on the show lot at Erastina Woods, the tents were decked with feathers, with flowers, and at night with the city lights shimmering across the water, we felt even more like a far country that had washed up alongside real life in the night: high life, in this case, the capital of the big blasé East. Beyond our tent there was noise and movement; inside a hush, her face chalky against the web of hair on the pillow. How she had looked forward to this opening, how she had wanted to be here.

I sat watching her, hearing the sounds from the lot, smelling medicine and illness, and I felt a terrible fury at her for bringing this on herself, bringing it on with her own stubbornness, with a slyness too—all because she couldn't miss a goddamn parade. The fury in me; the sorrow. In the half light her new trunk sat up tall, the new Heckert & Miesel theatrical trunk she was so proud of. It opened out like a dresser, and I could see her scent bottles on the top, the light wavering inside one, and her hairpins, her combs and earrings, the greasepaint she put on for the arena, the cream to wipe it off, the corset I had unlaced from her that lay still formed by her breasts—all the tender chaos of her coming over me so strong it blurred in my sight; chaos she never would have permitted if she'd been well.

It had begun as an earache, perhaps an insect bite inside the ear, worsening as we'd worked our way up toward New York from Washington, D.C. I'd no idea how bad it was, she'd never said a word. I only knew there was pain by the extreme of her silence, the set of her jaw, and the night we shook down on Staten Island, the night before the big Broadway parade, her skin had blazed against me in bed. By next morning one side of her face had started to swell, her eyes gone glassy with fever, and even John Burke agreed she shouldn't ride in the parade.

Her eyes followed me around the tent as I dressed; I was going into the city with the company, them on the ferry to the parade, me to find a doctor to bring back. Her eyes flickered from me to her costume, the new one she'd made especially for this day, working on it for weeks, cutting it out and piecing it together in the tents and trains. I knew how much she'd wanted to wear it and I swept it out of sight into the trunk. Her eyes showed no disappointment; her teeth chattered. She was lying quiet when I left her there, an Indian woman sitting by her in the darkened tent.

Cody and Nate and I clustered together on the ferry, speaking of her in low voices while we waited to start, and then I saw Nate's eyes widen, staring past my shoulder. I turned and saw her riding up the ramp on her horse. Over her sidesaddle her skirt spread evenly, fringe flat, pleats crisp. The roses embroidered on the side panels were perfect. The shooting medals glowed from her blouse like dozens of large coins. Her leggings, pale blue to match the costume, were evenly laced. Her lucky silver star was pinned, just so, to her hat-brim. Her hat was tilted to shadow the swollen side of her face, and her face was the color of ashes.

It was too late to send her back, the ferry was moving out into the water—as she had calculated, I realized. She didn't meet my eyes, not then, not lining up for the parade either; it was all I could do not to shake her as I sat a borrowed horse and watched a chill set her shivering in the saddle. But she stayed on that horse all the way up Eighth Avenue and across Forty-second, all the way down Fifth Avenue, down Broadway to the Battery, past the houses and offices and hotels, the crowds ten deep on either side, the Indians shriek-ing out ahead of her and the June sun flaring in her eyes. She stayed in line, back straight, she waved, she took the corners at the right angles and she passed out only after she was back on the ferry again four hours later.

"*Blood poisoning*: I heard the doctor say it," she told me. "But it made no sense, I didn't even know how I'd gotten back to our tent. And then I heard my voice screaming, screaming as he lanced my ear, I felt that pain in my soul. *Soup*: you said it and I'd forgotten what it meant, leaning against you, letting you spoon it in. Your face, always there, so serious, yours and Nate's. Nate there whenever you went out, I remember he sat and brushed my hair one time, braided it, didn't know what else to do. *Great little trouper*: that was Cody, his face there all of a sudden, he said that again and again. But I hadn't really done it for him, for the trouping. You knew that. I'd done it because . . . because I wanted to be out there. Well, it was New York! It was the only parade of the summer. And I just had to be out there, in that costume of mine, I wanted that time. Looking back now I see how godamighty stubborn I was. I see how I always guarded my good times . . . so that nothing could touch them, nothing. And I guess as they got better, I held them even tighter, I'd have them no matter what. And if I had to lie there in the dark because of it, if I had to sweat in those sheets . . . if I had to scare you, scare everyone, maybe risk my life, well, I would then. I remember lying there, holding onto my costume. Running my finger over those embroidered roses. Figuring, figuring: How many shows I'd miss. How long I'd be down. Back then, I thought all you needed was the will to do something. And if you worked, you could have whatever you wanted. Work, will . . . all it took, I believed that then. Dying? I heard the doctor, I didn't believe him. I felt so strong. I would will that fever to break, I'd be back out there in five days flat. And I was. Oh Jimmie, I wasn't even sorry for scaring you like that. I didn't even think about it, not till you went silent-mad on me like you did . . . and even then I never said I was sorry, couldn't . . . but I'm sorry now, thinking back on it. That silent time, two days . . . if anything scared *me*, that did . . . that silence . . . all the old silences came back then . . ."

And she trailed off, her face saddened for a minute.

For a minute. Until I reminded her how the silence ended.

It was the second day I wasn't speaking to her, getting on for the evening show. It was time to get ready, get dressed, so I put the ropes up around the tent, dropped the flaps, and stripped down to my skivvies to shave. I could see her there in her old calico housedress, watching me, her shoulders hunched, hands pleating her skirt over and over; eyes so big, so miserable. From the corner of my eye, I saw drops of water from her bath clinging to the frill of hair at her neck, her hair up in a knot on her head. I was starting to weaken. I didn't want to weaken. I lathered up and looked in the mirror and started to shave. I guess it was a few minutes before I realized we weren't alone.

There was a couple just inside our tent. A lady and a gent with their Cracker Jacks, their programs, gazing around hushed and reverent as if they'd just walked into a church. Another instant and they were edging slowly around the tent, stopping to look at everything with that polite little half-step people do in museums; somehow they'd missed the rope outside, figuring, I suppose, that this was like the Indian tepees, Cody's tent—this was one you went through. And there they were, so polite, gazing at the pile of dirty laundry in the corner, the fold-up canvas bathtub, the bed—and then there they were, standing by Annie right in front of the washstand, standing with her watching me shave. I glanced at her. There was a glimmer in her eyes: she wasn't going to spare me this and tell them to leave, she was going to wait till they made me talk. I was damned if I'd break down. I went right on passing that blade over my chin, and they went right on watching, as if I were some Remarkable Shaving Man in a waxworks exhibit. I remember the *scrape-scrape* of the razor; the *munch-munch* of their Cracker Jacks. From the side of my eye, I saw Annie's shoulders beginning to shake with silent laughter. In the mirror I could see her eyes, brimming with it, and it was starting to catch, to tickle through me too; how I didn't cut myself I don't know. Finally, shaven clean, I blew the lather off my razor—and the lady and gent applauded politely and filed out. Then we couldn't hold back anymore, the two of us laughing, gasping, bending double, our eyes running, starting all over again—and she was back in my arms, that was the end of my silence.

That laughing, that giddiness: that's what I think of now when I think of New York that season, not sickness, not fighting. That whole year felt like that, our first smash year, all of us giddy all the time after that, knowing we'd done it, Cody crowing over and over, "Damn, we're good, we knocked those city people right out of their *hand*-sewn, *hand*-starched *drawers*."

And so we had.

The tall silk hats on the city gentlemen looked grand that year but not quite as grand as the Wild West's stetsons. The new electric arc lights in the city's streets looked stunningly bright but not quite as stunning, not quite as bright as the new electric spots and floodlights in our arena. The brownstones in Murray Hill, the Marble Row houses in the East Fifties were fashionable that season but not quite as fashionable as our tents and tepees. All those imported sparrows in Central Park, the new Brooklyn Bridge and the new Statue of Liberty's right arm waiting in Madison Square—those things were lookers but we knew we were too. Somehow we felt equal to the sights of the city, and somehow that year I think we really were. To the critics, to the crowds, to the reporters who slept on the show lot and wore their hair like plainsmen, there seemed no comparison with anything else in town. That summer on Staten Island they couldn't get enough of our bivouac a half hour from City Hall; that winter they packed big bulky Madison Square Garden, making it echo like the train depot it had been. That winter what outshone the new Metropolitan Opera House was the Garden with our Badlands backdrops, a block long, our new production of Custer's Last Stand, and our cyclone machine blowing tumbleweed from Madison to Fourth.

There was a place nearby called Ritzman's with a show window full of cabinet-sized photographs of celebrities. When we'd opened on Staten Island, I remember, the pictures were all of Lillie Langtry and Lillian Russell and Albert Niemann. By the time we'd opened downtown all the pictures were ours—Cody, Buck Taylor, Chief White Eagle and Jack Red Cloud and in the center, gazing gravely out over the words PEERLESS WING & RIFLE SHOT—my wife. We came to expect to see their faces. We came to expect to see our Indians stopping traffic on the way out of Macy's. We weren't surprised that the biggest swells wanted to take Cody to dinner at Delmonico's and we weren't even surprised when Western fashions started appearing on the streets, popular as the roller-skating craze that year. We saw skating parties in fringed jackets, we saw people skating to work in stetsons, we saw feathers in the hair of children. And not just children. We saw the names of our company in the papers with the names of Stanley and Livingstone and Teddy Roosevelt, and we knew, almost mystically that year, that New York belonged to the West.

Every show we sensed it from the stands. Every night we saw it in the walk, the stance, the look of the crowds streaming out of the Garden, and we felt it ourselves, watching as we often did from the back. When you left the Wild West arena you knew you'd been somewhere. Somewhere far. You came windburned from Madison Square Garden—windburned, weathered, lean; and tough, unquestionably tough. You were in stride, in charge, indisputably in the right. You moved from the stands with a certain freewheeling authority. Maybe you loped, maybe you roamed. You might even ramble. And nobody best mess with you. Newly brave, suddenly laconic, you hailed a cab with a jerk of your head. You got along home, confident of the straightness of your spine, the clarity of your purpose. And that night you'd lie back on your bed that was a bunk that was a bunkroll, and through your ceiling you'd still see the stars, smell the gunsmoke, hear the hoofbeats; that night and a span of nights to come.

We saw that in the people, we sensed it in ourselves, and we knew we were part of something bigger than a press agent's mirage. We were part of something bigger than we'd ever expected, going farther than we'd thought. We were going, at the end of that season, on the steamship *State of Nebraska* all the way to London, to play for the queen.

WHO can say how much they were with her then, those hidden times? During those years it must have seemed she had outrun them, gone out of their reach, but I never really knew; sometimes I think the only window I had then into certain quarters of her soul was certain hours, certain nights.

I remember waking after midnight in London to a sound in our rooms. I reached for Annie; I was alone under the quilt. From the bedroom doorway I saw her in the sitting room in the lamplight at the scrolled writing desk. Above her hung jubilee posters of Victoria; she fascinated Annie, this widow queen, her black-garbed figure and motherly face gazing down, fivefold, on the room. Under that gaze, spread out on the desk, were all the gifts the English people had sent since we'd opened: fans, handkerchiefs, gloves; a bracelet, a brooch, medals she'd won at the London Gun Club. The medals gleamed like crimped gilded tea cookies on their velvet tray; from the brooch a sharper glint, from the pearl-handled opera glasses a soft shine. Her fingers moved over each, touching them, holding them up to the lamp, turning them in her hand, these gifts she never wore, never would; they were too precious to her. She would keep them, watch over them in the nights as she did her new guns—her guns, of all her gifts, the only ones she would indeed use.

She had moved to the gun rack, selecting one of the shotguns custom-built for her by the great London smith Lancaster, a hammerless twenty-gauge weighing less than seven pounds, its grip checkered and its lock-plates inlayed with gold. She stood barefoot on the cabbage-rose rug, her hair loose to the middle of her back, the lace of her nightgown spilling over the forestock of the gun in her hands; she weighed it, balanced it, left hand under the barrel, right hand on the grip, cheek down on the comb, walking through the act. Down on one knee, her knee on a rose. Up at a crouch, face shining. Forward, faster, up and light, over the low sewing table, earrings bobbing. Big smile. Quick turn. Without the shots, the props, the band, the act's seams and stitches showed: the effort, the breathing, the sweat on the lip. Without the vast arena around her, she looked tall. She looked strong. She had power. It was her magic, this dance that kept back the darkness—Annie in the lamplight, swinging with the gun, spinning with it smooth and fast, holding it out, now as a woman would measuring curtains, now as a girl would learning a waltz, and how light it was in her hands, how it snapped and swept and fit to her, her gown circling white around her, the wink and shine of her treasures over her shoulder.

So many nights in London I saw her in the sitting room and in the mornings there would be shadows under her eyes, her hair tangled on the pillow, and it would take her longer to pull herself from the bed. Every morning even so, she was splashing her face in the basin by eight, calling to me through the rush of water, What offers had come in, don't turn any down, she'd take them, take them all, she'd do more today than yesterday.

There in London she was as well known as Cody. She wasn't what the English had expected of a "lady shootist," not some loud rough rawboned girl, and they were charmed by her; the shops copied her costumes, ladies took up shooting, perfect strangers sent marriage proposals. My blotter was piled with requests for lessons, private exhibitions, matches, even a drawing-room theatrical. She put a .22 through a proposal and sent it back; I booked everything else, between performances with the Wild West, and even when it started to tire her, tire me, we couldn't stop. I was signing deals, she was signing autographs, and none of this was happening unknown to our pockets: by July we were pulling in seven hundred and fifty dollars a week. And by the end of July something within the company had changed.

That April of '87 when we'd first arrived, still reeling from the rough crossing and feeling lost, everyone was up in our rooms every night—Cody and Nate and the company and crew, up there in our suite in the Metropole Hotel on Northumberland Avenue, near Charing Cross. Every night the suite would fill with laughter and smoke and the clink of beer bottles, me tying neckties for the cowboys to slip over their heads, Annie sitting in the big flowered easy chair, sewing on buttons, helping them write letters home, firmly marking the envelopes *Dayton* and *Denver* and *Dakota Territory, U.S. of A.* There was a rowdy hum of voices and the flutter of maps we'd pinned on the walls and stretching below the window, a thousand chimney pots and twisting streets, and from the open casement a smell of dampness and soot and mutton, the lilt of peddlers singing *Gingerbeer* and *New cheese*—London, so big, so old, grumbling, ringing, clattering out there all around us. It was good to see our own faces peering out at us from posters through the fog, good to be finding our way through the streets, grand to be topping our New York success in our first season abroad. But after a while, as the city grew more familiar, as the invitations came in, our rooms grew quieter. Johnny Baker still came, older but no less shy; Nate came, but never Cody, fewer and fewer of the cowboys. Nate, homesick, would spread out pictures of home and steer the conversation elsewhere whenever Annie asked him about Cody's growing distance.

When did it start? she'd ask, and Nate would only shake his head and show another picture.

When did it start?—I knew exactly. It was that very first time she was singled out that season; the first time she was ever singled out in public at all.

* * *

In her hands was the Stevens sporting rifle, smoking from the last shot. In my mouth was a lit cigarette rolled tight in Lucky Lady paper. From the side of my eye I saw her walk off the thirty paces; then spin, turn, snap the rifle up—and the cigarette was out. From the stands came the cheers as always, but not quite as always, *hurrah, hurrah!* She made her leap over the gun table and we heard them again: *hear, hear!* We swung into the last stunt, the glass balls, and I saw the spray of crystal in the sky above the ramparts of Windsor Castle.

The show was set up on the misted water meadows before its east gates, us with our moose and mules and steer, camped like invaders before this home of the queen and the Chapel of St. George and the Knights of the Garter. "You don't turn your backs on royalty, you bow out, understand?" Cody had shouted at us behind the backdrop; this was a command performance ordered by Queen Victoria herself, summoning us from our exhibition grounds at Earl's Court in Kensington where she'd seen us with the Prince of Wales. "You bow but you don't scrape, got that? We're the ones won the Revolution, remember, we ain't scared," he'd yelled, taking a swig from the flask in his hand; we were playing for most of the royal family and several crowned heads of Europe as well, there to celebrate the Queen's jubilee, but "never mind who's out there, damn it, we're Americans and just folks and proud of it, you hear?" Everyone in London that season, including the royals, seemed completely taken with "the Yankeries," but Bill Cody's yelped speech stayed in our minds nonetheless till the very last step of our act.

As we turned to the Royal Box at the end, the queen motioned us nearer. I made my bow; then Annie stepped forward and Victoria leaned down to her. With a rush of pride I watched my wife, her back straight and her cheeks flushed, holding her short skirt out in a perfect curtsy; those two small women together, the black bonnet bending toward the stetson with the star, the fringed black shawl leaning toward the fringed blouse, the ruler of the entire British Empire—and Missie. As soon as we went off behind the backdrop a liveried messenger appeared, inviting us to watch the rest of the show from the Royal Box. Next thing, we were following him behind the stands, Annie's hands flying over her hair, sleeves, skirt, smoothing and tucking, the whole of her quivering with the hopeful fear of a girl meeting her first beau. She flashed me her Oh Lord look; I flashed my Not Bad look, and we were there, halfway through the Indian Buffalo Hunt, taking our seats on spindly gilded chairs in the box behind a dozen other guests and the queen's flounced black skirts.

They were transfixed by the show, we were transfixed by them. We sat stiff and prim, as if in church, breathing in delicate sips; they were rustling and whooping and stamping their feet, slapping striped trousers and leaning from the box, even Victoria, in her widow's weeds, and nothing she did escaped Annie's eyes. Past the ridges of silken shoulders, past the queen's beaked profile we saw our arena stretching out ahead, the big open oblong warbling with Indians, and beyond the stands the castle rose, its gray stone like some massive windowed bone, its battlements layered behind the red-gold buttes of our backdrop. As the cowboys came bucking out on horseback, hats in hand, hands in the air, the queen's pale hands clapped and clasped, fluttering on the box's rail like doves on a perch. Chairs scraped back around us, sashed shirtfronts slipped by as Prince Edward climbed into the arena with four of the guests: the kings of Saxony, Belgium, Denmark, and Greece. With the prince riding shotgun up front and the kings leaning, crowing, from the Deadwood Stagecoach, Cody sent his long whip snaking out on the air and behind the mules the coach rocked off, once around, twice, three times, the prince waving his hat, "Yahoo, Mother, yahoo!"—the queen herself rising to wave her handkerchief, for an instant like a prairie wife waving at a passing wagon. She stood again for the Grand Finale, bowing as Cody rode forward with Old Glory, him as streaked with dust as any knight who'd ever borne a banner there; and above him, above the pins and pegs and pennants of the arena, the castle watched, sunlight slanting across the Round Tower like a great sundial. As we rose to leave the queen turned to us, saying in her high girlish voice how clever Annie was, presenting without flourish a small box. Inside it, on a bed of cotton wool, was a pair of pearl-handled opera glasses: a tribute to the sight of a performer, a sharpshooter, said Victoria, and Annie's eyes filled with unexpected tears.

When we came in through the flaps behind the backdrop, Cody was slouched up against the canvas, his eyes moving past the Indians, the horses, sharp as tacks on us. And after that it wasn't the same. After that he looked her sharp whenever she came in through the flaps, dressing her down and faulting her act in ways he alone could see. I remember him standing there, a mist of whiskey around him, rocking on his ice-bright boots, watch in hand: ". . . ran a minute long, Missie . . . you makin' *love* to them out there or what? . . . slow, Missie, *lackluster*, dull . . . limelight got you *dazzled*, eh Missie? . . . you can do better, *do* better then . . ." She never said a word, pretending to ignore him, her back turned, shoulders tight, pumping the unspent rounds out of her rifle, *cha-bink-cha-bink*; the sound repeated sharp as a retort, all the while stagehands stepped uneasily around them, and feathers and arrows flashed by in the arena. Cody's own shooting had started to suffer from the whiskey, and I began to spot a trace of satisfaction on her face, back behind the drop and hidden from all but me, whenever he missed a shot. She'd stand there smiling on Johnny Baker's new sharpshooting act, his round choirboy's face red with effort, his eyes straying to her, lighting up as she'd nod *go ahead, good*. Patiently, precisely she'd groomed him, taught him, but that was different, that trusting younger brother of a boy; that wasn't Buffalo Bill.

She'd never admit how she competed with Cody, as much as he with her: he had certain skills she couldn't hone as sharp in herself, but they weren't skills of the arena. She was the one praised in London for her shooting, sought for her craft and art, at exhibitions and matches. He was the one lionized for his showmanship, sought for evenings of drinking and talk at suppers and pubs. He had an easy way with him, a way with people, always glad to share "a glassa greeting," to lavish money on everyone, anyone within reach of a toast, a traded secret, a shared tear in the eye. It wasn't her way, it wasn't her strength, and it pricked her sharp for the first time.

It's a wonder to me now that I didn't try to stop it turning out as it did, but I was full of myself as an impresario then, smoking cigars and signing contracts. I came to favor the idea of a split, but though she knew it, she couldn't let go easy. Nor could she let go what galled Cody most: the press, the extra work, the extra money—money she noted carefully in her ledger with expenses, just as she had in those boarding houses on the breadbasket route through Ohio.

It wasn't the fame, she said then, not the fame she held to.

It wasn't the fame, she says now.

"It was the money, Jimmie. Thinking back, that's what I couldn't part with. Just having it, not spending it. Not throwing it away like he did. All those years *not* having it . . . years and years . . . what it meant to me, I can't say. . . . And Cody, well I guess I just figured he'd change once we left London. You know, we'd seen it happen so much in the business, heads turned, sometimes it passes. And I still thought it might that fall, season winding up. I didn't plan for it to come out like it did, that last day, that day he had me up to his suite.

"I still remember those rooms of his, that hotel in Picadilly—all his windows looking out on Hyde Park. Wood paneling. Marble fireplaces. Those andirons shaped like lions' heads. And then that valet of his, that hired valet with a face like a prune showing me through the bedroom—some actress asleep in the bed—and through the bedroom into his dressing room. And then I was madder than when I came in. All this talk he'd done about being just plain folks, I can hear him now—'Me, I was just a poor Pony Express rider, me, I was just a poor buffalo hunter out on the plains'—and how he was carrying on now. Airs. Valets. That honorary 'Colonel' in front of his name. Claiming descent from Irish kings. And me waiting there in his court, I guess, that dressing room was big as our sitting room—tall pier glass, enormous wardrobe, a chaise, and this row of silly hats on a long shelf. Whole place smelled of liquor and cigars. All I could see of Cody at first was this one hand holding a glass of whiskey, the rest of him behind this screen painted with a scene of hunters riding to the hounds, I remember. I don't know what the valet thought, he was there through it all, eyes on the rug.

"Well, then there was that voice—'Now Missie, glad you

could find the time to come, all them engagements you got and all, real glad you could squeeze me in.' I didn't say a word, and he came oozing out from behind the screen, real slow and elegant, leaning back on his chaise in his skivvies . . . just waiting for me to look shocked. I wouldn't give him that, not for this world. He poured himself another drink, offered me one. I shook my head. Looking back now, I see how stiff and prim I must have seemed—I didn't see it then. I wasn't feeling prim inside either, I wanted to choke him . . . him sitting there, pointing out clothes for his valet to take from the wardrobe, me standing there in my cape all the while.

" 'This sideline business, Missie'—he glanced at me—'I just know you'll quit it now, you didn't realize it crosses your contract, ain't that right?' He pointed at a pair of fresh drawers, and I just snapped that I knew my contract, it allowed sidelines if we didn't advertise, plain as print.

"He pointed at a dress shirt, a satin vest. 'Sounds like your husband talkin', Missie,' he said. 'Never could tell with you two, which one's got the brains, which one's got the balls.' I looked him straight. 'That's because they're spread so even between us,' I said, surprising him—surprising myself—and he threw back his head in a laugh.

" 'Now Missie,' he said, 'let's talk like friends here. You don't want to take away from your own show, your own outfit, your own *family*, Chrissake, heyhey, come on now.' I wouldn't let him jolly me along. 'Publicity for me's good for everybody,' I said, and I guess we could both hear the edge in my voice. He didn't look at me then, just downed his whiskey real slow and pointed to a big felt hat with a white plume. 'You know, Missie, you 'n' me, we both come up the hard way, you 'n' me both. You don't say, you won't talk, but I can figure from this and that, you come up hard. I been poor, I can spot poor. You're same as me, no better, hear me? You and me, we both know what it means to have nothin', we both know what it means to have it all. Leastways, *I* do, *I* do,' and he swept behind the screen with his clothes.

"The whiskey was making him mean, making him poke for tender spots. I should have realized that, God knows I remembered how drunks could be, what they could do to you.

But all I could hear was that voice roaring out from behind that screen, going on, getting louder. 'I know you, Missie, I know you, I can read you like a book. I know you love your *dollars* so damn much you ain't even able to *spend* 'em, no drinks for you, no nights on the town, no out with the boys, no *cabs* for Chrissake, you got no gift for *life*, Missie, got no gift like mine.'

"My face was hot. I put my hand out. I took that screen and so help me I knocked it down. It folded slowly, crashing over to one side, and there was Cody, naked as a jaybird, covering what he could with that plumed hat. I didn't blink. 'Say it, you want me to quit my extras, just say it,' I rapped out. And he hollered right back, 'You bet I will, you quit it all or you're out.' I said nice and clear, 'Fine, you lost us,' and I turned around and walked out.

"I was so ice-cold mad then I could have skated on it. That got me to the street. That got me blocks and blocks away. I was walking fast, head down, not looking where I was going. I can't say where I was when it started to sink in—I wasn't going back to the Wild West. It wasn't out there for me anymore, it wasn't where I belonged now. All of a sudden I felt tired. Chilled. And I kept making wrong turns. And the streets kept getting narrower. Darker. Smelling like vinegar, like garbage. There were no more muffin men, no more pie men. No more flower sellers. There were old women picking through the dustbins. A blind man with sores on his face, a harp in his hands. He called to me. I walked faster. More peddlers. Trinkets shaken in my face, jubilee charms, tin spoons, funeral plumes for cheap, for cheap. I walked faster still, faster, I walked right into them—the beggars, all around me, dirty children, sharp eyes, fingers picking at my skirt, my sleeves, fingers all up and down my cape, 'Penny for bread, mum, penny for bread.' On the show lot I could last this out, I could stay calm. But there was no show lot now, I was lost, the Wild West was gone. And those faces so close, blurring, faces like mirrors, 'for bread, for bread,' I couldn't breathe. I was pushing forward, grabbing for my purse, a penny—anything, anything to make it stop, that chant, that rhyme, and I could see the schoolhouse again, the steps, the door swinging open, stop it, stop it, *no one knows where she gets her clothes-es,* I could hear it, the circle around me, the smell of pitch-pine desks—chalk—puke—*got no rag to blow her noses,* oh God stop it stop can't breathe, the faces closer, closer, *Moses Poses Moses Poses,* and then somehow I was pushing through them, past them, I was running. I ran till I couldn't hear them, not looking around, not looking back, telling myself I was near our hotel, had to be, please God be, I ran till I couldn't run anymore.

"I looked up the street. Looked for the Metropole, for you, Jimmie, and half a block off I saw a man— Had to be you, I thought. That was your jacket, your shoulders, that was your bowler hat. I tried to catch up, too winded to call out, but the man went down a narrow iron staircase, behind a sort of railing—I figured it for a shop. I ran down the stairs after him, then on through the door, it was marked with a pointing hand.

"Inside, first thing I noticed was the floor. A mosaic of tiles with green leaves in a border, pretty, a little stained, damp. Second thing I noticed were the fish. Goldfish swimming in big tanks, eight maybe ten of them, the tanks set up high on the walls near the ceiling, greenish, pretty, kind of strange. Next thing I noticed were the urinals. They were ranged along the walls, each in a stall, eight, maybe ten of them, each one under a tank. I saw the copper ball in each tank then. I saw the waterline in one of them drop all of a sudden. There was a rushing sound, and the man I thought was you walked out, staring at me.

"That was when I realized where I was, what I'd dodged into—the shock of that almost broke the shock of those beggars. I stood there dazed, and I was still shaking, feeling all spun around when the cab pulled up to our hotel.

" 'All the world can't make a racehorse of a jackass'—I remember that was the first thing you said when I told you about Cody. What a relief—you seemed so pleased about the split, pleased with me, with yourself. And then, those new contracts, Berlin, Paris, we were free, we were on our own, glad of it, I can just hear the two of us going on like that, there at first. We didn't need Cody, oh no, didn't need the Wild West, didn't need anyone, we'd knock the world flat on our own.

"I guess the Wild West was on the train up to Manchester the same time we were on that train to Berlin. How quiet we were by then too. How different it seemed. Remember, overnight on that train, raining outside, our clothes all wet? What a pair we were, the both of us looking so beat-out, rumpled, I remember my eyes so red in the mirror, you needed a shave. And all around us, Europe like some kind of big dark sea, cold and strange. You know, I think that was the first time we really felt far from home . . .

"And then Berlin: So overcast. So damp when we got there. That room with the dark drapes, no heat, where was it, somewhere on Potsdam Platz. . . . Seemed like all the sounds of the Wild West were still in my ears there. The canvas. The horses. The voices we knew. Seemed like the tiredness of that whole season was in my bones too, and yours—us both flat out on the bed in our coats, waiting to drag ourselves up again and load those guns. It looked like it was getting ready to rain by the time we got out to that arena in Charlottenburg. I half hoped it would.

"You know, Jimmie, there we were, in sight of another palace, playing for more royalty. And all I wanted to do was go back to bed. There was the sky like lead, that crowd dead quiet. All those rows and rows of army officers. All those spiked helmets. I kept thinking of Weilert's, the music and noise Over-the-Rhine in Cincinnati. And all I could hear were the guns clicking, those clay birds breaking up. I felt so small in that arena. Stranded there. Still listening for the Wild West, I guess, for the Indians, the band. Every shot seemed hard. I could feel every bone in my corset. Seems to me it was like that the whole way, pushing it, right up till we did the cigarette stunt—till all of a sudden there was Prince Wilhelm, walking into the arena. I'll never forget it, him in that hussar uniform of his, right next to you . . . the way he drew out that cigarette . . . that gold case he had, remember . . . how he tamped it, tucked it in his teeth . . . jerked his head for me to shoot. And I was standing there thinking, if he moves even a little, what will they do to us. For a second I had his mustaches in my sights. My heart was so loud. And then there it was, the crack of the shot—and the ash, flipping over in the grass, I could see it glowing there. I remember the cheers. I remember shivering through the rest of the act. And curtsying, curtsying. And then both of us being bundled back to our room, chilled clear through.

"Well, I guess it's no wonder we were sick next day, no wonder we got packed off for home, not Paris—me arguing with those doctors, arguing till the last. And I still wish it had come out different. Paris. Cody. Everything. All the way back on the ship I thought about it. All the way back I felt scared, shaky. I kept hearing what Cody had said. I kept seeing those beggars. And I kept wondering, what if I'd made some bad decision for bad reasons. The wrong reasons. A decision that would ruin everything. Not just for me, Jimmie. For us, for you."

JUGGLING, I've always found, is the best way to concentrate my mind. I began as a boy with pebbles and now prefer ninepins, getting two in the air first, then adding a third, and if what's on my mind is serious, a fourth. It was juggling I did in our rooms nearly every evening after we got back to New York, thinking while she pressed the costumes, the flash of her iron in the light and the whisk of four pins in the air.

I arranged a series of matches for her, the first of which she lost to a champion English sharpshooter, her timing off, standing on her mark tight and tense, a winter wind from the Hudson blowing her birds and her hair. We came back hushed that night, the words and the wondering held within us. Sleet streaked the windows. Our room was in shadow. We undressed quietly by the fire. In the half light her body looked pale and suddenly very fragile, shining at me like a dimming lamp. She put down her hairbrush, put down her nightgown, and put out her arms to me. So tight she held me, so tight, her lips on my shoulder, her hands pressing me to her, and she was wet as a halved peach, and it was as if we'd never touched each other, the way we touched each other then, all night holding each other so tight, so tight.

We didn't speak that night or any other of the losing, the fear of losing again, nor would it have helped. The next match she won narrow, and the next one by more, and then she was winning a streak; we were working steady when the Wild West came back from England in May. We couldn't help noticing it, the paper was filled with its news. We couldn't help wandering out to Staten Island one Sunday, out to where we'd all been together on the lot at Erastina Woods, just to look through the gates, just to catch a glimpse of something we couldn't name filtering through the crowds. We stood there a good while, she on a crate, straining forward like a child at a parade. I could feel her homesickness for it, and mine, rising sharp as a bellyache. Second thoughts, stored speeches drifted on the air around us, but in the end our pride was too strong. We looked at each other a long minute, then turned and went home. It seemed good to get out of the city after that, to try another Wild West show, Pawnee Bill's, but it wasn't the same. It wasn't polished, it wasn't prospering, but more than that it wasn't the people, the family we'd known.

We drifted out to Illinois to see my brother, to Ohio to see her sisters, her mother: another of those visits to that plain frame house near Greenville, where the weather was discussed and the show business never mentioned; we drifted back to New York. Strange. We had always felt so at home wherever we'd been on the road for years, and all at once we felt not quite at home anywhere. I couldn't explain it, though I seemed to feel it less than she. Soon I was waking in the nights to find her out in the sitting room again, with the lamp. But this time she wasn't walking through the act, wasn't looking at treasures. This time she was at the desk, shoulders tight, her pen scratching fast across the paper— paper that was always cinders in the fireplace by the time I waked in the morning. When I'd ask her what was wrong, she'd only say she couldn't sleep, and after a month or so the writing stopped. She had moved from the desk to the window, watching there in the dark, watching something definite, it seemed, that I could not see. I'd come and stand with her sometimes before I'd take her back to bed, but all I could make out was the quiet street below and a row of brownstones across from our hotel. What was the matter, I'd ask again. Just thinking, she'd say, just thinking.

"I was thinking, what if there'd been no Wild West," she says slowly now. "What if there'd been no vaudeville, no act. Suppose we'd just settled down there in Cincinnati. In a house, in one place. I wondered then. I'd fought that so hard, all those years, I was ashamed to admit it. But that year I thought about it every night.

"I'd think of my sisters. I'd think of women who came back to see me after shows, matches. Women with children tagging behind them. How they'd look at me, so wistful. Envious. And something else. As if I was another breed. That year I felt it sharp for the first time. I was so different from them. These women, they had houses to keep. They had all these cupboards they filled up, and butchers, grocers, who knew their names. They had kitchens—and children. I was nearly thirty years old, and I'd never had that, any of it. Maybe if I had, I thought, I'd be smoother inside. Maybe I wouldn't have old things floating in my mind, wouldn't have time to remember.

"That year in New York, I started watching a house across from our hotel. Just a small house, narrow windows. Wrought iron gate. Nothing fine, like a thousand houses in the city. I don't know what there was about it but I watched it all the time. There was something about the washing on the line. All those shirts. A set of white napkins, flapping away. The lights, how soft they came on, early evening. How the teakettle whistled, late afternoons. I could hear it when it was warm out, windows open, I'd listen for that. And at night, how fast asleep the house looked, shades drawn. No lights. No one awake there, walking the floor. I used to sit and wish it was mine.

"Days, I'd look for the woman who lived there, I'd see her coming in and out. Tall, blonde hair, about my age. I'd watch her working in her garden that spring—a garden, we'd never been anywhere long enough for a garden. And I'd see her coming back from the market with her basket. With lettuces, bunches of leeks. And big round buns. And sometimes a leg of lamb. And her children hanging on her skirts, two little girls. Their high black shoes, the sashes so smart on their dresses, blue ones, green ones. And this one song they'd sing, 'If you knew my Jenny, if you knew my gal' . . . and in the afternoon, the teakettle.

"Watching that house, it gave me such a feeling. It made me forget how I'd felt before. And I made up my mind, if we ever had the money we'd have a house—with a flower garden, with a wrought iron fence. Well. Of course when we finally did have the money, when we finally did build our own house—of course nothing was that way. How long was it before we figured out we'd never be around long enough to raise those flowers? When did we realize we'd built that whole place without any closets—the two of us living out of trunks, just like always, there in our fine new house. Hiring housekeepers, firing them, them quitting—I never could get it just how I wanted it, just perfect. I guess it just wasn't our way, housekeeping. They say you never know a theater till you work it. Well, we worked that house and it just didn't play. I was so relieved when we finally went back to hotels! But sometimes, ever since, when times have been troubled, I think about houses again. I wonder about that life, I start wishing for it all over. Until I remember. I think of us clearing a chimney with a shotgun, oh Jimmie, I have to laugh. But if I'd known how it would be then, sitting there in that window, I'd have been heartbroken. That dreaming, it got me through that time, I think. Got me through till winter, till things picked up and we moved downtown. And I started sleeping nights again."

We might have weakened that winter and contacted Nate, but Buffalo Bill's Wild West had left New York. Then there were more matches for her, top billing at Tony Pastor's, and a part, mostly shooting, in a Western drama downtown. It was during the run that we came back to her dressing room after a show and found Bill Cody there; he was sitting at her table with the bottles and creams and boxes of shells, one of her shooting gloves in his hand. His old fringed jacket hung over a plain denim shirt; his hat was on his knee. He looked older, cold sober, his face puffier and his hair thinning. A silence dropped over the room like the lid on a trunk.

"Saw the name out front," he said after a while. "So I came on in."

"Good, good," I murmured and the silence came down again.

"Maybe you read about me," he said, his eyes on the glove. "Down in Washington? In the inaugural parade, President Harrison, you seen that?"

Sure we had, of course, we repeated each other softly, awkwardly, How fine.

"We, we went out to the Island, Staten Island, last summer it was, last summer," she said, and wanting to add something more, suddenly offered him the soda-fountain glass in her hand. Cody took it, balancing it on his knee with his hat, gazing into it an instant or two.

"Never touch phosphates," he said finally. "Specially lime. After a while, you get to know that about me. That, and you get to know I don't mean what I say when I touch the other stuff, don't even remember it, I like people to know."

"How's Nate?" she blurted out. "How's everyone?"

"Nate misses you. Misses you both. Would like for you to come see him, Frank. Talk business. Talk Europe. We're headed back, three-year tour, looks like."

He glanced at Annie. On her face was the look she'd had that day on Staten Island, that wishful straining in her eyes, her yearning in the air like perfume.

"John Burke, now he'd like that too," Cody went on. "Cowboys, Johnny, Buck, they'd like that. Think about it, you both." He put down the drink, then the glove. "*I'd* like that. Like for you to come back, Missie."

If he'd stayed a second longer he would have seen the tears in her eyes.

That April when the steamer *Persian Monarch* sailed from New York with the company, we were aboard. After the confetti and the streamers and the send-off, the Cowboy Band was still playing, playing on as we all sat down to supper at the red-and-white tablecloths from the mess tent, passing the plates and talking at once, like a noisy family together again. And through the voices, through the clatter of dishes, the clink of cutlery, we finally noticed what Nate had signaled the band to play: "The Girl I Left Behind Me."

BECAUSE of the lemon she knew it was summer.

Spices for autumn; jasmine for spring.

Ambergris for winter, and coats.

Because of the sachets she tucked in her trunks, she knew what season it was wherever we were, whatever the climate, whatever the weather, in all those years of traveling, of losing bearings, of forgetting the day of the week, the month, sometimes even the year. And because she knew, I knew.

Lemon was summer; witch hazel was evening, late afternoon. Wherever we were in Europe, that high thin smell was always there after each show when she'd give herself a rubdown, then lie back in her bath, that collapsible canvas tub we had in the Wild West for years. Morning was starch and hot cloth under her iron, then gunpowder as we hand-loaded the day's shells. Midafternoon it was tea and greasepaint, and late night, the chamomile rinse she'd have in her hair, the snap of her hair fifty times through the brush and the rushed murmur of her prayers.

These were things I came to expect, to rely on. These things she always did, same time, same way, kept my house and made me at home, clocking the days for me no matter where we traveled; they gave a shape to our life, a constant thread, even as the countries blurred and the show changed around us.

"What we got in mind," Cody said in the mess tent, somewhere along the Rhine—or was it the Rhone, that second sweep, or was it the third?—"What we got in mind's a bigger outfit, foreign-type riders, international-type flavor, understand? . . . Lined up right now we got genuine Cossacks, soon's we get 'em through customs, you make 'em welcome, hear? . . . All right, we also got genuine mounted French chasers—"

"*Chasseurs*," said Nate.

"Y'all listen to Nate le Salsbury, never mind me. We also got lined up some genuine mounted German—"

"*Ulans*," said Nate.

"—those'll be the boys in the iron helmets, treat 'em right, and next, Argentine Gauchos—thanks, I can say that just fine—and the British Lancers, we got an eye on some fancy riders from Araby—"

"Bedouins," said Nate.

"Way we see it, they'll get three, four numbers, ride in formation, circles, crosses, race each other, and at the end they'll all come out with their flags. We'll call it—"

" 'The Wild West . . . *and*,' " John Burke boomed out, " 'the Congress of . . . Rough Riders . . . *of the World*,' it's new, it's big, it's sophisticated, it's—"

"It's still *Buffalo Bill*'s Wild West and so forth, if I ain't mistaken," Cody said. "Now look, allya, no long faces over this, don't show me that. Wild West's still first, nobody's number's cut. Got lady riders now, Missie ain't kickin'. Still got all the old standbys, Deadwood Stage, Pony Express, Custer's Last Stand, just a bigger show is all. World got smaller, we got bigger, well I figure you oughta feel proud."

In Europe the show got bigger; the show got richer. We didn't walk on grass in our tent anymore, but on a wideboard floor covered with an Axminster rug. We didn't travel catch-can anymore, but on a sleek train with two sections and gold letters, modeled on the one back home, our stateroom fitted out comfortably with a brass bed and easy chairs; Cody's with chandeliers, a chaise longue and a bar. We had six trunks now, not two, filling up with foreign medals and Paris gowns, capes and camisoles and a Scottish kilt. Our gun trunk still held the muzzle-loader and the Damascus and the Stevens with their wooden stocks and plain open sights, but there was another Stevens, silver-plated now, and a pearl-handled Smith & Wesson .44, and a Winchester 30/20 with a gold-plated receiver. And tucked into all the trunks, in every corner, as plentiful as the sachets, those little bundles of gunpowder, Schultze Smokeless, a brand she'd tried in England and the only one she'd trust—and like Sanborn's Starch and Harmony Witch Hazel, one she refused to do without; she even packed our hot water bottle with Schultze and wore it as a bustle through French customs.

The show was bigger, richer, but a family still; a family in Paris, no heads turned by our first success there that summer —that summer of '89, the centennial of the French Revolution. I remember sitting with the outfit at a café, watching the celebrations on Bastille Day: wherever we looked there was a sunny spaciousness, even with the crowds, even as above us hundreds of hydrogen balloons lifted into the sky, baskets swinging, and before us on the Champs Elysées, hundreds of men were dancing with lit candles in their top hats.

"Candles," said John Burke, "nice touch."

"When's Missie coming back?"

"On her way." A cowboy spat tobacco juice and winked.

"Got confetti in our *vino*, 'nother round, Nate, ask him."

"... *garçon, encore du vin* ..."

"Think he knows who we are?"

"That stetson may give him a faint idea, Johnny."

"Hell, everyone in Paris got a stetson by now."

"You know, Frank"—Cody leaned over—"Missie's in top form."

"... everyone in Paris got *spurs* by now."

"Top form, Frank, tops, want you to know that."

"More *vino*, Nate, what say?"

"Anymore *vin*, gentlemen, you'll fall off your *cheveaux*."

"Fact is, Frank, the King of Senegal wants to buy Missie."

"Wants to what?"

"Offered me 100,000 francs for her after the show."

"Go on with you."

"Wants to take her back, protect his country against tigers."

"Never heard such a tale."

"God's truth, Frank, I swear. I said she ain't for sale."

"*L'autograph*, Monsieur Buffalo, *s'il vous plait?*"

"There she is."

"Lookit Missie with that parasol."

"Brand new, very proud of it too."

"Balloon rides." Annie held up a fist of tickets. "One each."

The cowboys looked pale.

"Hell no, not me . . ."

". . . me either, I'll puke."

"Come, gentlemen, a try, give it a try."

"On your feet, boys," Cody said. "Can't turn down a lady."

"Great exposure, gents. Balloons—nice touch."

And we were floating up over the Tuileries in a fleet of pear-shaped balloons, the city sailing below and the great grilled needle of Monsieur Eiffel's new tower rising alongside, and beneath us, dwindling, the sweep of streets and parks blurred in a sudden snow of tricolored confetti, voices from below calling, faint and high, "*Vive, vive le Wild West.*"

We were a family through France and on down through Spain, our links to one another strengthened by that terrible death-ridden winter in Barcelona.

We had come in December, the days sunless, the stands empty. Nate cut the ticket prices and the stands still didn't fill; bullfighting was more honorable than our bronco-busting, we were told. All through the chill weeks the arena was quiet, strange, an eerie frame echoing our act, but the show lot was busy with beggars. They came in swarms, crushing around the cook wagon and the mess tent, sleeping in bales of hay and Indian blankets, and for every coin we tossed ten more of them appeared; swift, skinny, insatiable, picking our pockets and stealing our garbage. Within days, the city seemed to surround us like some unwalled prison, smelling of fish and bones and fire ash; we couldn't leave it, we couldn't keep it away. At night we heard the beggars rattling in our bins and bags outside and I would wake to see Annie sitting straight up in bed, back stiff, listening, listening. Once I found her kneeling over her trunks in what seemed a fit of shuddering prayer; she was crouching there with her hands over her ears. She looked so white, so remote, as if she'd coiled herself deep inside her clothes, I thought she might be ill. In fact I feared it as, by twos and threes, places fell empty in the mess tent and the enclosure, and more of the company took sick.

The beggars cleared out as the illness moved in: smallpox among the roustabouts, influenza among the rest. Within a week of Christmas six Indians and three roustabouts had died, and more than half the camp was down with fever. A deep hush roofed the lot, broken only by the snarling of stray dogs and the Indians' chanting. The ground was grizzled with frost. There was a smell of rot and mold, a sound of rats scuttling behind the canvas. I remember Annie taking soup to the cowboys' tent, her lips pressed as if to hold some frightful word in her mouth, her cloak flapping in the clammy-handed wind, me beside her with extra blankets. The show lot spread around us as it had that first evening we'd seen it, like a village, but now a ghostly one. Now it was sheeted in mist, the sky lowered onto it like a vast dirty quilt, the tents huddled beneath, everything the color of ashes and iron. Now there was no movement, no voices; even the bleats from the corrals seemed whimpers. Now for the first time there was shabbiness, unheard of before, loose pegs, slack ropes, rust and grime, like some down-at-the-heels circus. I could feel a chill crawling up under my skin and shook it off, dreading the feel of it coming again. We set down the soup and blankets outside the quarantined tent, hearing only a faint reply when we called inside, and as we turned away we saw the flaps down on Cody's tent, Nate's as well. We went into the next one, shared by John Burke and our announcer Frank Richmond; they hadn't been as bad off. Burke was curled in a ball on his bunk, his heavy body shivering under the blankets in an uneasy sleep. Richmond was on his back, his handsome face like the profile on a coin, his dark hair plastered with sweat to his forehead. There was something about the way he lay there that made us move closer, Annie quicker than I.

"No?" she said, "no?" as if asking to be contradicted, and then she reached for him, his hand limp and his arm tumbling over the edge of the bed. She leaned toward his face as if to question him, as if to catch some word, his thick-lashed blue eyes staring up at the roof. "Missie," I said, my hand on her shoulder, "he's gone, I'll call someone, come on." She ignored me, staying by the bunk, her eyes wet and her face stricken, though Richmond was one member of the troupe she'd never known well, nor had I. Without his megaphone he'd been silent, withdrawn, hard to warm to and easy to overlook. And yet she sat there weeping helplessly as if for a tight friend; then she reached out and quickly, expertly closed his eyes, straightened his arms, bound his chin with her handkerchief, and pulled up the sheet.

I looked at her in surprise as we left the tent, my face hot by then, the fever starting its spin through me. Beside me, she was a queen in her cloak in the dusk, she was a sealed battened ship floating through the haze in my eyes: stern, sweet, secretive, shy, stealing herself from me still in ways I didn't understand; nor could I try to just then.

I was coasting into our tent on my fever, an odd gloried rush of it before the worst set in, feeling the same lightness I'd felt in that balloon over Paris. It seemed a mirage now, that ride, but all the same I smiled to it, hummed to it, allowing her to peel off my shirt, prize off my boots and put me to bed, her eyes fierce and frightened, her hands firm. I remember little of the next few days except the feel of her shoulder, surprisingly hard and muscled under my head as she forced broth through my lips, and the strength of her arms wrapping me in blankets, and her face floating watchful, wistful above me. She was one of the few on the lot who didn't succumb; she didn't escape into the fever, couldn't get away from Barcelona that Christmas as I did, and she says she'll always remember it.

"I remember them burning Frank Richmond's mattress. His clothes. His sheets. On the edge of the lot, that big sad fire. I looked at it and I walked away. You could smell the stench of the feather tick burning up all that day, the day after he died. It was Christmas Eve. Next day there were blankets heaped on the fire. Two more Indians had died, two of the Pawnee. I could hear the churchbells from the city, pealing, pealing for Christmas. And I could see that fire. I could smell it when the wind blew the wrong way, even in our tent, sitting up with you.

"I sat there and talked to you. Told you about the fire, about the bells. About how it felt like maybe it was getting ready to snow. Your eyes were closed or they were somewhere else but I couldn't not talk to you. It seemed to soothe you. Sometimes it soothed me. I couldn't get sick, would not, I resolved that: would not get sick, would not let you get worse. Would not let them burn your mattress. But oh Jimmie, I was so scared for you, you so limp, so heavy against me, my strong husband. I'd wring out cold towels and lay them on your head, but I couldn't get you cool. Then I couldn't get you warm. I'd stir up the brazier. I'd wrap you and rock you, sitting behind you like . . . like I was rowing you, I wanted to rock that fever right out of you, rock it away. In the nights I'd hear you breathing in the dark, I'd listen for it. Sometimes I'd find I was breathing with you. One of those nights, they were all alike, I got up and lit the lamp, and I cleaned all the guns, just the way we'd done together so many times. I kept holding that beautiful English gun, I could remember when you put it in my hands. I cleaned it—cleaned them all. As if that would help, somehow. As if that could set you to rights. The smell of the gun-oil, it was so matter-of-fact. And then I just sat there with that Spencer pump across my knees, looking at you. Your face so white. Your beard coming in. And I said, 'Well, Jimmie, the wind's blowing up some.' And 'I think there'll be eggs for breakfast.' And all the while I thought, I just have to hold on.

"Everything looked so strange, different. No shows then, at the worst of the sickness, the arena's lights on anyway at night—like a house all lit up for company and no one home. And the show lot unearthly still. No one around, nothing moving. Cody down with it, Nate sick but up, dressed, everywhere. Trying to get doctors, trying to nurse the boys. He looked so thin, thinner than ever. Not like himself. Like an old man in Nate's fine coat. I remember how he leaned on my arm, that morning we went to bury Frank Richmond.

"It was just me, Nate, and a priest. The cemetery cold, windy, filled with fresh graves. Nate looked down on the coffin, turned his hat around and around in his hands. Finally he said, 'Here was a man who had a fine voice.' And the priest made the sign of the cross and walked away. Nate kept standing there, leaning on me. 'I couldn't think of anything else,' he said. 'I just realized, I knew his voice, not him.' He shook his head. 'I know all the numbers. How many it takes to chase a wagon train, eat a hundred pounds of steak, wear a hundred yards of denim. But do I know them?' He did, I told him; it was true. But he just kept standing there. Nate, always in charge—he was trembling. 'I always think of them moving,' he said. 'On their feet, on their horses. Not lying down, lying ill, and what can I do? With my own children, I read to them when they were sick, at least I did that.' He let me lead him away then—he was hot with fever. But that evening I passed the cowboys' tent with your supper, and I heard his voice. Jimmie, he was reading the program aloud to them. All the numbers. The descriptions. The profiles of the cast. He was with them all night.

"Next day he was too sick to get up. You were too sick to leave. I looked outside. Everything hushed. The lights still on in the arena. The tents starting to sag. I looked at it again. It wasn't the Wild West anymore. I didn't know what it was, I'd lost my bearings. Had we really been in Paris? Were we really *magnifique*, were we really *le plus grand spectacle*? I could remember Johnny Baker and Buck going down the Rue de Rivoli, their arms around four girls, pouring wine on each other's heads . . . you and me and Nate up in that balloon . . . it seemed like it never happened. There were more blankets burning. I could smell them. What if everyone died? What if this was the end of it, all of it, here in this strange place?

"I looked at you. I looked in the mirror. I saw lines in your face I'd never seen before. I saw lines starting in mine, at my eyes. John Burke had kept my age at twenty-four in the program for years—we'd none of us get old, we'd none of us die. I'd half believed that, I think. Not anymore. No matter how I wanted to, after that.

"That night I started having the dream. I had it every night that week. In the dream I was out on the show lot. And it was dark, it was cold. I looked in all the tents. I listened to the breathing. I drew the sheet over the faces and turned to go outside—very slowly. Because I knew that outside they were waiting for me. In the dark I'd see their faces, the faces of the beggars standing there. Their hands dirty. Their clothes dirty. And all of them had my face. They were looking at me, and they were laughing. And then on the edge of the lot I saw him. A man, standing there, watching me. I knew him. I'd seen him before. I'd seen him the last time in that theater in Lima, sitting in the front row, watching me and knowing who I was, remembering. And now he'd come back for me. He put his hand out. The beggars saw, the beggars laughed. And I felt the pull of them, of him. I was drifting towards him, he was reeling me in. I couldn't hide from him. From them, I'd have to run. I'd be running as I woke up. Shaking in the dark. Lying there, listening to your breathing.

"It came back, the dream, strong like that until your fever broke. Then it got fainter, came in pieces. By the time everyone was well again, thank God, it was just wisps in the corners of my mind. And when we finally piled onto that boat—when we steamed into the Bay of Naples, sky clear, Mount Vesuvius ahead, I knew it was gone. And I thought you'd never know."

I didn't know about the dream then, sick as I was, and I didn't know about it for some time. She didn't have that dream again, or others like it, until we heard that Sitting Bull was dead.

We were still in Europe when we heard the news.

We were in France when we first heard a rumor of unrest on the reservations back home and we were in Spain when we heard it again, but we didn't think much of it. We didn't think much of it in Paris because Paris was so giddy and we didn't think much of it in Barcelona because Barcelona was so grim, and there in Italy when we heard the rumor again, we still didn't pay it heed for long.

We were in Italy when we heard about the messiah.

It was in Italy, that spring, that the cities started to blur, up from Naples through Campania to Rome, up from Rome through Tuscany to Florence, Lombardy to Milan. It was there the cities merged into one city with tile roofs and washing on poles and church domes shining behind our tents, gleaming above the arena. In Italy some of our Indians slipped away to a ship bound for home and in Pisa we all sat together in the mess tent, opening mail and talking about it. Nate's wife had crocuses coming up in her garden; Johnny had a carrot cake from a sister in Omaha; Cody had the usual complaints from his missus and an unusual letter from his friends at Fort Yates. A prophet, he read, had been raised up among the Western tribes, foretelling the coming of an Indian messiah, a savior who would drive the whites into the sea and reclaim the ancient hunting grounds; his nearness had set off a frenzy. Even our own Indians were being drawn home to it, not telling us, it seemed, and we dropped our voices for the first time as we spoke of them, then talked back up to our regular tones, laughing at ourselves. A messiah. What could it really amount to?

We were in Munich when we heard about the Ghost Dance.

In Munich came word again from the Dakotas, of ceaseless tranced dancing to bring the messiah, circling the Ghost poles, chanting the sacred words—it still seemed far away. In Munich the crowds were big, the arena jammed; at every show they called "*Wunderbar*," and at every club Annie won medals. Somewhere the Ghost Dancers were spinning, but our West was undisturbed. Our West was dropping like a tidy compact world into the cities of Bavaria, their gables and spires ridged behind our canvas like paper cutouts; before them our cowboys and Indians battled daily, smoothly, on cue, then filed out together for supper. But in Munich there were more missing Indians, and in Dresden there were agents of the Indian Commission asking about them. In Hamburg there were more Sioux and Pawnee gone, shipping off from Bremerhaven to dance the messiah near. In Hamburg we began to think more about it.

Annie was spending more time with the Indians then, sitting with them in their tepees and before each show in their dressing tent behind the arena. I came with her sometimes, there to that big bright-lit space with the Indians drifting in, tossing lassos and chewing toffee, smoking and squatting over their makeup bags, spilling out their bowls and mirrors and jars of paint. They'd welcome us, smiling, making room for us on the blankets at the edge, where the women did their beadwork and a papoose splashed her hands in a basin of water. Annie always liked being there, the feathered head-dresses floating in rows above us from the tent-ropes, that wet-earth smell of paint on the air and the bowls brimming reds and yellows, set out like bright porridge on an old tablecloth. That fall Annie sat there, I know, as Sitting Bull's daughter, watching the Sioux stain their faces, asking them about the Ghost Dance, wanting to understand.

It will bring the messiah, said the young ones.

It will bring bullets, said the older ones, and looked away.

Sitting Bull, Sitting Bull, I'd hear her saying over and over, low-voiced—who had word of him, what would happen? She searched the striped faces for answers, assurance, but there was no word; and next town, one or two more of those faces would be missing. As we moved down the Rhine, more and more of the company came to sit in that tent, everyone pulling closer together there. We'd been abroad a long time by then, and would be longer, but it wasn't homesickness drawing us. It was a sense that the family was changing, some of it slipping away; some of us might not see each other again.

"I don't hold with it," Jack Red Cloud said quietly, mixing ochre with water off to one side. "Me, I'm showfolk, like my father, like half of them. But well, the rest . . ." His broad face, half-painted, was somber. "If I believed, I'd go home, pray, dance; maybe I'll be sorry . . ." He hesitated, looking from me to Annie; then he shook his head. "Those are old dances. For me all that's gone."

"And the others?"

"They'll go back, Missie."

"Hating us—wanting us driven into the sea?"

"No. They're glad the outfit's here, you know, so when it happens, when the messiah comes, you'll all be safe."

We all smoked the Indian pipes that fall, being especially gentle and careful with one another, sitting cross-legged on the ground in the makeup tent. I remember looking in from the flaps one evening and seeing a ring of bare backs and fringed shirts leaning over an enormous strudel sent in by a Bremen baker, its sugar powdering everyone. And I remember an evening in Vienna when Jack Red Cloud turned to Annie, his face streaked blood red and bone white, black serpents painted around his eyes, and his eyes on her troubled ones. He reached out with his finger, drawing wide red stripes on her cheeks, touching her lids with yellow, holding up the mirror on its cord around his neck until she had to smile. Sitting Bull, she'd been asking again, any word? In November, in Vienna, no one knew.

Our last stand of that autumn was a week in Strasbourg, and every night Cody and Nate and Annie stood together back in the enclosure, talking, half watching the show; I'd see their silhouettes against the bright arena, their voices drifting toward me, low and tight.

"It's going to be bad," Cody said one of those nights. He shook his head and down his white jacket ran a ripple of fringe. "Cavalry's there, Custer's old regiment's with them, you know they're just itching to move. Cavalry all around the reservations, watching, waiting."

Over his shoulder in the arena, the lights had come up on a settler's log cabin, surrounded by the creeping bodies of Indians. The paint on their arms and faces glowed under the lights; the ground seemed to wriggle, alive with their skin.

"Once we shut down for winter, I'm gone back," said Cody. "Lived with Indians most of my life, I know them. Go back, see for myself."

"Sitting Bull—could you get to him," Annie said, "talk to him somehow?"

"A fool's errand," said Nate. "We need you here; there's next season to advance, you may recall."

Warbled cries filled the air behind them, tomahawks swinging, arrows slanting and catching the light.

"Talk to him, just talk," Annie's voice was urging. "He's a medicine man, a chief, maybe he could stop it."

"He can't. Lost his sway with the young ones, the Ghost Dancers. And anyways, wouldn't matter now."

"Get word to him then." Her voice was fierce. "Tell him he has a place here—he does, doesn't he?"

"He may not want to come back," Nate said. "Missie. He's

an Indian, a Sioux. He may very well want to be just where he is."

"I can find out." Cody touched her arm. "I can get there. General Miles, he's as good as promised, he can cut me orders, old time's sake."

A smoke bomb went off over the cabin's roof beyond; screams rose from its windows. Around us in the Enclosure the cowboys pressed closer, mounted, dressed as scouts; a stablehand held Cody's white horse.

"Stay out of it," said Nate.

"I can't."

"He shouldn't."

"Mr. Cody." The shifters held back the flaps. "You're on."

A week later the show went into winter quarters in Alsace and Cody went home with the Indians, promising to talk to his pals at Fort Yates, to write. We were in London for a string of engagements when we had his first letter; it sounded so hopeful, so sure: he had orders for Standing Rock, he would bring Sitting Bull back, all was well. I heard the Chief's name from her more than I cared to that week, and then, the next week, I heard it again—Annie saying it in an odd flat voice, a voice not quite hers, saying a name not quite his, stammering on the *S* so it came out a hiss, and dropping a letter like a stone onto the bed; and me, unnerved by her face, the twist to her lips, asking over and over again what had happened.

"It seemed so strange to read it, not hear it," she said. "To read it from Cody like that. . . . Thinking back now, it all seems so strange. Cody riding out there. On that . . . that mission. And me believing he could do it. Stop the trouble, get Sitting Bull out. And not just me believing it. Everyone in the outfit but Nate. And you. Believing in Cody riding out there with those wangled orders—and a wagon-load of hard candy. Candy. Presents for the Indians. What was he thinking of? What was I? What was General Miles, when he wrote those orders? But right up till that last minute, right up till they recalled him, I'm sure Cody thought he'd bring it off. And me, reading that letter there in London, I could hardly believe he hadn't. I remember standing there, you know, looking at the letter . . . I couldn't seem to take in everything he wrote, not right then. Not till later. But one thing stayed in my mind, a picture of one moment he wrote about, that one split second on Sitting Bull's reservation—the Chief coming out of his cabin, going toward his horse. That horse he'd ridden with me all those mornings, our gift to him. Him saddling the horse. . . . The gunfire starting. Him falling, his shirt drenched in blood. And that horse starting to kneel, bow, paw the ground—going through all those Wild West stunts, cued by the shooting. I still can't get that picture out of my mind after all these years.

"Those weeks in London, the news coming in so slow . . . it was hard being far away then. Every letter with something else about the shooting at Standing Rock. The massacre at Wounded Knee Creek. And over and over I'd picture it. But not the Indians they mowed down. Not the children screaming. Not the big Hotchkiss guns. Only Sitting Bull, falling, falling . . . and that horse taking a bow.

"I couldn't talk to you about it. I kept it in. I told myself it was because of how you felt about Sitting Bull. But that wasn't why. I was afraid if I started to talk about it—about him—all those other things, those old things, they'd come pouring out of me. I'd spent so many years keeping it all in, Jimmie, holding it back. It was my way, always has been. If you don't talk about it, maybe it isn't true. If you don't think about it, maybe it never was. I guess the only time I cried, let myself cry, was in my sleep. I'd start to dream and I'd wake up shaking. And you'd be awake and the pillow would be wet.

"I made it fade. Told myself it hadn't happened. Told myself, that whole time we were in Europe, that the Chief was still out there at Standing Rock. I got to believe it after a while. I was able to keep on believing it till the show came back home. Till I saw what was inside the gates on the lot when we opened out in Chicago: Sitting Bull's cabin. It was a part of the West, Burke said, a part of history, people ought to see it, people got a right to see it. Maybe so, I don't know. But I saw those bullet holes in the walls and I turned around, walked away—got sick back of the cook wagon. I never let myself walk anywhere near it again. I just wanted to forget.

"When Sitting Bull died, there were no more fathers for me. I knew what I'd never have then, what I'd missed. But I couldn't think that, couldn't bear to. And I couldn't look at his cabin, couldn't let it remind me. Now I wish I had looked at it. I wish I had it in my mind now, his cabin, to think about. I wish I could remember looking at where he'd sat and smoked. And eaten supper. And talked about so many things. Maybe even about me.

"Remember or forget. Which is better? I don't know anymore. I used to think forgetting was best, but I was younger then. Now I'm not so sure. Now I do think maybe it's better to remember."

SHE never thought she would have to look at certain memories again. She thought they would finally, eventually leave her be; someday when she was old enough, famous enough, far enough away. And by the summer of '96, it seemed she was all those things at last.

Sweet fame. That season if you came to interview her on the show lot you would wait your turn. You would observe that she and the show were at their peak; you would recall them from Ambrose Park and the Chicago World's Fair. You would compare the Wild West's popularity with baseball's, nothing less; you would ask her how it felt to be cheered by Roosevelt, painted by Remington, kinetographed by Edison. In your review of her act you would add "still" to your praise—her eye still sharp as a field glass, her finger still quick as a watch spring; still matchless, peerless, still magic. You would know she wasn't still twenty-eight, as the press agents said, but from the stands you wouldn't see the fine lines at her eyes; you would see her with her hair loose, her waist slim, still looking like a little girl down there, a tiny innocent with deadly aim.

How charmed, how untouched by time or misfortune she must have seemed to Cody that year, and to Nate. Cody, at fifty, sodden, tired of the show business, unable to break out of it; and Nate, at fifty, never tired of the show business, filled with plans he could never break in. Nate: sitting there in his wheelchair, lamed by a stroke, his shining speech slurred, but his eyes still the eyes of a pastor; kind, cagey, thoughtful. He had time on his hands, Nate did, that summer, his last traveling with us. He'd given up its management to that circus man Bailey, watching helplessly as sideshows were added, schedules changed; even so he couldn't give up his interest in the show, his ideas for it and other shows beyond it. These, the productions he knew he'd never see, he played out against the walls of our tent that season, talking them through—"a whole new one, Missie, I'd call it 'Black America,' Negro music, dance, history, Missie, can't you just see it? . . ." His voice, thinned and blurred, held a thrill of excitement. On the arms of his wheelchair his long delicate fingers lay like pale vines rippling with his words, and his hollowed face was lit from within. Nate seemed to have fine edges and angles to him that year, as if his mind's keenness were whittling him from the inside out, sharpening his nose, quickening his hands, distilling his eyes to the color of ale on ice. And as he talked, he saw things; he listened. As the show train moved on into the Midwest that June, down toward Lima, down toward the old radius of bad dreams, he seemed to sense a quieting in Annie. He couldn't see what players mimed behind her eyes but he could see some trouble there. I had learned to let these times run their course in her like fevers, but Nate was a doer, a fixer; a producer. His mind grew busy, delighting in his private plans to cheer her, and like the best managers, he stayed behind the scenes, letting his plan unfold as a surprise. She didn't know who had circled the one-show stand at Picqua, Ohio, on her calendar. She didn't know who had arranged for her mother to come see the show there—to see her perform for the first time in all her years in the show business.

"I remember how I stared at that calendar," she said. "Just watching that date get closer, it was set for July 4. I couldn't have said how I felt, didn't understand it myself. My mother. I wanted her to come . . . I didn't want her to come. I wanted to tell people. I didn't want to tell a soul. I should be happy, I told myself. What ailed me, I should be glad. 'My mother's coming,' I'd hear myself saying in the mess tent. My voice so bright. So strained. 'My mother's coming,' I'd tell the cooks. My voice would crack. My mother. It was bound to be good. It was bound to be bad.

"Why was she coming, after all that time? . . . I didn't know. I didn't really even know why she'd never come before. Well, I knew what I'd told myself . . . it was on account of the show business, the Quaker in her, that was why. I'd held to that excuse, you know, but I knew better. Maybe she'd felt that way at the start but that wasn't all of it. I knew that. I knew she hadn't held much with her faith, hadn't raised us in it. That excuse. Just an excuse, a tale I told.

"Two weeks away, Rock Island, Illinois—that baseball game on the lot, cowboys against the cooks, I remember watching it. And not really watching it, I was the only one didn't know the score. A week away, Fort Wayne, I was so tired, up nights. And that night before, on the train going into Picqua, I lay there with my eyes open, shivering. I didn't want to feel like that. I wanted to shake myself, shake this . . . this feeling off. I was too old for it. I was a professional. Just another stand, I told myself, just like always. Out to the lot, tents going up, crowds coming in. Just like always, don't think, just move, out into the arena, into the act and through it . . . like always, always. And then it was over. And . . . not like always . . . there was my mother, waiting for me in our tent.

"I remember how I stood there outside the tent for a minute. Just stood there. Then I opened the flaps. I saw her standing in there, in front of one of the trunks. Saw her black bonnet and dress like a shadow in there. She turned, she looked at me. I saw her face. Why had I thought it would be any different?

"A dry kiss against my cheek. A rustle. That old rustle I used to listen for. That rustle that meant Mama. I offered her a chair. She took it. We sat together, across from each other. I saw myself in her face. That broad straight nose. Gray eyes. But her mouth so tight, her face so hard. Not like mine, that hardness. Why had I thought she'd be pink, excited, the way other people were, back here after the show? Sitting there, she seemed to pull away from me.

"I can just see her, how she put her head to one side, looked up at the walls. 'All this . . . just folds up . . . ?' she said, and I heard my voice going on and on, explaining. Filling up that air. I couldn't believe she was there. In my tent. My world. This wasn't how it was when we visited her, with her garden to look at, the house to look at—the talk of them covering up so many things. So many things we didn't say. So many things we could pretend never happened.

"'Canvas, well,' I said, 'we even have a canvas bathtub.' My voice sounded so high to me, silly. I couldn't take my eyes off her. I knew she didn't really want to be there. But I wanted her to be there. But I hated her being there. I wanted to ask her why she couldn't smile. Why couldn't she say one word about the act, the show? I wanted to say, Mother, people come from all over to see me, they come again and again. But all I asked was if she was putting up her plums again this year, was she still making her own soap—just as if we were in her house, not mine.

"'Did you get that last check we sent?' I said. And she smoothed her gloves. 'Always glad of the extra money, Phoebe Ann.' Old names. Old words. I could see her looking at me wondering, Who is this woman, why does she have my face? Looking at me, I knew all she could see was old times. Hard times. And me—I could see her, dark-haired, young again; sitting in that parlor, pulling away. Looking away. Oh Mama, I wanted to cry to her, look at me. Mama, why didn't you come see me, all this time, Mama, I am thirty-six years old, and '*Mama*—' I said aloud. But then there was this burst of laughter from outside—there were my nieces, nephews, they were running in through the flaps, all of them talking at once. And then my sisters coming in after them, and they were all pulling me back out onto the lot, wanting to see this, see that. And as we came out I saw Nate sitting just beyond the tent in his chair, watching us. And smiling, smiling.

"I guess I went through that next hour in a daze. And then they were leaving, piling into that wagon, they were waving good-bye. And again, I hadn't asked what I'd wanted to know, it was too late now, and still . . . still, I couldn't get it out of my mind, her face. Her face, young, dark-haired, coming back and back at me, *you see how she's different*, oh Jimmie. It was like . . . like her face, it had somehow made a hole in my world there, my good safe world. And through that hole all the old times were spilling, *trouble, different, Phoebe Ann should go*. I didn't want to remember these things, not now, not ever, and still they kept coming, coming. And I remember whispering to myself, Stop it, stop it. I was too old. I was too far away now, it was over. Stop it. And there was Nate wheeling up alongside me, and suddenly it flashed in my mind—him smiling like that outside the tent, waiting there, of course it was Nate who'd arranged it. And I turned on him, it burst from me, 'How could you—how could you do this'—my voice so sharp, harsh, I heard it and I said it again, 'How, *how* could you'—and the hurt in his eyes, all at once, so deep, so deep.

"Oh God, Jimmie, how it hurts me, remembering that—that look on Nat's face—dear Nate, I can't stand thinking of it. How I hurt him—because those times had come back so strong, because he'd made me remember. . . . You know, there are certain things, things you put away from you. And you get past them—most of the time, then you turn around, there they are again. And you just pray they'll go back where they came from. And you pray they won't come again. You pray they won't sneak up and steal any more time. Especially your good times. Your best times. Like my Greenville day, like that. That day, Jimmie—I just wish I could remember it free and clear, free and clear."

"Big day, big day": Cody had said that the night before we played Greenville and she had trembled in her chair. Greenville, her hometown, our first show there ever: "Big day tomorrow, you bet."

I remember sitting in our stateroom with her and Cody the night before, coming in on the train. He had joined us with his whiskey as he often did after Nate retired; it was almost as if he were warming himself by us then. I remember him slinging himself into the rocker as if into a saddle, there by the table with the lamp. The lamplight fell in amber circles around him, catching in his glass, flashing on Annie's needle as she stitched the costume in her lap. Colder, sharper lights flickered past the window, making the room seem even more of a hearthside, as squalls beyond a window can do; beneath us the train grumbled and groaned like earthbound thunder. Cody glanced from the homemade curtains to the quilt turned down on the brass bed, and he sighed, running his hand through his thinning gray hair. The night before in the arena, waving his hat to the crowds, he had accidentally lifted off his toupee; with great dignity he had continued on around the ring without a pause, and so great was his presence that no one, behind the flaps or before them, had laughed. There were folds of loose flesh at his mouth and neck now, his gut hung over his belt, and heaped in that rocker he looked like a great rundown mansion, sagging, peeling, worn—but a lingering air of grandeur remained. His diamond flashed from his neckerchief, his crimson shirt still draped his shoulders like bunting; his eyes, bloodshot that night, still said *look here*. But his voice, moist and deep, had saddened, softened, and was softer than ever as he spoke to us.

"I envy you, Missie," he was saying. "You never get tired of this damn road, never get tired of the shooting, I can tell. . . ."

There was a gurgle of whiskey as he poured himself another drink. Annie looked at him, her face polite, her eyes absent. Her hands, I could see, were trembling over her sewing; she seemed scarcely with us in the room.

"—tearing around the country, all the sham worship, I get tired of it, maybe it's my damn age. But you—with you it's different, you got a craft, see, well I never did see myself as much of a craftsman. . . ."

Past his hunched shoulders I could see her glancing out the window, up at the clock; Greenville was coming closer through the night, she could feel it nearing, I knew.

"Tell you what, Frank," Cody went on. "Thing I fear most's dying on this damn road, middle of nowhere, night like this—and they don't know what to put in the obit, see, so they say 'He died in the middle of nowhere.' That's what I'm afraid of, but you two, you ain't . . . ain't afraid of much, I don't guess. . . ."

He couldn't see it in her, the fear, not as I could; not as Nate had sensed. The only way to know it was to sense it: she wouldn't talk about it, not a word. The tightness in her shoulders, the wing-like shadows under her eyes were plain to me—but not to Cody.

"—different now. No big hero ridin' off to war, don't figure myself for that now. Now I think, if I had what you two got yourselves, that's all I'd need. Me and Louisa, been so bad so long, only thing left's divorce. . . . Well, like I say, I envy you, I do. . . ."

He envied her; wistfully, not vengefully now. She was still opaque to him, perfect. He smiled on her and rose unsteadily to his feet. "Big day tomorrow, better let you get some shut-eye. Bet you'll be seein' a lot of old faces, bet everyone'll come from miles around . . . they'll remember you from way back when, eh? Big day, you bet, get a good nighter now."

I saw the look on her face as he said that. I saw how she was after he'd gone, getting ready for bed: the jerky strokes of her hairbrush, the shaky clash of her cream jar, her fingers pleating her nightgown. I tipped her face up in my hand.

"Missie—" I began, but she swiftly shook her head, as if the act of speaking itself would cause her to shatter. I sighed, knowing she wouldn't talk; I went to bed, dimly hearing her move about the room. From time to time I opened my eyes to see her sitting by the table, her hair falling over her shoulders, a shawl around her; sometimes her fingers were pressed to her eyes. She was sitting like that at dawn as the train pulled into Greenville, and she was sitting like that inside our tent as soon as it went up on the show grounds. It was then that I discovered she'd somehow contrived to keep her name off the posters in town, off the newspaper advertisement as well; Burke was fuming, furious, until he saw her face. She looked desperately, frighteningly ill: too ill, she said, to ride in the street parade—she who never missed a parade, who had ridden fevered, delirious. Burke went off with a low whistle, worried. I stayed with her, watching as she sat there, silent, head down, drawn into herself. Gazing. Thinking? So white-faced, Christ, so white.

"I was thinking," she said. "Thinking of what Cody said. 'Big day, old faces.' I was thinking of the faces. Of their eyes on me. 'They'll remember you from way back when, eh?' I could hear his voice saying that. And I could feel myself trembling all over, gone cold. Thinking of it, thinking of it, those faces from long ago. I didn't want to remember. And I couldn't stop remembering now. Maybe with my name off the posters, I thought, maybe with it out of the papers, they wouldn't come. People I knew. People I used to know. People I'd known once. From the house, the school. From the Infirmary, from then. They'd see me, they'd say . . . oh God, I couldn't stand to think of them here. Here in this place that was mine.

"I heard the outfit riding off to the parade. I tried to picture the show lot in my mind. Quiet. Peaceful. Protecting me. The canvas, the paths, the corrals. And even so, the old faces kept coming in. The faces—and me, in their eyes, how I was. That face in the audience, that time in Lima . . . and if he was gone, his son remembered. They all remembered. I'd been here visiting so many times, but never like this, on show. . . . I looked around at the walls, those safe walls, our tent—I saw the old walls with the handprints, and all around the voices, all the time. I saw that and I knew this would be worse than Lima. This would be worse than Picqua when my mother came. This would be worse than all the worst times.

"I tried to think of all the medals I'd ever won—I counted the ones pinned to my costume. I counted them, I counted the records I could remember: 4,772 glass balls in 5,000 broken in nine hours, 984 in 1,000 in an hour-fifteen. The numbers—I held to them. The numbers—the name. I fixed on it: OAKLEY on the gun rack. OAKLEY on the trunks. OAKLEY, OAKLEY. I held to that hard as I could, getting dressed, walking to the enclosure—waiting to go on. To that; to your hand. And then it was time. I was in the saddle. The Grand Entry was over, we were on alone.

"Once I was out there, I thought, maybe I'd be all right. I always was. But not that time. Oh you know, I made my shots. But it was like shooting into a wind. My palms wet.

My hands sliding on the guns. And every step, I could feel those eyes on me . . . *Moses Poses Moses Poses* . . . eyes on me, old eyes, all the while I swung, aimed . . . *got no rag to blow her noses* . . . mud on my boots, splashed on my skirt . . . *no one knows where she gets her clothes-es* . . . I was losing myself, sliding back into the old time. Annie Oakley, who was she—who did I think I was? Why did I think I could get free, get away with it? Dirty Annie, bad'un Annie, it was showing in the lights, the silence, they were all seeing it again. And when it was over all I wanted to do was get off, get back behind the flaps.

"But the applause kept going on. And there you were, taking my hand. I'll never forget how you lifted it up and up, over my head—and then I saw that man coming out of the audience. That man walking across the arena into the light with me, a man in a new-looking brown suit, something in his hands—and then I saw it was just a lawyer from town, name of Anderson. I was so relieved there was this pained squeezing in my chest. I saw him through a kind of haze. I heard him calling me 'our Annie Oakley, Greenville's own.' And he was smiling at me, smiling, and suddenly my eyes were filling. And he was saying 'Annie Oakley, our native daughter,' and I could feel the tears spilling over, I was crying in public, I didn't care, 'She has made all of us proud.' I saw he was handing me something, slipping it out of a cloth, and there was that silver loving cup, there in my hands—so cool, heavy, shining, shining. I was still crying when the applause started again, and I can still see it: That afternoon so bright. Bright as my guns on the table. That cup in my hands. I can see it, Jimmie, I can still see it now."

She paused, her eyes alight with tears, remembering. Then her gaze came back to the dim hotel bedroom, and to the clock face that read three in the morning. She ran her hand over her eyes and looked at me.

"After that," she said, "I thought there would be no more bad times—no more bad times coming back anymore. I'd made the changes and they'd lasted after all. My whole life I'd wondered if they would. I'd prayed they would. Swore they would. Jimmie, I know that sometimes the old things, they've come in, broken in. I know, I know, and I couldn't tell you, couldn't explain—I know you saw. But I've always wanted to think that mostly I've outrun them—my God, I believe that, I *have* to believe that." She moved to the window, standing there very straight, her white nightgowned figure in the light from the street lamps. She lifted her hair off her neck, let it fall. When she spoke again, her voice shook. "But now, with the detectives coming around—poking, digging in Greenville, everywhere—now it's all come back stronger than ever. And if they find what I tried to leave, tried so hard, so hard—if they bring it out after all this time, how they'll use it, they'll twist it—Jimmie, I just couldn't bear it is all."

I came to stand with her at the window. Below us, across the street, we saw the detective's slouched silhouette, cigarette glowing. She watched him, saying nothing; only spread her hands on the sill as if to strike a chord on some invisible keyboard. I knew that motion, I'd seen it before: at the end of an evening, a conversation; before trying a new stunt, before buying a gun or a hat. Her back straight, her hands spread: her sign of decision.

PART THREE

NEWARK, NEW JERSEY
NOVEMBER 30, 1905

HER back half turned from me in the dark.
Her fingers steepled before her face.
"When I was eight," she said, and stopped.
Eyes down, fingers locking, unlocking.
"When I was eight."
A shake of her head.
"Damn."
Head low, shoulders tight.
Then, a breath, her eyes on me.
"When I was eight, Jimmie. I was taken away, one morning, in the wagon. My hair in tight braids. Dress starched. My things in an egg basket, covered with a cloth. I was taken in the wagon to work. To work in this place. I was to work there, to stay there, until they came back for me. They said it wouldn't be long.

"The walls of this place were whitewashed. There were handprints and scratches on the walls. The prints and the scratches didn't come off. There were windows. But nothing to look out for. There were voices, all the time. Even in the nights. Ones that moaned over and over, 'Ahh-ah.' One that sang, no tune, 'Sally go round the mulberry bush.' One that always laughed, one that always whined. Voices, all the time.

"At the sewing machine there, my feet on the treadle, if I could go fast enough, I wouldn't hear them. Wouldn't hear them, wasn't like them, I said that to myself. They were left there, no place else to go. No one to keep them, no one to want them. I wasn't like that. I looked out the windows. I didn't lean on the walls, didn't scratch them. I worked there. And someone was coming back for me.

" 'Someone's coming back for me,' I'd say upstairs at night, up in the long room with the rows of beds. I'd sleep with the others, second bed down, left-hand row. Rows of heavy iron bedsteads, all alike, china nightpots beneath, all alike, and gray blankets, folded, all alike. At night I'd hear the voices, all night long, 'Sally go round,' and the whimpering, 'Sally go.' I'd hold my cloth bag in my hand and I'd feel for the button like a ruby, the stone like a half-moon, my sister's old thimble, and the hammer from the rifle. I'd hold onto them till I fell asleep, but I'd always wake up in the middle of the night. And sometimes the sheet would be wet. I'd lie there, the sheet sticking to me, feeling shamed—I was too big to wet my bed. I'd bunch up the sheet and carry it down to the hamper at the end of the hall, hoping no one would see. And I'd pick my way back, through the voices, the dark. I'd sit up, the blanket around me, and I'd take out my bag again. I'd look at the stone. The button. The hammer. I'd squeeze them in my fist. And I'd wish on them, on all the power I knew they had, to make two years disappear. To take me back, two years before. Before Maryjane died. Before Papa died. Because I knew I never would have been taken in the wagon to this place, if they were still there."

She understood her father was dead when the pump broke.

It had hung on all through his illness, through the bad month of January, it had even hung on through the funeral supper when there was so much company, so many trips for water in one day.

But the next day she'd gone out there first thing in the morning and it had been dry. Mid-morning she'd tried again and it gushed all of a sudden, drenching her skirt, then dried up again. Next day its handle flew up and hit her in the chin, hard enough to draw blood. From then on it was usually like that, behaving just enough to be used at all. Her father had always been the one to coax it, especially in the early mornings; she'd never thought of that before. She couldn't explain to herself, at five, how the pump knew the touch of different hands just as she did, or why it had held on through the sad sick months just past. She had heard of clocks stopping when people died but not pumps, nothing about pumps. But after a month of its coughing, spurting, and outright sharp smacks in her face, she understood: the pump knew somehow that her father was dead, and so it must be true. He wasn't behind the curtains hung across the far end of the cabin. He wasn't in the woods, on the road, in town. She had seen them put the coffin in the ground but that hadn't been him, not to her, her father couldn't be in a box. It had been February and the ground had been hard, hard enough to clang when a spade fell over during the eulogy. But her father wasn't in that ground, the minister said. Her father was in eternity. She hadn't understood what that meant and no one could tell her and until the pump broke or changed or sickened itself she had thought maybe they were all wrong. She had thought maybe he would be coming back with the wagon at noontime, calling out to them, fetching in for them the twenty pound sacks of feed, flour, sugar, and coffee he'd gone to get the last time she'd seen him stride out the door.

That had been October. The cabin had smelled of paraffin from the tops of the mason jars, of cloves and allspice and the apple rings strung over the hearth. All the things that meant autumn were there: the wood stacked high to the mantel; the fresh plaster daubing in the log walls; the quilt with the three red stars spread on the bed; the lamplight getting yellower, earlier, pooling on the floor; the new shoes lined up at night, their hides still stiff, the heavy floss stitching still white. These were the things she could count on to happen every year, every time. These were the things that told her all was right with the world. It seemed impossible to her that her father could go out one morning to fetch in supplies as he always did, every year, every time, and that night be carried in past the apple rings, past the wood, through the lamplight, his new shoes still on his feet and his eyes rolled up and the red-star quilt stuffed under his head.

"I heard the door bang open," she said. "Banging open, hitting the wall. It woke me, it was late at night. I got up—I remember how cold the floor was. I looked past the edge of the curtains around my bed. Snow was blowing in through the doorway, but no one was there. Everything was quiet. There was only the light from the fire, and from the lamp on the long pine table. And I felt this big rush of fear, you know, all of a sudden . . . the door open like that and the wind in the cabin, everything so still. And then I heard that sound—a sound like something heavy being dragged along, like a log across the ground. I came closer to the fire, my fingers in my mouth—and I saw my mother and my oldest sister carrying my father inside. I remember how their skirts swirled out on the wind. And over their shoulders, my father's arms. And his legs out straight, dragging on the floor. His head rolling like an egg on a spoon. Oh *Papa*—Papa, it couldn't be. He was a mail carrier, he always went out in storms, always came home all right. He was the one who always carried us . . . tall Papa, his head in the rafters, his laugh so big. Standing there, all of a sudden, I could feel how he'd swept me up off the floor just before he'd gone out—'going to get the snow sugar, Annie,' up up to the beams, his voice below me like this great big net, 'snow-sugar, Annie, what say?'

"I can still hear him saying that. And I can still see him, how he looked that night. His head rolling, his hair, that gray hair, falling over his face. I can see my mother: her hair black, in a long braid down her back, her face flushed. And stern, so stern, mouth tight. My sister Maryjane: red hair loose on her shoulders, eyes wet. Their talk, snippets of it, coming to me, '—watch it, got him—' and a little further into the cabin, '—hold him, oh Jacob—' and that sound of his boots dragging, all the way to the curtains around his bed.

"No one had seen me. I stayed there on the hearth, feeling all sick in my stomach. Watching their shadows, my mother's, my sister's, on the curtain. Slowly, slowly, I crept over—afraid to look. Having to look, all the same. And oh Jimmie, my father's face, propped up there—it didn't look like his, so white, it looked like a mask. The eyes rolled up. The mouth open. Spittle, strings of it, at the corners. A cut across his nose, blood running down one cheek. He was shaking so hard the wooden slats in the bed were rattling, I'll never forget that sound—so strange, you know, almost jolly, like a wooden toy I'd once had. And my mother, her face close to his, talking to him all the while she piled on the quilts. Talking in this terrible voice, low, more frightening than any scream: 'Did you listen, I begged you, begged you not to, did you listen, I said it could wait, said it would storm, did you listen, Jacob,

Jacob, no.' Her face scared me almost worse than Papa's. I put my hand out, holding her skirt. She looked down, saw me there, I think, for the first time. 'Go on, go on,' she said, brushing my fingers off. 'This minute, mind me.' I shook my head. She turned to me, her eyes so sharp. *'Phoebe Ann!'* Her voice, still low, still that terrible whisper, it sent me back out to the fire. I climbed up on the table by the hearth. There was a bowl of walnuts, half shelled there, I remember that—my mother must have been shelling them, waiting up for him to get home. And I remember sitting there, putting pieces of the walnuts in my mouth. And sucking on them. And watching the shadows on the curtain. Listening to their voices. And thinking of his voice, *snow-sugar, Annie,* tall Papa, up to the rafters in his hands, *Annie, snow-sugar, what say. . . .*

"Snow-sugar: The taste of it. Eating it. Making it, every year, right after the first big snowfall. Going into town with Papa on the wagon, just me, the year before. Going to town to get the molasses, sitting up with him on the seat. The snow, thick across the fields. Papa, that soft squashy wide-brimmed hat on his head—head back—singing, 'drink to me only wi-ith thine ey-eyes,' not caring who heard. In town, everyone greeting him, knowing his name, stopping to talk in all those dark stores. Me, feeling so proud of him, him introducing me around. Having him all to myself, that almost never happened. And on the way back, I remember, him talking about this inn he and my mother had run back in Pennsylvania, before I was born. Before it burned down. Weary Pilgrim's Inn, he'd named it himself, he'd started making his snow-sugar there, 'best inn on the pike, Annie, best candy too, you bet, good years, good years.' I could imagine it, the inn, hearing him talk. Could imagine my mother, registering the guests. Seeing to the keys, the sheets. But I knew it would have been my father making people feel welcome, at home, pulling up chairs by the fire. I remember sitting there on the wagon, thinking about that. And leaning against him, smelling his tobacco, his pipe. Listening to his voice, more than the words. Tasting that snow-sugar already. And then we were home, his voice calling 'Look what I've got, look here'—the laughing, the scrambling to get to him first. My sisters, my brother, all over him, hanging onto his legs. Me up on his shoulders, my hands in his hair. His hat on my head. 'Where's my kettle, tell your mama to get my kettle on,' the sound of his laugh, his boots, his voice just filling the cabin up. 'Now . . . sugar . . . now molasses . . . now, who remembers what comes next?' And all of us yelling 'Walnuts!' —crowding around him at that big old cast iron stove, handing him spoons, cups of nuts, the kettle steaming while he stirred it. 'Best snow-sugar this side Cincinnati, stand back, stand back, ready now.' That sweet smell rising off that kettle, everyone jumping up and down, pushing, shrieking, out into the snow after him, him with the kettle in his hands. 'Whole secret's in how you throw it, Annie, watch now'—Papa rearing back, tipping the kettle, more, more, and suddenly, with a snap, all that hot syrup on the air like a curtain, falling over the snow—thinning out, setting, hard in an instant. And we were galloping around it, our ears bright red, breaking off pieces, cramming it in our mouths—all of us, even my mother, smiling, smiling. And me up on Papa's back again, riding him over the fields. And down there, that wide-open laugh of his, and that candy, all spread out like a cape on the snow . . .

"Oh Jimmie, that's almost the only clear memory I have of him. I have so few, so few. I can remember his laugh. But not his face. Not really, not anymore. Not how he looked that day, it's a blur. He's like a big shadow to me, he was gone so soon. Sometimes the closest I get to remembering his face, it's how he looked when he was sick. When he died.

"All the while he was sick, there was the terrible sound of breathing, his breathing, all through the cabin. And then one morning when we got up, it had stopped. The cabin had gone quiet. My mother rode off on the wagon with the doctor to arrange things. And I remember how we all sat on that bench by the hearth, staring at the curtains around his bed. Just staring. No one saying much. After a while, Maryjane gathered up his comb, his shaving things, a basin—she went behind the curtain with him, and I followed her, she let me stay. She let me hold the basin while she washed his face. I remember looking at him, staring at him. Strange, you know, he looked so much better than that night they carried him in. Calm, almost contented. The cut on his nose had healed. He had some stubble on his chin. One of his eyes had come partways open. It gave him the look he used to have sometimes, dozing off by the fire, half watching us while we played under his chair. I reached out to touch his face. The lather from Maryjane's rag came off on my finger. He was being washed, he was being shaved. He couldn't really be dead. Maryjane closed his eye, bound up his jaw—I combed his hair. I remember how his hair felt, thin, fine, like a child's. I combed his hair and I didn't cry. I didn't cry later, when the neighbors came to see him. I didn't cry in the graveyard. I didn't even cry later, when the pump broke. When I finally believed he was dead. I just couldn't seem to cry. And off and on, I still had this same dream, the one I'd had all the while he'd been sick—all the while I lay there, listening to his breathing. I had that same dream, now and then, for maybe three years.

"I'd be dreaming that something was caught in Papa's chest, and if I could just get it out, he'd be well, alive, everything would be all right. I'd be fishing, dropping this long line down and down. And reeling in whatever was caught inside him. It was some kind of dark shape, hard to pull in. I'd brace my feet, I'd get it in close enough to see what it was. It was always one of those twenty pound sacks from the wagon. And as soon as I saw it, it would start spinning away from me. The line would snap. The water would go dark all around me. And I'd fight to wake up."

Clack-snap.

The wooden clapstick woke her every morning at five, up in the room with the long rows of beds, up on the third floor of the main building of the Darke County Infirmary. *Clack-snap*: the sound bit the air and she lurched awake, her eyes opening on the cracks and whorls in the whitewashed ceiling. With another lurch she remembered where she was; the remembering as sharp as the clapstick snapping on down the row. Instantly her hand felt beneath her for a wet place on the mattress; then she propped herself up on her elbow, the rough scratch of the blanket on her legs, and looked out across the row at the children who slept here with her. Through the ashen dawn light, through the bars of her bedstead she saw them getting up, the one with the crutches, the one with the harelip, the simpleminded ones, the orphans: nineteen in all, all of them wards of the county and full-time inmates of this place whose name she hated to say. She watched them as they reached up, arms high, pulling off nightshifts; reached down, legs spread, squatting over chamber pots. She tried for an instant to see them as her sisters waking in the morning at home; she couldn't maintain the illusion for longer than that. There were the sounds that didn't fit: the babbling of some, the whimpers of others; the beginning of Ellen's chant beside her, "Sally go round, Sally go." In the next nearest bed she was coming awake—Ellen with her slanting eyes and slurred speech and slow heavy body, reeking of the diapers she still wore at ten years old. Ellen was nearest: better Ellen than certain others. Farthest away, ten beds down, stood the dreaded Pug, fully dressed, hands on hips: at thirteen, the oldest in the room and its unquestioned tyrant. Pug had grown up in workhouses like this one: due to her superior age and know-how she had charge of waking them with the clapstick and goading them into their clothes. Pilfered cinnamon sticks bulged her cheek like tobacco; she chewed and watched and laid down the law: "Jenny, you ten now? You don't learn to move faster, you won' tsee eleven . . . move, Maureen, get dressed or you die of new-mony like the last girl, I been here, I know . . . slugabed's askin' for trouble." . . . Annie felt Pug's eyes and the burn of that gaze propelled her from bed, her heart beginning to jump. Moving swiftly, she covered her mattress with the blanket and stripped down to her undershift, facing the low pine shelf behind her bed. To calm the needling of fear inside her, she fixed on the things before her: hairbrush, soap tray, stockings, drawers, the dress she had come in, the dress she'd go home in. The footsteps stopped behind her. She pulled her rough dayshift over her head, over the cloth bag around her neck, and kept her eyes on the folds of her good dress, the dress she'd go home in any day now, any day.

"Wet the bed again, snot-nose?"

Annie kept her back turned.

The clapstick snapped next to her ear.

"You hear me, sheet-pisser?"

Annie's hands closed on a pair of stockings.

"Too shamed to look me in the eye, piss-bed?"

Silence.

Clack-snap. A streak of pain shot through the lobe of her ear as the clapstick bit it, and she dodged away, pressing her lips tight against the yelp in her mouth. Pug stood watching her, arms folded, eyes aglitter. Her name was clearly derived from her pug nose and round face; a face as hard as a fist, punching forward on the air, chin thrust out, elbows and pelvis thrust out below it, her skin freckled and her hair, the color of licorice, bobbed as short as a boy's.

"Said you wet your bed again, you still want mama?"

Annie turned to Ellen, who sat gazing up at them, confiding her rhyme to herself in a whisper.

"They're coming back for me, Ellen"—Annie began a high fast patter—"maybe tomorrow, maybe today, coming back real soon—"

"Tell us, piss-bed."

"—real soon, Ellen, coming back for me in a brand-new buggy, buggy with red wheels, matched horses, that's right, wait till you see it, Ellen, give you a ride, they're bringing me a brand-new dress too, dress to wear home, yellow with a—"

"Sure they are, shit-face." Pug shoved her. "Ellen believes you, acourse Ellen believes it's Sunday every day if you tell her so, don't you, Ellen—God, she stinks, you two make a real good pair, Annie-Fannie, both you need diapers—oh no? You telling me no, well look here."

With a snap of her wrist Pug flipped the light cotton blanket off Annie's bed and into the air, exposing the stained mattress to the line of girls forming in the aisle. "Piss-bed-piss-bed," she hissed, sidestepping as Annie lunged at her and sprawled on all fours; a moment later the blanket dropped from Pug's hand over her head.

"Piss-bed-piss-bed," Pug whispered, pulling her line of charges from the room, and Annie, face flaming, fists clenched, had to join them or miss breakfast. *Piss-bed-piss-bed* down the hall, down into the mildewed dimness of the stairwell, the grown inmates joining them there; down the steps amidst the slow scrape of worn shoes, the flap of baggy pants and sagging shifts, the rising rancid odor of them, *piss-bed-piss.* Down with the deaf ones, the drunks, the half-wits, the old ones, the lame, the whole shuffling company closing in around Annie, moving her along, taking her in, marching her down to the long pine tables in the shadowed dining hall. Her hand lifted in rhythm with theirs, spoonfuls of oatmeal rising to their lips, to hers, the grayness of their sleeves the same grayness of hers, and as always at meals she felt a flash of panic, seeing herself sinking into this drab silent army. Beyond this meal the day stretched wide and the sewing machine waited in the basement—but before the basement there would be five minutes of delicious respite.

Between breakfast and the commencement of work there was a narrow crack in the day, and every day she slipped through that crack, slipped away alone up to the attic. She made sure no one saw her as she went; it wasn't a haven she wished to share. She shut the short hutchlike door behind her with care, listening before she started up the spindly staircase. She would climb, holding her breath, up into that dusty gabled space, its roof only high enough for a child's head, its floor littered with old sewing forms and moldering boxes and, curiously, the rotting keyboard of a disembodied piano. The place had come to hold for her the magic of a cave or a candy shop; its light seemed golden, shimmering with dust motes, catching in the cobwebs by the small diamond-shaped window. She would stand at the window, looking out over the Infirmary's grounds, watching some of the gray uniforms appear there: a man helping to slop the hogs, a woman sprinkling corn for the chickens, a line of children starting to hoe the vegetable garden. She would see the lumbering shapes of cows in the pasture, the haze of green on the fields, but it wasn't any of this that held her eye. It was the curve of road that ran past the gates, following along the dark line of trees and disappearing there out of sight. It was the road that led up toward Greenville, up toward Versailles and Wayne Township, up toward home. Every morning her eye would trace the road; every morning she would stand there and put in her mouth her allotted sugar lump from breakfast, saving it with greedy excitement for this moment. As the sugar began its delectably slow melt on her tongue, she would imagine her mother on that road, her mother coming back for her in the wagon. She would draw the image so vividly in her mind she could almost see it there: her mother's gray bonnet, the one with the long ribbon-like ties. Her mother's brown cape, the one with the black buttons in the shape of berries. Her mother's black hair, put up the way she'd seen it done a hundred times, with the eight hairpins and the two wooden combs. Her face, so like the face Annie saw in her own cracked mirror every day, but pink, pleasured. Her mother would come smiling. Her mother would come whistling. Her mother would come speaking in that soft Quaker way, the old way, that tender way faintly recalled from earliest childhood.

It was the nature of this reverie that it lasted as long as the sugar cube did. It would coast her back down the attic steps, down the three flights of stairs to the sewing room, and it was only there, after the last misting of sugar had faded from her mouth, that harsher thoughts would strike her. Her mother seldom smiled like that. Her mother no longer whistled. Her mother hadn't talked Quaker to her in years. Her mother, moreover, was the one who had placed her here, knowing full well all the while what it would be like.

"My mother," she said. "I wanted her so much. Wanted her coming for me, holding out her arms, wanted that so bad. And I believed in it—for a while. The things you want to believe. The things you make yourself believe.

"Every day I'd look in the mirror. I looked more like her than anyone else. I was in her image—surely, surely, that had to mean something. I'd see her eyes in the mirror, I'd see her nose. Her mouth. I'd make the mouth smile. I could almost smell that almond oil she put on her hair. And I'd whisper to the mirror, 'Take me home, take me home, why do I have to be here?' The mirror would just mist over with my breath. And I'd hear her voice saying, 'You know the answer to that, Phoebe Ann.'

"Seemed like she said that every question I asked after Papa died. She never smiled easily, my mother, she smiled even less then. And I missed that lightness around her that

came when she'd whistle, washing clothes, cooking supper—
songs my father sang, 'Drink To Me Only,' 'Old Folks At
Home,' songs like that. Sometimes I wondered if she even
knew she was whistling them. They didn't seem to fit with
her, exactly, but it was good being near her, those times. She
never whistled after Papa died. And she never talked Quaker
at bedtime again. I remember her *thees* and *thous*, how soft
they were. How safe they made me feel. 'Get thee in . . .'
she'd say, 'lay thee down. . . .' Bedtime, it was the only time
she said them. And then she stopped, except with my brother,
the only boy among us girls. He was nearest my age. His bed
was nearest mine. It hurt me, hearing her with him. But
bedtime, well, that was the least of the changes that year.

"I remember my mother going off in the wagon, those first
times. Her bag up on the seat next to her. One of the lanterns
hooked alongside. That gray bonnet hiding her face. She
didn't like good-byes, she'd never turn around to wave. And
we'd all be standing there waving to the side of her bonnet.
I'd watch her till I couldn't see the wagon anymore, my throat
so tight. Wondering if it would be the way it was with Papa,
her going off in the morning, being carried in at night. She'd
ride away and be gone for days, sometimes weeks, taking care
of sick people across the township—the county paid her, she
was what they called a district nurse. She didn't know
doctoring, never claimed to, but even so, she got to be
known.

"I remember one time when she was home between her
'cases.' A man banged on the door, asking for her—hollering
for her. His cart was out front, could she come quick, he said,
his girl had fallen off a horse. My mother rushed out, me
after her. I can still see her skirts flying out behind her over
the grass, the cart tied up to the gatepost, and that terrible
screaming coming from it. There was a girl lying in it, she
was maybe about ten, lying on an old quilt. The quilt caught
my eye, it looked so like one of ours, with a red pattern—
then I realized some of the red was her blood. Her arm was
lying crooked beside her, like it wasn't hers. Then I saw the
white splinter of bone sticking out above the wrist. I felt a jab
of sickness, looking at it, but my mother was already up on
the cart—the girl screaming, panting, shivering all over, my

mother so calm. She called for me to fetch another quilt and the sugar jar. By the time I got back with them the girl had quieted, lying with her head on my mother's lap. My mother leaned over, talking to her. Held her. Stroked her face, smoothed her hair. Swayed back and forth, crooning, crooning. She spread our quilt over her. She dipped her finger in the sugar jar, held it to the girl's lips—let her lick the sugar off. And how that girl clung to her, that hair, blonde blonde hair, all over her lap. . . . My mother couldn't set the bone but she rode in to the doctor's with them. And I'm sure that girl's head was on her lap all the way.

"The sight of her there, my mother with that girl in her arms, how that stayed in my mind. How I wanted her to hold me like that, oh God, ached for it. How I longed for her to croon to me, lay her hand against my cheek that way . . . just one time, just once. I must have seen her holding that girl, over and over in my mind, every day I was at the Infirmary. I'd never seen my mother like that with anyone before . . . except maybe my brother. And I guess I thought about it whenever I saw her getting ready for another week or two away, out with her cases.

"I'd know she was going when I saw her bag sitting out on the bed, the one she always took with her. Her clothes laid out. That soft white flannel nightgown. Her big old checked apron. Her underwear in a muslin sack tied with a ribbon. Once, when no one was looking, I pulled the nightgown on. It smelled like her. It felt so good, as if I'd gone inside her skin. I was standing there in it, looking through her nursing bag, that time she caught me.

" 'Don't touch that'—her voice made me jump.

" 'I wasn't.'

" 'Take that off.'

" 'Oh Mama, do you have to go, *have* to?'

" 'You know the answer to that, Phoebe Ann.'

" 'Stay? Just this one time, just this once?'

" 'Why do you plague me like this, child, I believe you lie in wait for me every time I step foot out that door. Your sisters, even your little brother, they don't pull at me like that. Let go now, you ought to be glad of that money I'm fetching in, you truly ought.'

139

" 'Maryjane says it's getting ready to snow again.'

" 'Nonsense.'

" 'We'll make snow-sugar when you come back?'

" 'Snow-sugar—that was your father's folly, Phoebe Ann, *take* off that nightgown.'

"I took it off slowly and handed it to her. As soon as it touched her hands she was folding it. I watched her hands, those long fine hands. The hands of a tall woman. And that's how she appeared to me, tall, though she wasn't any taller than I am now. There was something about her. Some air, some . . . dignity. She was always so far away, all of her hidden, held back. She looked so beautiful to me right then. Untouchable. I wanted to touch her. I wanted to put my fingers on her face, smooth out the lines on her forehead. Wanted to draw the mouth into a smile. And, same time, I wanted to pinch her—it's true—wanted to push the flesh on her face into ugly shapes, to hurt her. For her coldness. For the way she let her voice cut me.

" 'Don't you look at me that way,' she said, sharp. 'Don't you ever let me catch you looking that way again. And don't you let me hear any more complaining.' She smoothed the folds of the nightgown. 'What do you have to complain about? You're here, safe. I'm the one has to go out sponging down strangers. It wasn't supposed to be this way for me, you know. I was the one supposed to have the nursemaids, your father always promised. *My* father always promised. Back in Pennsylvania, a dressmaker made my clothes, did you know that? Now just you look. The doctor-lady's coming, they say. You think I enjoy it? Doctor-lady! I clean up their puke. I pour broth down their throats. Sleeping on God knows what-all, that's right.' Her hands shook out the nightgown, folding it tighter, talking more to herself. 'Well, some places are better than others. Some places, helping with the babies, it's better. Over to Frenchtown, that time. Nice place. Clean. Curtains. Lady there, real grateful. Held to my hand, wouldn't leave go. Grateful. . . .' Her eyes came back to me. 'Some people are plenty grateful for what I do, you try and be. Every time I look at you, you're giving me those eyes. Like you're blaming me. Don't you blame me, this isn't my doing. Your father's the one went out in that storm, your precious father.' She snapped her bag open, dropped the night-gown inside. 'Comparing me with him, that's what you're doing, isn't it? Listen to me, I'm not your pa. I'm not your pa, Phoebe Ann, you understand me? No one else expects me to be but you. I can't be your pa, you hear? Everyone can't pet you and love on you like he did, make you the little special one. Be grateful you have a mama. Be grateful I'm able to feed you. Now take that look off your face, Phoebe Ann, you got more to do than glare at me. Get about your sewing, I fetched in those two jobs for you, that lady wants her dresses Thursday week, I won't tell you again. You're to stay here and sew, help out, understand? Go on with you now, I said go on, mind me.' "

SHE was to stay there and sew.

She was to stay there and sew for the money.

She was there, in the basement of the Darke County Infirmary, at the second sewing machine, Domestic brand, with its six drawers and its monogrammed treadle, every day from six in the morning till five-thirty in the afternoon, to sew shifts and drawers and pinafores for the inmates under the age of fifteen, to sew at the machine for twenty-five cents a week that would every second Monday be sent home to her mother.

In the sewing room, in the basement, it was always damp, and her nose always ran, and the best light would filter in through the high windows near the ceiling, making small squares that slowly moved across the floor. The room smelled of machine oil and cabbage; cabbage was grown in great quantities on the grounds, flooding the building with its smell and accompanying every meal except breakfast—she could never eat cabbage after that. She would sit at the machine and she would wipe her nose on her sleeve and she would adjust her chair. She knew to sit with her back firmly against the wall so she could see everyone who came in or out. Early in her first week there, she'd learned the value of walls at her back in a place like that; as she'd bent over a seam, she'd felt a sharp thin pain near her shoulder blade and spun around to find it was Ellen, placidly, curiously inserting a pin into her flesh. She always looked for walls after that, and seated against one, she'd prop the back legs of her chair on blocks of wood, leaning closer, lower; it was the only way she could reach the treadle and the needle at once. Finally she would hear the hum and clatter of the machine, and under her hands the simple dresses would begin to take shape: gray, gray, always gray, made of the same coarse cotton that scratched her back as she leaned over the machine.

Sometimes people from upstairs would wander in as Ellen had, touching things, tearing things, talking to each other and to themselves, but more often there was a kind of peacefulness to the sewing room. Sometimes, as the sunlight moved up the steep side of the afternoon, she would have a few moments that approached ease, if not contentment; a feeling she never had anywhere else there except in the attic. Part of the peacefulness, she knew, came from Clara, with whom she shared the room: Clara, who worked on the other machine, was a middle-aged black woman, a mute, and a skilled seamstress. Under her gray-flecked hair, her broad face looked tranquil and her heavy figure, creaking with corset stays, was somehow comforting. Her large bosom and capacious lap jutted from her like a series of balconies, and across that bosom gleamed rows of needles and pins, thirty or forty of them, stored there for easy reach and glinting from her like jewelry. Sometimes she would hold up a piece of work for Annie to see or she would nod at work in Annie's hands; sometimes she would produce a piece of stolen food, pilfered expertly from the storage bins—an apple, a pear, a wedge of cheese. Once she had brought forth from the folds of her dress a jar half filled with marmalade and she and Annie had devoured it together, making little whinnies of pleasure. Above their heads, that afternoon, ordinary sounds had drifted through the windows on the spring air: the clang of tools, distant voices—not the voices of this house, its rooms and corridors, but the voices of the world beyond it; voices that spoke matter-of-factly of hoes and rakes and ham for Sunday dinner. The memory of that afternoon remained with Annie a long time.

Sometimes in the quiet of the sewing room, her thoughts would turn dark, disturbing: the dreaminess possible at the window in the attic was never possible here. But sometimes other thoughts came, other memories. Sometimes, sitting with Clara, the sewing would put her in mind of her sister, Maryjane, who had taught her to sew. She would think of those times then, those good times; times with Maryjane and the sewing, with Maryjane and the rifle.

"Maybe it's the way you see things, that age, you know, close up, but I was always very mindful of Maryjane's smile. She had perfect even teeth, they got all mixed in my mind with those polished white buttons she used to sew in rows on the dresses she made. That smile of hers . . . I have so little of her, but I always like to think I have her smile." She sat silent for a minute, her eyes filling. "So many, many memories of Maryjane—that thick red hair she had. The way she could whistle, real loud, piercing, to call us inside. Those mint leaves she chewed, they grew by the door and that smell was always around her. . . . She wasn't gentle. Or 'sweet-faced,' her made-up word for some of the ladies we sewed for . . . sewing was something we had together, she and I, more specially ours than anyone else's. After Papa died my mother started bringing in sewing jobs for us, and Maryjane, she taught all us girls to sew fine. I guess she spent more time with me than the others because I was younger. Like I said, she wasn't gentle. But she was gentle with me.

"I thought of Maryjane as nearly grown-up, almost sixteen that year. Mostly she ran the household after Papa died, my mother away so much of the time, off on her nursing cases. She ran it less strict, Maryjane did, less fussy. But still, with her you always knew where everything was: kettles, cups, brooms—the winter clothing up in the loft, the summer clothes out in the lean-to. You knew when things would happen: meals, lamplighting, bedtime. Papa was gone, my mother was away—everywhere you could feel them missing —but Maryjane was there and things were going on. So many memories of her . . . but then again . . . not so many. Not enough. Not near enough . . ." And she stopped, sitting silent again, eyes wet.

Her memories of Maryjane that last year lay in her mind glimmering like the slivers of a shattered mirror, each reflecting back to her a separate image of the whole. They had been so long locked within her, hoarded, treasured there, she spoke of them haltingly at first, but she could see them clearly; so clearly I could see them too. Maryjane sitting with her in the doorway, heads bent together over their sewing. Maryjane kneeling on the cabin floor, pinning up on a chair a long float of a wedding dress, commissioned by a lady in town: the whiteness of the dress shimmering in the dimness, light from the open door slicing across it; the coppery spill of Maryjane's hair bright against the pale skirt, the scissors sparkling on its cord around her neck. Maryjane, her angular frame bending toward the dress, her long face rapt in concentration, all the while directing the setting of the supper table behind her, completely by ear. "I only heard five spoons set down, Sarah Ellen," she called, back turned, her hands submerged in yards of silk. "Lemme hear two more, that's it." A crash, a cry: her hands unfaltering, pinning up lace. "All right, all right, just sweep it up then." Nodding her head at the sound of the broom, clowning for them, a scrap of lace on her hair, whistling loud as a shout, "Here Comes the Bride."

And another sliver, brighter, broader: that summer, her mother gone, the days so long, so hot—so hot at night they'd sit in the doorway, catching what breeze there was, nodding, drifting, and falling asleep there, her head leaned back against Maryjane. At dawn they'd wake and gaze out over the rustling flatness of the fields around them, low picketlike rows of corn on one side, a sweep of wheat on another, here and there the red rise of a barn, the whole vast green expanse rippling, swaying, leaning toward the faint horizon line.

No place to go, that summer, no wagon to ride in, not much to do, except to watch Maryjane fire off Papa's rifle. She'd take it down from its pegs over the hearth to clear the birds off the vegetable garden, measuring the load as she'd seen their father do, all of them gathering near her on the grass. Annie would sit there, hands clasped around her knees, waiting breathless for Maryjane to fire the rifle—listening for that sound: a sound to her like distant thunder, rolling thunder, thrilling her and threading down her spine a raptured tingle. She'd ask Maryjane to do it again and again, as if she were setting off a great firecracker, and soon Annie had taken over that task of scaring off the birds.

"The first time I did it, that rifle felt so heavy my younger brother Johnny had to hold the barrel up for me—one hand under the muzzle, one finger in his ear. And how that rifle kicked, hit me right in the nose. The baby, Huldie, she burst into tears and toddled off on her fat little legs for the house as fast as she could. And Maryjane, lying back on her elbows in the grass—her hair, I remember it, so red in the sun—she barely kept from laughing. And how I loved her for not. 'You must have dumped in enough powder to kill off a buffalo,' she said, getting up. 'Well, never mind, try it again . . . jam it real tight into your shoulder, Annie, no, like this . . . all right, now cock it, and when you squeeze, squeeze easy, *easy* . . .' I squeezed. And there it was, that great noise again, that noise like thunder. Some blackbirds flapped off a tree. I let out a whoop at them. I let out a whoop at my sister. She was standing there, smiling at me, and before I could even ask for it, she was handing me a fresh cap and the powder flask, knowing I was going to have to do it again.

"I have so many pictures in my mind of me standing there with that muzzle-loader, Maryjane beside me, watching, directing, her apron still on—us in the vegetable patch, then at the fence, plinking at a row of cracked mason jars. And then I wanted to hit more than mason jars. My arms weren't strong enough yet to hold the rifle up for birds, but I knew I could get a rabbit, a squirrel. And after that I was out all day trying for them. One time I was on this old wagon trace and I saw something move in the grass alongside. Something brown, a haunch was all. And I knew—how did I know?—that was my rabbit. I loaded up real quiet, I capped the rifle—the rabbit gave a hop and *there*, I had it, I'd dropped it, my shoulder was tingling from the rifle's kick. And right then there was this sound, far off, some farmer's wife ringing a dinner bell . . . this low peaceful clanging, I always remember that. I remember listening to the bell, looking at that rabbit—and feeling raised up out of myself, big as the day.

"When I brought the rabbit in to Maryjane, she was at the stove. And I just stood there, holding the rabbit out to her. I couldn't say a word. I was so proud, I was near to tears. Maryjane had a wooden spoon in her hand, stirring this ever-lasting lentil stew we had every night—she just tossed that spoon over her shoulder and swept me up off the floor. 'Meat!' I still remember how she said it, that low firm voice of hers, trilling up at the end: 'Oh Annie, *meat!*'

"Well, what had started out as a game—making our own thunder—had turned into putting meat on the table. I was out with that muzzle-loader almost every day after that, chasing rabbits, squirrels . . . and the more I was out there, the more I wanted to stay out. Out in the fields I forgot Papa was dead, forgot my mother was away. Out there I started to have this feeling . . . that the fields were mine . . . I could wade into them, deep, deeper . . . and out there with the rifle, everything was right. That feeling was so strong, you know, even my mother's anger couldn't stop me. She went white the first time she saw me with the rifle, she shook me . . . even so, I couldn't stop. I just waited till she went off again, and she was away so much I didn't have to wait long. My sister was always glad of meat on the table, pleased to see it, pleased with me—whenever my mother was gone, Maryjane would reach the rifle down for me in the mornings and prop it against the wall. She never said right out that I could take it. But she'd smile and leave it there . . . and when I'd look back at the house from the fields, sometimes I'd see her waving from the doorway.

"And then that next spring, there was the week when the rifle stayed up on its pegs. Just a chill, Maryjane said from her bed, it was nothing. But soon again there was that terrible sound of hard breathing in the cabin. I used to lie awake listening to it. I remembered. I knew what it meant.

"Sometimes I'd wake up whimpering and see Maryjane standing there by my bed. Her hair would be in two long plaits. Her hands would be hot but as soon as she'd touch me

146

I'd feel calm. Her eyes, big hazel eyes, they looked green in the nights. She'd lead me over to the hearth . . . she'd sit me up against her. And we'd look at the banked fire and rock there together. Sometimes she'd cough. But pressed up against her like that, I liked to think I was helping her to breathe. Every time she took a breath I'd concentrate and take one too. I'd feel her chin on top of my head. I'd feel her arms covering mine. We didn't say much. At the time, I never thought I was doing anything to comfort her. I thought all she was doing was comforting me.

"When she died I was stunned as I'd been over my father. But this time I believed it. And I was angry. She was so strong, I thought, she could have fought it. Could have—should have. I helped lay her out . . . it sounds terrible to say, but I wanted to slap her face. I kept thinking of all those things we'd never talked about . . . never would. Beaus . . . parties . . . our own wedding dresses. . . . So many things I wanted to ask her about the rifle. . . . I took the handkerchief I'd been embroidering for her birthday and . . . I did something still shames me. I ripped the stitches out of it, turned it into this horrid ugly piece of cloth all pockmarked with little holes. It was so hard to look at—I was so ashamed of it—I took it and threw it down the well. It wasn't till after the funeral that the anger let go. It was each day missing her made me cry till it hurt. And after that nothing was the same.

"There were doctor bills, funeral bills . . . but I didn't really understand about them, about money, not then. What I understood was the empty place in the barn, one morning, when I went in with the feed. Pink, our cow, was gone, sold. Pink: we'd all grown up riding around on her . . . sitting on her neck, her tongue licking our feet. And then another empty place, Huldie's crib. I kept staring at it, couldn't believe it. My mother had taken her to stay with a neighbor, she wouldn't be living with us for a while. With Maryjane gone, with my mother working, it was better that way I guess, but it sent a shock through me like a slap. We'd played with Huldie like she was our doll, all of us, tickling her, lugging her around . . . and now she was gone too.

"Empty places. Everywhere I looked I saw them. Papa was gone. My mother was away. Maryjane was gone. And Huldie.

Even Pink. It went around and around like that in my head. I couldn't seem to make sense of it. How could everything be so different in such a little time? The house had stopped, stopped like a clock. It was coming apart, nothing was sure anymore. Inside it smelled of spoiled milk, spilled lamp oil. Things broke. No one fixed them. Things got lost. They stayed lost. One day I couldn't find a ladle, next day it was the winter nightgowns. When I finally found them, moths flew out of them. Mealtimes were different every day. There was no bedtime. There were no more apple rings over the hearth. No smell of allspice, paraffin. The red-star quilt was stained with bootblacking. The shoes under the beds were worn out. Even the lamplight didn't look as yellow, and sometimes the lamp wasn't lit at all. Sometimes we'd eat supper in the dark, me and my sisters and my brother, and no one would talk. I'd see them, hunched like shadows around the table. Quiet. Spoons clinking. That scared feeling sitting on us all. And I remember thinking, when Papa died, it was the pump that quit working right. But when Maryjane died, it was the whole household.

"I kept waking up in the nights. My teeth would be chattering. There'd be a knot in my stomach, something sour in my mouth—I'd run out, retching, to the privy. When I'd come back in, I'd stand in the doorway, listening to my sisters, my brother, breathing there in the dark. I'd be so afraid the breathing would turn, change. Or just stop. Mostly then, I'd go over by the hearth. I'd sit there like I did with my sister. I'd sit there and rock, my arms around my knees. Rocking, holding on, whispering over and over, 'Be all right, be all right.'

But it wasn't all right.

She said that haltingly, almost apologetically, quickly adding it wasn't all bad. She didn't want me feeling sorry for her. There were some times it was better, times when her mother was there, not so bad then.

It wasn't all bad. But it wasn't all right.

Not even when her mother married again, a man by the name of Dan Brumbaugh, a widower with grown children, nearly as old as her father had been. It wasn't all right: it was worse when they moved to his cabin, a cabin like the first, pine table and cast iron stove, a vegetable patch and still no money; it wasn't theirs, wasn't home. The house was strange and everything around it was strange as well. The man up at the general store didn't know her, nor did the girl teacher down at the schoolhouse. The fields had a different lay to them; she couldn't so easily conjure the spirits of father and sister moving over them. And there was a new dark-eyed man casting his tall shadow on the curtains drawn across the end of the cabin, across her mother's bed. Many nights he was there alone, her mother still out nursing, and that was strangest of all. He didn't seem to belong there. He didn't seem to belong to them.

"He'd never belong to me," she said. "I knew it that first meal, first one we all had together. I remember us all sitting there, around the table, my mother saying the blessing. And then us children, we were supposed to go around the table and say something to welcome him, each one of us. We'd been drilled in it I don't know how many times. And it started, 'Welcome, Papa Brumbaugh' . . . 'Glad to have you, Papa Brumbaugh' . . . till it came around to me. I looked at him, that man, her Mr. Brumbaugh, sitting at the head of the table—my throat just closed over. My mother nodded past me at Johnny. 'Hope you'll like it here, Mr. Brumbaugh,' he just sang right out, perfectly rehearsed. My mother's eyes came back to me. Her smile faded. And I still couldn't speak. Everyone was looking at me—I just glared down at my plate. Not shamed—mad. Mad that she was making me do this, making any of us. And after a minute, she made this little click in her throat, finished the blessing and started ladling the soup. She didn't look at me for the rest of the meal—and my stepfather, he couldn't seem to stop looking at me. He was tall and stringy, gray-haired, balding. I remember he had knuckles that stood out like knobs on his fingers when he cut his food up, chopping at his plate like he was splitting kindling on it. He was clean-shaven, but his beard made a shadow, coming in on his face. His eyes were so dark you couldn't see the pupils and they kept passing over us. And kept fastening on me. I could just hear him thinking, This one'll be trouble. I didn't care. He'd been a neighbor for years, I'd seen him from my father's horse. He'd been short-spoken, hard-eyed then—I'd never taken to him and I wouldn't now. Most of all, I was afraid him being there would keep me from the rifle. I didn't dare take it down when he was around, but he started going off on carpentry jobs around the county, and there again, we were mostly left on our own.

"The household was still half stopped, those times. Half dark. I still kept waking up in the nights, teeth chattering, wanting Maryjane. But I knew if I could get out in the fields next day, it would be better. I'd think about it: Pulling that burlap sack over my hat . . . pinning my hat on . . . reaching down the muzzle-loader . . . and that feeling I'd get, like coasting, running out the door with it . . . I'd think about it and I'd be able to sleep then. Out there in the fields, everything else still seemed to roll off me. Out there, the smell, the feel of the house, it didn't seem to matter so much. I didn't know why, but out there I was far far away.

"Sometimes if my mother was home, or my stepfather, I'd go out there without the rifle, just to sit. Sit and be there, letting my eye follow the birds. That's where I was the day Mrs. Eddington stopped in to visit my mother—the day everything changed. I was called back in, so were my sisters. We were told to go over by the window and work on our sewing, while my mother and this guest of hers sat at the table, talking. I remember the nightgown I was smocking. And the sound of their coffee cups, their voices, my mother and this little plump woman in a flowered dress . . . it was too tight on her, I noticed, made her look upholstered somehow. She had a way of cocking her head at us, watching us sew. Watching us close. My mother had done some work over at her place, she said, they knew each other fine. . . . Something in her voice, I couldn't say what, made me look at her again. She stood up, patted our heads. And over our heads I saw her nod at my mother. I saw her eyes, that appraising look in them. Snatches of their talk came back in my ears—about what a fine place she had, any child would be happy there. And I grabbed up my cloak and ran outside—I stayed there till I was called three, maybe four times for supper.

"That night I heard them talking behind the curtain. My

mother. My stepfather. 'She should. Phoebe Ann should go.' They didn't think I could hear them, but their talk seemed to fill up the cabin. 'You see how she's different. Trouble. Best she be there.' I couldn't close my eyes for the whispering. 'Soon . . . trouble . . . she's the one should go.' Next morning they told me it was arranged. I was going away to where Mrs. Eddington lived. I'd sew and make money and the money would be sent home. It was only a visit. It was only so I could help. Only a visit, such a help, I should be proud.

"I sat out in the fields all that day, waiting till night. After supper my mother went behind the curtains around her bed. My stepfather hadn't come in yet. I went and pushed the curtains aside. My mother was sitting on the bed in her nightgown, that soft flannel nightgown I'd put on that one time. She was taking down her hair. The quilt was turned back. I ran to her, climbed on the quilt, hung onto her. I didn't want to go, I started to say, and then I felt the tears spilling over. She told me to be a big girl now, they were counting on me. I hung onto her nightgown with both hands, my face pressed into it, Let me stay, let me stay. The smell of the nightgown was so close, I was wetting it with my tears, I couldn't stop. My mother's voice came over me sharp. She uncurled my fingers from the flannel. There was a silence, a strange one. I looked up. My stepfather was standing there where the curtains were parted, unbuttoning his shirt, looking at me. After a minute I crawled out of their bed, crept away.

"That night, I took the rifle down and pulled the hammer out of it. I put the hammer in my cloth sack and hung the sack around my neck. I would have it to remind me. And while I was gone, no one else would be able to use what I'd come to think of as mine. There was nothing more to be done. Next day I was taken away in the wagon. It was January. There was snow on the ground. It was the year I'd turn nine."

It was the year she learned to keep a wall at her back. It was the year she learned to hoard sugar and treasure dreams. It was the year she learned to empty twenty chamber pots for a hundred people in half an hour, that half hour of free time between sewing and supper, at the end of each day at the Darke County Infirmary.

It was another of her jobs: at five-thirty the sewing machines would fall silent, their covers put on, and she would be up on the third floor again, passing down the dim corridor to the "idiot room." The room was so named because it was the day chamber for the twenty grown inmates who couldn't work: the insane, the very old, the three who were blind, and though it was empty at that hour it always held a deep terror for her. Its door swung back slowly at her touch, a special door of heavy oak. Inside the air smelled like sour cheese, overheated by the coal stove in the corner, the windows nailed shut, shades drawn. The room would swim in faded yellowish light, and she would force herself to move forward into its silence, a silence like none she had ever known, as if the room were under some ominous spell. The objects within would seem suspended in the silence: the bench with the toys, the faded red ball, the china doll with its face rubbed away; the old slat-backed rocker in the deep grooves worn in the floor; a gray shawl, its fringe plaited over and over into tiny braids; the two tall chairs with the straps on the arms and seats. The close rancid smell of the place made her stomach quiver as she moved about with her bucket, emptying the china pots, trying to stand clear of the splash and the stench. Her eyes fixed on the streams of urine rather than the bench, the chairs. She did not want to wonder if she would one day sit in this room, staring at the handprints on the walls, and at the needlepoint motto nailed high on one: *Blessed Are The Meek*. She did not want to wonder; she always did. She would move toward the door with the weight of the room upon her, and once she was out in the hall there was a new terror: this hallway, this time in the afternoon, was often the province of Pug.

Pug's daily task was to help in the "idiot room" and for some reason unknown to Annie, she was its good angel, showing a gentle side to its inmates she showed no one else; it was rumored her sister had died there, but rumors like that were common. At any rate, after the room's inhabitants had begun their slow descent to supper, Pug sometimes stayed in that hall sweeping up, and though she never menaced anyone in the room itself, the hallway was fair territory. As Annie stepped back into it, she stopped, listening, glancing about, hoping that this afternoon she would be spared: before supper she wanted to ask Mrs. Eddington about going home.

The hallway crouched over her, dim and windowless and long, echoing faintly as she lugged her slop bucket toward the dumbwaiter. Again she had the feeling of being underwater, passing slowly through the shadows, her eyes fixed on the floor threading out ahead of her. She had just set down the bucket on the dumbwaiter when a hand fell on her shoulder.

"What you up to, piss-bed?"

Annie turned quickly, setting her back to the wall, staring into that brittle face, those mocking blue eyes.

"Think you're too good to talk to me—don't you."

Pug waited a moment; Annie set her jaw, refusing to reply.

"Think you're so godamighty different?"

In the silence she could feel Pug's hand tightening on her shoulder.

"You ain't, you hear?" Pug reached out swiftly and, with sharp precision, pinched Annie's nipples through her shift, one, then the other, her fingers snapping like pinking shears. Gasping, Annie wrenched free, and as the hand reached out again she took the nearest exit she saw—she dodged headfirst into the dumbwaiter. Crouching on the platform by the bucket, she reached up and yanked the rope; the dumbwaiter sank down the shaft, leaving Pug's startled face hanging above her. But almost as soon as she was completely enclosed in the blackness between floors, the dumbwaiter gave a violent jolt and lurched to a stop.

"Got you now, shit-face." Pug's laughter pelted her sharp as stones. The dumbwaiter shivered and jerked on its rope in Pug's hands, spilling the slop bucket and sending a warm wash of urine over Annie, crouched beside it. Something sour rose in her throat; a stream of turds slid over her legs. Trapped there in that stinking square of darkness, she choked, she gagged, pounding the walls, and through her panic spiraled bright as flame. The darkness seemed to thicken, crowding close, dense, and then there was another voice slicing through it: a voice calling up through the shaft from the safe world below, a sharp voice demanding, reprimanding, and as soon as it knifed up to Pug, she let go the rope. The dumbwaiter began to slide down the shaft, and with shaking arms, Annie hoisted it the rest of the way.

When she finally emerged, dripping, reeling, she didn't look around. She ran out back, whimpering to herself, shivering, her knees wobbling as she dragged the bucket behind her. Listing unsteadily, she dumped it down the privy and then crouched by the pump, trying to clean herself off; trying to stop whimpering, trembling, and could not stop. When another hand fell on her shoulder she lurched forward against the pump handle—above her was the stern face of Mrs. Simms, a tight-lipped long-necked attendant known as the Serpent, who marched her in to supper.

She took her place at the long table, watching the others lean away from her; she sat within the smell that still rose from her, choking down salt pork, looking around for Pug. Across the room she saw her bobbed head—she pictured that head breaking off at the neck, rolling forward onto her plate. She pictured Pug crawling to her down the upstairs hall, crawling through slops and piss and vomit, crawling painfully and begging her pardon. No more the proud Pug, her body lean and hard, her hair a shining cap on her head: this Pug was haggard and shriveled, afflicted by some terrible blight that had withered her hair, wasted her limbs, and humbled her face while she, Annie, stood in a new yellow dress ignoring pleas for mercy. . . . Her thoughts seemed a scream in the quiet dining room. The grin on her face felt jagged, slashed there, evil. It faded; the images shredded away. Inside her the darkness deepened again. The only thing that could change it would be going home.

As soon as supper was over she was running for Mrs. Eddington's study, ignoring the damp patches on her shift, a faint odor of soil still hanging about her. Something was powering her on, pushing her over the threshold, across the thick rug and up to Mrs. Eddington's desk. The words rushed out of her—could she go home, she didn't want to stay, couldn't stay, when could she please go home.

Mrs. Eddington's plump wren-like body seemed to hover

behind her steel-rimmed spectacles were kind, their gaze filtering down through the early evening light.

"Didn't your mama tell you, child? . . . you're to stay here with us a good while, she must have told you that."

Annie shook her head, her fingers gripping the edges of her shift. "She said it wouldn't be long."

"Are you sure she didn't tell you, Annie? We talked about it very carefully. Why, she was here all one afternoon, I showed her through. She saw where you'd sleep, where you'd take your meals, where . . ."

"No—she couldn't have—*couldn't* have."

Mrs. Eddington hesitated a moment. "Perhaps you just don't remember? There are no arrangements for you to go home, Annie. We'll be your home now, how is that? Isn't it fine to be able to stay and help your mama? What a fine thing that is, being able to . . ."

She didn't hear the rest. She turned and ran for the door, the hall beyond blurred by her tears. She didn't bother to keep near a wall, she didn't look around, she didn't care. *You see how she is.* The smell from her clothes, forgotten in the parlor, rose around her again. *Trouble, best she be there.* The smell seemed to stem from deep within her, from some darkness there; a darkness her mother could see, Pug could see. *Think you're so godamighty different?* She was here in this place for people no one wanted, and she wasn't different from them, not anymore.

Her legs carried her up the stairs, to the second floor, to the next, and kept on going. She had never been there before in the evening but she knew, as she reached the third hallway, that she was heading for the attic. She could barely see it as she emerged into the sloping space; it was bathed in twilight, its forms and barrels looming ghostly around her. She paused, hearing a sound: the scuttle of a rat. Something drifted past her cheek; she brushed the cobwebs back and moved toward the window. For a moment she stood there, looking out at the curve of the road against the dimming land. And then she put her fist through the pane of glass, not minding the sting of her knuckles, listening for the faint tinkle below on the brick path to the spring house. Now her view was ruined behind the desk, as if on some invisible perch. The eyes forever. Now she would never be able to moon at that road again. She would not even be tempted.

"After that night, Jimmie, I never went up there again. I didn't tell Ellen anyone was coming for me. I didn't let myself dream on that another time. I got listless. Dragged around, didn't care. I could feel it, the way I moved, walked, I was getting more like the others. There was just one little string of things that I did, that I held to, counted on, every night.

"Every night I brushed my hair fifty times.

"Every night I rinsed my face ten times.

"Every night after I was in bed I took out my cloth bag and shined the button, the stone, the thimble, the hammer.

"Every night I went over in my mind the sewing I'd done that day, picturing each stitch, making sure each one was even, right.

"Every night I said to myself the names of everyone in my family, living or dead, not the way I did in the prayertime but slowly, imagining each face as I said the name, to make them remember me.

"And every night I went over in my mind, very slowly and carefully, the exact steps for cleaning, loading, and firing the muzzle-loader that was still over the hearth, to make sure I didn't forget. I did this last because it was the best, and I made it go on as long as I could, until I finally fell asleep.

"That got me through the nights. I don't know what got me through the days. Maybe it was Clara, being near her. Maybe it was the sewing. But I was like a sleepwalker. No wishes, no will. I knew I could stop feeling that way if someone would come for me, but no one would. I'd always be like that, I thought.

"So maybe you can understand, Jimmie, how much it meant to me when this man drove up and asked to see the girls, to see them for hiring, and took a shine to me. You can see why I wanted to go with him, get taken into his home. There he was in this handsome coat and driving gloves, this tall fine-looking man, smiling, boyish, with that big laugh. All us girls were lined up and he looked us all over. He looked at Mrs. Eddington, he looked at me. And I'll never forget what he said. He looked at me and he said 'Perfect.' He said it twice. 'Perfect. She's the one I want.' He wanted me. Someone wanted me. He said that, and he put his hand on my shoulder. I felt something raise up inside me. Someone had come for me, someone had come at last."

She said that and she winced. And for a few moments she didn't say anything more; she bent her head into her hands and she just sat there, the light from the street lamps catching in her hair.

Sulfur. Slippery elm. Wild honey.

Spring medicine: she's never forgotten it, that sharp sweet smell all through the Infirmary the day he came for her. It was brewing in the kitchen that day and she could smell it in the company parlor, as she stood on the Turkey carpet by the window, waiting, waiting. She could smell the traces of sandalwood soap lingering about her, could see the paper-white rims of her fingernails, could almost feel the shining pinkness of her ears after her bath the night before. The feel of that bath, the warmth of the water, the gentle hands of Mrs. Eddington—it all eddied around her like a faint breeze as she watched the yellow buggy come into sight, growing larger, clearer, on that curve of road she had gazed at so many times.

"What a chance," everyone had said; Clara had beamed, and Mrs. Eddington, and Mrs. Eddington's husband, the superintendent himself: "What an opportunity." The other girls were envious; out of all of them, she had been chosen. She would be riding off in that yellow buggy, a buggy that even surpassed the one in her stories to Ellen: brand-new, polished to a high shine; brass headlamps, nickel plating, black wheels. And it was coming there for her.

The man on its seat had driving gloves the same color as the buggy, a rich honey color. She saw the fine weave in his jacket, his shirt, she saw the gleam of his watch chain in the sun. She remembered noticing the watch chain and smelling the medicine and looking out on the crowd around the buggy: the buggy that was here to take her away; to take her on, Mrs. Eddington had said, on to better things. The buggy —and the man. The man, she said, who would be like a father to her. Looking back later, she saw that the Eddingtons must have arranged this for her, but at the time all she knew was that she had been chosen; someone had seen something special in her that no one else had found.

She was breathless climbing up into that buggy, speechless all the way to the new house. It wasn't far, not much above a mile from the Infirmary, but it seemed a vast distance to her, crossing a line into a different land entirely. The fields slid past them, enchanted, April green, and then the house was rising up before them, a fine brick house sitting back from the road, sitting back on its land. She was breathless, speechless, as she crossed its threshold, passing slowly through its rooms: The parlor. The dining room. The kitchen, the pantry, the lofty halls. The coolness of the house fell over her, fragrant with furniture polish and fresh flowers. It spread before her, serene, silken, revealing to her bookcases and andirons and fringed lampshades; everything so beautiful her eyes misted over and she swallowed hard.

Of all the beautiful things in that house there was one more than any other that seemed to embody the hope she felt shining within her. It was a chair in the front hall, covered in horsehair and trimmed with small brass tacks. Its arms and legs were polished oak; its body was glossy, rich. It had a proud look to it, dignified, but the way its arms curved, they seemed to be reaching out to her. It was this chair that took her eye more than any of the wonders in the house that first day, and that night she slipped downstairs to it after all was still. After an instant, she climbed onto the chair. She knelt on its seat. She put her arms around its back. She pressed her cheek against the smooth smooth horsehair, feeling cradled in some great lap, and she whispered to the chair all her hopes, her hopes for how everything here was going to be.

"My first evening there," she said, "I did just like I'd been taught at the Infirmary—I set the places for the family in the dining room and set a place for myself in the kitchen. But after I came in from drawing the water at the pump, I saw that my place setting was gone from the kitchen. It had been moved out to the dining-room table—I was invited to take my meal with the family. I can't tell you how big that table-cloth looked to me—like a snow-covered lawn. I sat down carefully, at the very edge, and I remember staring at the silver. How it gleamed there beside each place, like jewelry. I remember the roses in the center of each china plate. And the weight of the fork in my hand, balancing it. And those faces there in the lamplight: his, so boyish, so handsome, the gray just starting in his hair. Hers, pale, delicate, under that mass of fair hair she had. I thought they were the most elegant people I'd ever seen. And they had chosen me—these people with a name everyone knew. A good name. An old name. I knew he was a bank trustee, a country commissioner. I was told she gave parties, played the piano. And their son, just a year or so older than me, he knew the names of all the presidents of the United States by heart and in order and also the correct way to peel table fruit. These were the people who had picked me. Who wanted me. This was the family I was eating supper with.

"And oh that supper, that food. How it tasted after all that salt pork at the Infirmary, salt pork and cabbage. The taste of that lamb—cold, roasted before I got there—lamb with rose-mary. And tiny new potatoes. And a spread of pickles, rel-ishes like I'd never seen. White flour rolls, not bread. Straw-berry pie with a lattice crust. I could feel my eyes tearing up, it tasted so good. It was all I could do to chew everything slowly, not gulp, not slurp. I don't think I'd ever seen—or tasted—such a supper.

"They waited until I'd finished eating before they spoke much to me. I was grateful—each forkful took so much concentration from me, I thought somehow they knew that and spared me distractions. Even their boy seemed to be helping me, sitting quiet, passing me the salt before I'd even asked for it. Everything was so calm. So smooth. All I could hear was the breeze in those dried flowers on the sideboard.

"I can't remember the exact words, when they finally talked to me about being there. They dazzled me so, I heard them in a kind of a daze. They were glad to welcome me to their home, they said. They hoped they'd be able to offer me more than employ—more than just the fifty cents a week agreed upon. They hoped they would be able to 'bring me along.' He had certain ideas, certain theories—it could be done, it could be done. It only took the right approach. And the right child. They'd had other girls from the Infirmary before but none was quite right. Until now. Now, Mrs. Eddington had assured them, I was the right one. The right girl. They could see it themselves. *The right girl.* I said it over and over to myself, I could feel my face flushing with the joy of it. I looked at them, there at the table, in the lamplight—my new family. And my throat ached with all I was feeling.

"That night, I went to bed in my new room—a tiny one, but not the one I'd expected to have, the one off the kitchen. This room was upstairs where the rest of the family slept—it looked out over the garden. I remember standing in that room in my nightshift, after everyone had said good night. Standing there, gazing around. There was yellow wallpaper on the walls, patterned with flowers. There was a yellow spread on the bed. There was a lamp with a yellow shade, and the light coming through it was pale pale gold. I tried out the bed. After the Infirmary's cot, it seemed like one big soft sponge cake. I caught a glimpse of myself in the pier glass— I'd never seen myself full length in a mirror before. My face was pink. My eyes all lit up. In that lamplight—in that mirror—I looked different. New. And fine, pretty fine. Not the girl from the Infirmary. Not the girl who got sent away. Not there. Not anymore. Suddenly I thought of my sister, of Maryjane not being able to see this. She would have loved this room. She would have wondered how they'd done the wallpaper. 'Maryjane,' I whispered, 'I'm here for us, Maryjane . . .' I tried to see her face, her hair. 'I'm here for both of us, Maryjane, I'm here for you . . .'"

And she trailed off, her voice dwindling. It was as if she didn't want to go past the shine of that night, that memory, and it was a few moments before she could continue, slower, speaking of the next day: the next day when, through cool slices of morning air, she was startled to hear the sound of arguing. The man's voice, the woman's. It jolted her; that sound didn't fit with this house. She hurried over the bed she was making, the bed in the master bedroom where she had already spent some time studying the silver-handled brushes on the dressing table, the leather-bound books on the nightstand. If those voices didn't seem to belong to this house, they belonged even less to this room, falling perilous as cinders through the air over the peach bedspread. As she flared the spread she seized on an explanation. They weren't arguing. They must be reading aloud. That was it, had to be. She ran her hands down the bed as if to cheer it, patting here, plumping there. And still she heard the voices in the hall, rough angry voices fitting no rhyme, no patterned printed sentences. She came closer to the door, stricken, pressing her face to the keyhole. As she bent nearer the doorknob suddenly rattled, the door swung open. Her master stood there, his fair hair rumpled, his collar not yet on. His face held a look not even hinted at the night before: the eyes penetrating, the mouth set in a mocking smile.

"What are you doing, Annie?"

"Sir? Making the bed, sir."

"Of course you're not."

"Sir?"

"Don't lie, they all lie."

"No sir."

"You were listening."

"No *sir*."

"Just like the others."

"*No* sir *no*."

That was all she could remember saying. Her master's shaving cologne filled the air, confusing her. The harsh voice was astonishing, the very suddenness of it all turning her slow and dumb as she stood by the door, wishing she could cover the keyhole like an ear, the keyhole that had started this. She was lying, she was caught in her lie; the dirt on her soul was showing up in the superior light of this house, its luminous people, so soon, so soon.

She stammered, she backed away. The bed was made wrong, she could see it now that she stood back, the spread was wrongside out, at the foot the sheet hung down—her master saw it too, pulling it apart, layer by layer, till sheets and spread were a pile on the floor. If she'd been making the bed and not listening at the door, then why was the bed all wrong? Was this how she meant to begin? The last sheet cracked through the air like a slap.

She remembers running out of that room, running in terror, in tears, wanting only to get away from that ruined pile of white and peach and those words, repeated, demanding an answer, "*Is this how you mean to begin?*" She ran into the hall, her shoes loud on the stair, her breath coming fast, running and hearing his steps coming after her. He caught up with her as she skidded on the bottom step, catching her, and she clung to him, babbling excuses. His face was above her; for an instant, in desperation, she saw him again as he had looked at supper, as he had looked saying "Perfect." He bent down, his hand on her shoulder, and it was just as she quieted that he hit her across the mouth.

She reeled back against the wall, too stunned to cry, and then she was running again, everything passing her in a haze; the next thing she clearly remembered was washing her face out by the pump and running her finger over her teeth. If they were loose, she deserved it, she had lied through them, she had babbled lies, she had run on those polished hardwood floors, now they would surely send her back—her chance, her chance, ruined, spoilt, in just one day.

The morning passed in silence. She struggled to do the things she'd been told the night before, trying to remember them all, desperate to do them right—afraid to ask a question. She pushed through the silence to dust a mantel, sweep a floor; she stepped through the trembling air into the kitchen to start noon dinner. At last the boy came in, sidling, and leaned against the stove. He had a smile on his face, a smile that seemed it might singe her if she looked at it too long, sly and oddly pleased. His eyes flicked over her as if for fleas. He said she was wanted upstairs in his parents' room, and he sidled off.

With great dread she climbed the stairs. Her feet felt like

dead fish. The slaps they made against the steps alarmed her; she would trip, she would dislodge the carpet rods. But it didn't matter. She knew what would happen next, she'd be given her bundled clothes and told to leave, declared unsuitable for this position. She would shame Mrs. Eddington, she would shame her mother. She would not be here for Maryjane or anyone else, and she would never again sleep in a yellow bedroom with wallpaper. She moved slowly down the upstairs hall as if she carried within her a slop jar about to spill.

But when she went into the big airy bedroom, there once again was the kind and gracious master from last night's supper, smiling at her. Forgiving her. Telling her he understood it was her first day, but really she must try not to lie, it was something he placed great importance on. She must try to take her reproofs calmly and do better; that was what she must promise. He still had great hopes for her. He knew she wasn't like the others, he knew that she would make him proud.

She served noon dinner in a pink flush of gratitude, again taking her place at table. That afternoon she was shown a book of *Aesop's Fables*, watching the woman's long fingers trace the illustrations, the fox, the crow, the grapes; for a long time those images were suffused with the scent of expensive perfume. That evening she was shown a map of Ohio, watching the man's strong square fingers point to the capital, the rivers, the largest cities. "And you are here," he said, pointing. "You are here." Here I am, she thought, here I am. She was shown other maps, other pictures. *Here I am.* She felt like a child in a picture, a picture where there is always lamplight, always a clock ticking and a fire laid. This was how it was supposed to be, this was how it was going to be. She had already forgotten the quarrel, the slap. It didn't fit the picture. The picture was what was real. *Here I am, here I am.*

Here she is, in the buggy going to town, on a morning as plainly outlined in her memory as a flower pressed in a book. Here she is on a dim narrow day of low clouds, a day which seems to her fine and high-skied because her master is swinging her up onto the buggy seat, him in hat-waving spirits, ruffling her hair. There is a grand airiness about him this June Monday and it comes over her as well; they are joined by it, it is along for the ride. The fields open before them and the road lifts the buggy through the morning, through the fog that clings in shreds to the ground, the grasses. Water shines in the rutted wheel tracks, reflecting back to her the quilting of clouds; the air lies against her cheeks soft and cool. They pass through waves of smells: fresh-turned earth, wild flowers, ham from a farmhouse kitchen. She notices them all, savoring them, listening to the jingle and creak of the buggy, the harness; ahead of her she sees the mane blowing down the neck of the mare and now and then she feels behind her, like a gentle tapping hand, a spattering of earth on her shoulders. To the left a stretch of woods rises, deep, mysterious, white flowers threading under the trees, and beyond the woods is the Infirmary. She watches it loom up, fortresslike, armored in its brick walls; she feels no fear of it, not now. Serenely, she watches gray shapes float on the clothesline, move in the garden, and squinting, she can make out the attic window she had gazed from. She can't tell if it's been mended, doesn't care; now she is on that curve of road she had stared at, she is riding in the buggy she had looked for.

The Infirmary falls away. Farmhouses rise up in its stead, worn red, faded white, squatting by the roadside; a straw-hatted farmer lifts a hand in the air, "Mornin, mornin," calling her master by name. She breathes in the morning, the greeting, the respect, smiling to herself and glancing at him sidewise.

"See that oak, Annie? My father owned all this land one time, from that oak all the way back. . . . Came out here in a wagon as a young man, made his mark on the county, sure did. . . . Built that school near us, did a sight of building . . . Abraham, my father, patriarch's name, well it did suit him . . ."

She watches him as he talks: his face tilted back, the jut of the cleft chin, the upturned nose; as always she has the impression of a grown choirboy, an angel's face framed with graying fair hair. His eyes, eyes the rich brown of syrup, move to her, smiling at her, the wings of his nose faintly pink with excitement as he talks.

"Now that bridge, we just had that built there last summer, I pushed that motion through the county board, used to be you just had to ride through the water, well, you bet they thank me for it now. . . . I do things for the people, Annie, that's what counts with me. . . . Most important thing, I teach my boy this, it's having respect, most important thing, Annie, remember that. . . ."

She sees from the side of her eye his honey-colored driving gloves, the reins in one hand, the other in the air. His gestures are wide, spacious, almost intoxicated, and he talks faster, his excitement eddying around him in invisible circles.

"What I most want to buy for Greenville's a new clock, put it up on the courthouse, that's what I'll do—clocks, now that's my true passion, how they work, how they look, how they *sound*, it's the sweetest—you wind them up, you can count on them more than most people, know that? . . . First clock I ever fixed, it was my father's pocket watch; he gave me a gold piece, I still remember . . . my father, a hard man to please. . . ."

She listens to him, awed, thrilled that he is telling her all this, his deep voice resounding like a preacher's, like a president's. She sees him as he looked in his study the day before, behind his desk, a clock before him and a long tweezer in his hand. She had shown in a visitor and he had motioned her to stay; she had stood by the door, watching the gaunt farmer approach the desk. The farmer's hands twisted his hat behind his back, his graying head bent, his trousers sagging from his suspenders. She noticed that he had hair in his ears, sad long-lobed ears, and a smell of earth and manure hung about him. He was coming to bring thanks, he said, thanks for seeing to it the bank didn't foreclose on his farm; "You're a great man, sir," he said, and the words sent a tingle of pride through her. "A great man, yessir." That was who had chosen her.

Now she sits beside him on the buggy, his knee next to hers, the solid knee of a powerfully built man, the fine weave of his coat encasing a massive shoulder. She is sitting next to a tall chimney of a man, strong, angled, anchored in the land, sending his high spirits up, up, like smoke to the sky. The straight white teeth flash a smile at her, he tilts his head back and sings: "When Johnny comes marching home again, hurrah, hurrah" . . . his voice, full and rich, rings out over the fields, the song rushing from him faster, almost feverish, "We'll give him a hearty welcome then, hurrah, hurrah." . . . She listens to him and thinks of her father singing on his wagon, on the wagon back from town; same town, different roads, different men, but here she is, another chance, another chance.

Ruffling her hair, he breaks off, catching her smile. "You're different all right, Annie, you are . . . we'll show them, you and me, we sure will . . . all right, honey, let's go through it now."

She clears her throat. He has been teaching her for two months now, teaching her facts and poems to remember, to recite, furthering her education, he says. For he is an educator, he tells her, with the most forward-looking theories unrecognized as yet, but that is due to change and soon; she is proud that he takes the time to tutor her. He has called her his pupil; he has called her quick.

"The first president of the United States was . . . ?"

"Washington."

"Good, the second . . . ?"

"Adams."

"Good, the third . . . ?"

"Jefferson."

"Good, good, we'll have the rest later, now the sonnet, the sonnet, let's have it."

She takes a breath.

" 'Full many a glorious morning have I seen
    Flatter the mountain-tops with . . . sov-er-eign eye,
    Kissing with golden . . . face the . . . the . . .' "

" '. . . the meadows green,' " he prompts, " 'Gilding pale streams . . .' "

" '. . . Gilding pale streams with . . . with heaven . . .' "

And she falters, the sonnet is still new. He smiles and declaims for her:

" 'Kissing with golden face the meadows green,
   Gilding pale streams with heavenly alchemy. . . .' "

Another smile. It's all right this time. "We'll try it on the way back," he says. "Good girl."

She smiles, warmed by the praise, sitting back pleased and still, clicking the words through her mind as they near Greenville. Around them the road fills with carts and wagons and ahead of them Broadway spreads, muddy and ribboned with curving ruts. The courthouse shoulders up taller than the other buildings, and she sees the light reflecting off the store windows, their arching lettered signs, KATZENBURGER BROTHERS, LAMOTT'S, FITTS TAVERN, ULLERY & WESSON'S GRAIN HALL. She waits as she is told in the buggy, the horse tethered to a hitching post, while he goes into Katzenburger's; soon he emerges, face flushed, waving one arm at her, a fine joyfulness effervescing from him as he bounds over—"For you! For you!" He thrusts a parcel out at her, asking her to open it, his voice glittering. "For you!" Yards of pale blue lawn cascade from the brown paper, blue lawn sprigged with tiny leaves, and spilling out with it a hair ribbon to match. He holds it up to her, tying the ribbon in her hair, and she gasps in delight, in disbelief, making his laugh boom out warm and pleased. With another bound he's off again, smiling over his shoulder at her, striding down the street to attend to his other business.

She always remembers that space of time—was it a quarter hour, a full hour, she'll never know—sitting in the buggy, hugging her parcel, smoothing her fingers over the cloth; picturing in her mind the dress she'd make, the finest dress ever, how proud he'll be of her then. This is happiness she can taste, brimming up in her like sweet cider, this is happiness so strong it almost dazes her. The blue of the material shimmers before her eyes, *for me, for me*. Around her there is a constant clack of heels on the sidewalk, a procession of bonnets and derbies, a dense smell of mud and manure and tobacco smoke—she hardly notices, intent on her gift, and on the return of the giver.

She searches the thronged street for him, looking for the slope of his shoulders, the slant of his hat, and when at last she sees him she feels something lift within her. And then the lift fades, as she sees the way he moves up the sidewalk—a different stride from the one he coasted off on: now his shoulders are stooped, his head down, now his pace is slow, his face dark. She pulls back; she has seen him like this before. It always comes on sudden, he can change so fast. Hoisting himself up on the buggy's seat, he doesn't speak, doesn't look at her; he slumps there, fingers drumming, gazing out at nothing she can see. The chill of his mood falls over her as if there's been a shift in the daylight. She sees the grip of his hands on the reins, the cords standing out in his neck. "They won't listen," he says, his voice low, furred, offering no further explanation. "Not to me. Never me." He shakes his head, still not looking at her, and when he finally drives away, he charges out into the street, forcing people to run from his path. She edges away from him on the seat, remembering; feeling obscurely responsible for this change, fearing that she has done something wrong to cause it. In the lengthening silence she glances at him, her hands tightening on her parcel. It is almost noon now, the day warmer; the sky, still cloudy, seems to press down upon them.

"Put that thing away," he snaps, his hand cutting a sharp strip of air near her parcel. "Right now—away. Work to do. Work to do."

Even before she has laid the yards goods down, his voice is nipping at her again:

"The sonnet, *all* of it this time, and maybe you'll pay *attention* this time, maybe you'll *deign* to, well, go on, I said, go *on*."

" 'Full many a glorious . . . morning have I seen . . . ' " His eyes needle her, numbing her tongue, knocking the next line into a far corner of her head.

"*Go on*."

" 'Flatter the mountains the meadows green—' "

"Wrong, *wrong*: again."

" 'Gilding pale streams—' "

"From the beginning, damn it."

Her throat is closing, her breath comes in jabs.

" 'Full many . . . many a morning—' "

"Goddamn it, all this time I spend on you, you're going

stupid on me, are you? On purpose, no doubt, I know that look. Sly, sly, like any little Infirmary brat, and I thought you were different. You mean to disgrace me, that it, *is* it?"

She shakes her head, her face hot, sweat seeping through her dress. He is swerving the buggy, pulling it over to the side of the road, drawing up sharp to where a mounting stone stands by a gatepost. With a rough sweep he lifts her from the buggy, stands her on the stone, demanding that she begin the poem, begin it again.

"Sonnet Number Thirty-three . . . by . . . by William Shakespeare," she hears herself start, her voice small. His face fills with blood, the eyes shadowed, his hands opening and closing on the buggy's seat. The weight of his stare seems to take her breath away; she whispers the first line.

"*Louder*, damn it, you *will* learn."

" 'Flatter . . . flatter with sovereign . . .' "

"Deliberate, deliberate, no excuse—" He is out of the buggy, he is beside her, and with one swift slam of his arm he has thrown her down on the rough bruising stone. She feels her knees tear open, and her palms—she stays there, cowering on all fours, the burning pain stronger, a whimper rising in her throat. At last she feels him moving off, hears the buggy creak as he climbs back in. Only then does she dare glance up. He is sitting on the seat, his head in his hands; as he feels her gaze, he looks at her.

"You didn't see that," he says, his voice thick. "That didn't happen, you understand?"

Slowly, she feels herself nod.

"Get up."

After a second she obeys, feeling the blood run down her leg, her hands moving stiffly as she shifts her weight from them. Something is whirling through her, spinning her head, weakening her legs. As she moves toward him, he blurs.

"Get in."

All the way back there is a mist before her eyes; all the way back she stares at her scraped palms. They ride through the same fields, past the same fences—but not the same, not this time. She feels heavied, sickened, wondering what she's done to bring this on. Something in her had, there's no other explanation. Something in her brought this out of Pug, something in her did it again today; she's better off not moving, not trying, she's better off alone in the kitchen. But as soon as she is back in the house, still clutching her parcel, she knows she will not be alone, even there. Her mistress is at the stove, clattering pans and ladles, her pale lovely face narrowed at Annie in reproach.

"You were needed here, you shouldn't have gone."

"Sorry, ma'am."

"What happened to you?" A glance at her dress.

"Nothing. I fell."

"What's that you've got there?"

"Yard goods. For a dress. Ma'am."

Her mistress sighs, pushing back strands of fair hair. In the noon light she looks frail and faded, like the worn porcelain figure upstairs on her music box: a pale blank-eyed doll moving in slow pirouettes.

"He gave you those yard goods, didn't he? . . . Him and his girls, you're the only ones he buys finery for nowadays. Well. It doesn't matter . . ." She trails off, glancing at Annie. "You encourage him more than the others ever did, you know that, don't you."

Annie shakes her head, baffled, afraid again, and the woman stands silent a moment, head bowed, her fingers making a slow intricate dance on the counter, as if piano keys lie there. Her hazel eyes stray to the spill of cloth on the table, her voice southern-accented, soft. "I can remember a time . . . a good, good time . . . he'd take me into town twice a week, buy me things, once it was yards of merino silk . . . beautiful, like cherries. Well. There was a time, you know, I'd have wanted to pinch the living daylights out of you, would have done it too. Well. Not now, no more . . ." Her voice is suddenly tired. "But I'm telling you this, whatever happens with him, don't you come running to me with trouble. I won't get caught in that again, you'd best see that right now. You're *his* experiment, you're none of mine. . . . Dinner in a quarter hour, the chops, the radishes, I think too . . . and remember . . . I don't want to hear about it." A rustle of skirts and she's gone.

Annie stands there in a wash of cloudy light, her apron

tied on, her knees stiff and her palms sore, the hot breath of the open oven on her face. From the parlor she hears the soft tinkle of the piano, her mistress playing some sad slow ballad she cannot name. Overhead she hears her master's footsteps, and all over the house she hears the metallic chorused voices of the master's clocks. *You're a great man, sir.* She turns the chops, closes the oven. *Good girl, we'll show them.* The salad greens bloom in a bowl, the radishes stir in their pot. *Perfect! For you!* The house is calmly moored in the middle of the day. There is no clue now to anything wrong except her stinging palms, her stiff knees. Maybe it really is as she said: she fell. Maybe, even better, it is as he said: it never happened at all.

It happened again and again.

Next time the punishment came down on her for touching things, a lure she never overcame, running her fingers over brushes and books and collar pins, opening closets to peer at the clothes waiting there like silent guests. But other times when she was caught at this she wasn't punished, she was instead shown more, given a silver-lidded powder jar to hold, a leather bookmark to take back to her room.

It was impossible to predict when she'd be punished for what, and she began to move through the house always listening, not only for footsteps behind her but for the sound of her own mistakes stalking her from room to room. They always found her, her mistakes, her failings, they always seemed to catch her unawares no matter how she tried. Whatever happened, it was her fault: so she was told, so she believed. She could always see the truth of that when it was pointed out to her, carefully and in detail; how she had provoked him, how she had brought trouble down on herself, how sorely this discipline was needed for her own good.

"You didn't see that," he'd say, even so, each time.

With the exception of that first slap, in those early months he didn't strike her outright; he would throw her down on her hands and knees as before, out back on the stone steps to the porch, out of sight. It looked as if she'd fallen; often the bruises on her knees didn't show at all.

"You asked for this," he'd say. "You make me do what I hate."

He was an enlightened man, he'd remind her. Of course she was to blame. Of course she must only learn to do better. And then it would stop as suddenly as it began.

She could feel it lift, as plain as a weather change, as striking as moonlight on snow. Suddenly she would be smiled on again, and though she was never sure of what she'd done to deserve it, she was always too happy to question it. This time it would last, she'd tell herself; this time she'd believe it. The tenderness she'd feel for the family then was so intense it would keep her awake nights; her master's attentiveness was heady and filling as a sip of ale he'd offered, one of those charmed afternoons. She remembers that afternoon, the sun dusting their faces like pollen as they walked to the fence at the end of his land. They stood there together, leaning on the rail in companionable silence, watching the house as it sat amidst its white porches like a girl with her skirts spread out on the grass. Looking at the house that way, she again felt her throat ache with sweet yearning—and when the next punishment came down on her, its pain was sharp and finite as a broken bone.

T HAT fall," she said, "there was to be a sociable at my master's house. And I . . . I was to be the centerpiece. So he said. Well. It was all to be so wonderfully perfect . . . even now, it hurts, remembering.

"It was to be a lap supper. A big one, a fine one. Each sociable had to outdo the last. Who had the most celery in the chicken salad. Who had the most, the newest kinds of cakes. There was to be a special set-out of cakes at this one: angel food, devil's food, spice, marble, lemon. But even more important than all this, he said, was his chance to present me. I would be introduced, I would show them what I'd learned—those 'county men' he talked of, the ones who'd respected his father but not him. The reason for his troubles with these men, these county officials, I never exactly knew, but even so I understood it was important. And my loyalty to him was real strong—together, we'd show them what wonders he could do, we'd been working toward this for months.

"I can just see myself, that morning of the party, standing in the kitchen with all those cakes. Me with my new dress on, the dress made from that new blue lawn. This small skinny girl I was, covered by a huge apron. My hair in two long braids. My eyes big. And happy, so happy. I had never, in the six months I'd been there, stayed in grace so long. I can see myself smiling into the mixing bowl. The kitchen sunny. Smelling of sugar, butter, good things. A secret bit of batter on my tongue. I'm mixing up the last cake, a marble cake, measuring for my mistress. And in my head, going round and round—chasing each other, almost—is a recipe and the new poem I'd learned. *One cup sifted flour*. I stir it in. *She walks in beauty like the night*. I turn my back on Ben, who leans on the counter mimicking me. *One cup sugar*. He can hardly stand all the attention I'm getting—well, I think, too bad. I'm sure of myself. Cocky. Protected inside my new dress, the dress so crisp, cool. *And all that's best of dark and light* . . . the curlpapers on my bangs crinkle. I smile to myself and look past Ben, out into the hall. The house smells of cake. And lemon polish. The floorboards shine with wax. Even the master's clocks seem to tick sweeter—the house is holding its breath. Everywhere there are bowls of chrysanthemums, gold and white. The supper is already spread on the dining-room table—the ham, glazed, shining, the chicken, the salads, all those big round rolls. Radishes carved as roses, carrot curls—the beauty of the food in this house just dazzles me. And behind me, all those cakes—the kitchen looking like a bake-shop, pink cakes, white ones. Gold, chocolate, honey-colored. Cakes on shelves, counters, the table, the stepladder, cakes sitting all over the kitchen like . . . like cats.

"Upstairs, my mistress is dressing. Outside, I see Ben wandering across the lawn, tired of teasing me. In the hall, my master comes in through the front door and stands there, looking at the house. Looking at it, I suppose, like a guest would. I remember him standing there—his boots shining, watch chain gleaming so. His head grazing the top of the doorframe, a bit of goldenrod in his lapel. To me he looks like a duke, a prince, standing there, the sun on him, his head so high—I feel a rush of pride. And longing. And dread."

She stops a moment, sighs. Pushes her hair back, looks at me. "Oh Jimmie, I remember that moment so plain. That feeling of . . . promise, big doings, some great thing waiting just for me. That hopefulness getting bigger and bigger inside me. Hopefulness—I found it in everything that day—all those buggies coming up the drive, that loud clear *rap-tap* of the brass doorknocker. And that hum of voices out in the parlor, the dining room. All these shoetops and trousers and skirts I saw, my first time around the room, eyes down, with a tray. Those beautiful skirts, silk moiré all around me. I repeated the line I'd been taught—'Good afternoon, pleased to meet you, ma'am'—but the rustling, the perfume, all those faces, they seemed to make the room tilt. 'Good afternoon, cranberry shrub, sir?' From across the room, my master's smile. I felt it like a hand on my head. Better after that, around once more with my tray, 'Afternoon, afternoon.' From the tail of my eye I saw the knot of men by the hearth: men with stiff collars, watch chains, double chins. The county men. My master standing with them, his face shadowed, this rumble of voices. 'Pleased to meet you, ma'am, cranberry shrub?' I felt a flash of loyalty. Us against them. And then I took my tray out to the pantry. My big moment was near.

"There was this tinkling sound: my master's spoon against a glass. He was introducing me, I can't remember what he said. I heard that tremor in his voice. Tried not to hear it. Stopped hearing it. Lined my shoes up on one floorboard. Pressed my hands together, as I was taught. Kept my eyes up above the heads, not looking at faces, also as I was taught. I felt a thrill, standing there, felt warm and pleased with myself. I cleared my throat. Took a breath. Began.

" 'She walks in beauty, like the night
   Of cloudless climes and starry skies . . .' "

"I looked up without thinking, looked up at my master. His eyes were fixed on me. His fingers were twisting his watch chain. His face was tight. I felt a flush of fear and the next line jumped out of me too fast, slurring.

" 'And all's best of darknbright . . .' "

"He moved suddenly, jamming his hands into his pockets. The words started to scramble in my mind, *stupid, you're going stupid on me*, how could this be happening? The sound of the silence got louder, pressing on my ears, *deliberate, damn it, deliberate*, I heard my voice starting again from the beginning. His face reddened, his face the only thing in the room I could see then, *She walks, she walks*, I could see the stone slamming up at me, feel my knees hit it, *She walks*, my tongue thick, eyes stinging, no more words, just letters left, oh God, I was sounding them out like a baby, 'She walks in bee-ewe-tuh-ee,' my voice like the deaf man's at the Infirmary, something sour in my throat. And then I was running from the room, a murmur behind me and one mocking voice, 'Not precisely what you promised us, George.' And laughter.

"I stood frozen in the kitchen. The stove was hot, too hot to touch, the oven lit, but it didn't warm me. My mistress, dishing up fruit salad, glanced at me. And past me. Next thing, my master was in the room. I saw him shut the door. I saw the veins standing out in his head. He moved toward me and I edged away, backing against my mistress—she flinched, stepped quickly to one side. And oh God, that silence, that forever it took his hands to reach me, the air thick as it is before thunder—and then his arm was around my neck, locking there. I heard him breathing, heard myself whimpering into his hand. He was twisting my arm behind my back, sharper, sharper, his body so strong, so hard behind me, his voice icy clear on the air.

" 'You know what you've done?' His breathing was louder. 'You think you could explain how you managed it?' Another twist to my arm, him panting now, and the room going red before my eyes. 'You have any idea of the pain you just caused me . . . you don't, do you . . . well, I'll try to make it clear . . . here's how much, here's what you made me feel—' And his hand grabbed mine, pressing it to the side of that bright-hot stove—the pain striking up through my palm, a burning agony up my arm. 'This, *this* is what you gave me.' And again my hand was on the stove, and I was choking, gasping, tiny lights snowing down the wall. He threw me from him. For a minute the kitchen shook, my mistress's face a white blur in the corner—then I was running out the back door, through the garden—running, running, my hand to my mouth, sobbing, gulping air, and when I fell flat in the grass, I stayed there. I lay facedown in my good dress, crying into my good hand. Tasting sugar. And dirt. And tears. The poem still ran in my mind all jumbled, *cloudless climes, starry skies,* like I was trying to find where it went wrong. My sobbing scared me, it was so loud, so wild. I couldn't stop it; '*Oh-nonono-ohhh,*' I wailed into the ground. Oh God, my hand, that hot chewing pain—worse than that, what I'd ruined, spoiled; disgraced myself, disgraced him, *starry skies, cloudless climes.* Oh please oh please, I prayed, make it this morning again, make it another time. The time by the fence. The time in town. The picturebook, the map of Ohio, that first evening, oh please. Make me better, make me someone else. I felt dark inside. Maybe it was true, I was stupid, a dumb Infirmary brat. Look what I'd done. Look at me now. I'd started to think maybe I was good enough. Good enough for this place. This chance. And I wasn't. I'd let everyone down. . . . I wasn't good enough to live in a yellow room. Or have a new blue dress. . . . It seemed to me I was where I belonged now. . . . Outside facedown in the dirt. . . . Away from people. . . . Away from everyone."

Her voice had sunk lower and lower. Again she stopped, her hands tight on the handkerchief in her lap. For an instant before going on, she closed her eyes.

"After a while I heard people leaving the house. The door shut again and again. And then there were no more murmurs, no more buggies on the road. The light changed, lower through the grass. I still didn't move. It was dark when my mistress came out and found me. She jerked me onto my feet and looked at me. I remember her face up above me, her white dress hanging there in front of my eyes. I wanted to bury my face in it. I wanted to run away.

"'All right now,' she said. 'You've been out here long enough. I did your work for you. Get along inside.' There was no expression in her voice, just tiredness. She walked me back to the house, and as soon as I got inside a terrible fear came down on me again. I smeared some butter on my hand, shaking too hard to eat anything, and I ran upstairs. I dropped my dress on the floor and stood there in my chemise in the dark. I didn't light the lamp. For a long time I just stared out the window, not seeing anything, waiting for the house to settle down. Only when everything was dead quiet did I dare come out, creeping down the stairs.

"I inched my way to the dining room. There was moonlight on the rug, the floor. I saw the silver shining on the sideboard. I saw the place on the floor where I'd stood to recite. That seemed so long ago. After a minute I went over and I stood there again. I stood there a long while, the tears running down my cheeks. I stayed there till I felt cold to my bones. Then I scuffed out slowly and shut the door, turning back to the hall. A light was on there, it hadn't been before. My master was standing by the stairs.

He looked so odd, beckoning to me, I didn't run. He was still dressed, but in his shirtsleeves, his collar off and his vest open. He looked unsteady, almost ill. He came toward me slowly, weaving, and as soon as he got close I smelled the liquor on him. He seemed so different from that man, that master I'd seen standing in the doorway that morning. So different from the master in the kitchen. Very gently he put his hands on my shoulders.

" 'Hurt you, honey, I hurt you?' he said. I couldn't speak. 'Didn't mean to,' he said, 'Didn't mean to, not a bad man.' His voice was thick, he swayed on his feet. Then he bent down and his arms went around me, his face against my neck. His face was wet. He murmured something, 'Sweetheart, sweetheart.' And his arms were still around me. I felt the stubble of his chin on my shoulder. And then he . . . he kissed my neck. Oh God. My neck, my shoulder, all wet. I was so stunned I couldn't move. I was so young . . . I didn't know . . . I just stood there, stiff, his arms tighter around me, his . . . mouth on my neck. He pressed me closer . . . the smell of his sweat came over me with the smell of the liquor. And then I saw Ben. He was partway down the stairs, crouched there, squinting through the railing. I saw him over his father's shoulder. I saw his face change—that seemed to jolt me somehow. My master's hands were on my back, lower, tighter. And then I broke away." Her voice shook. Her hands shook. "He saw me cringe back. He made a sound in his throat, a sound like a snarl. And then he slapped me, again, again, sharp across the face. It jolted through me like a flash of light. He pushed me away then, into that horsehair chair. He shuffled off. Ben's face was gone. I sat in the hall alone, sat in that chair, gripping the arms, my teeth chattering, until it got light."

WHENEVER I think of them now, Jimmie, I never think of their name. I've never told their real names to anyone. I still can't. Not even now. Not even to you. All these years I've always called them something else in my own mind. I didn't think of it right off, not for a long while. But now, whenever I think of them, they're always 'the Wolves.'

"I had a name for them—they had a name for me. Another name I've never been able to say. Oh Jimmie, how can I tell you this, I had a name I had to be rid of, get clear of forever—a name they hung on me like a sign of shame. And I had to change it, had to, for good and all. My name wasn't Annie Mozee then, the way I told you. It was . . . it was Annie Moses. I haven't said that name aloud in so many years. It's still hard to say it now. Maybe when I tell you what happened after that sociable—what happened in the school, and after that—maybe then you'll be able to understand . . ."

She broke off then, twisting the handkerchief in her lap, turning her face away. In the dim room I felt her moving off from me a moment, as if her spirit had drifted toward the door, seeking a way out. When she spoke again, her words seemed more directed at the door than at me, and what she said came out slowly, low-voiced, as if she were seeing again the house, the school; almost as if she had gone to walk through them, painfully, hesitantly, once more.

The schoolhouse down the lane had been built by her master's father and was attended by her master's son; a snug spare brick building that enclosed a single room and squatted by the edge of the road to Dayton. She had been sent there in disgrace before—"Out, out," he'd roar, "out of my sight." There she was sent the morning after the lap supper, leaden-eyed and stumbling from lack of sleep, down the lane in her gray Infirmary workdress and thick brogans, the wrong reader in one hand, a clumsy bandage on the other, her skirt and hair flapping on a breezy October rain.

On other days, sometimes, it had been a faint relief to escape the chaos of the house for the orderly schoolroom, the day sectioned into neat impersonal squares marked *Grammar*, *Sums*, *Spelling*. But gradually the schoolhouse had begun to envelop her in a misery of its own, bearable to her only by comparison with her master's wrath, which rendered it a lesser evil.

She can see it: the schoolroom with its whitewashed walls and rows of pitchpine desks, suspended in a kind of underwater light cast through the wide greenish-tinged windowpanes. The blackboard too has a greenish cast, a squeaking sheetlike expanse behind the teacher's desk, and standing beside it, chalk in hand, the schoolmaster: a balding young man with bad skin and storklike legs, his high voice scissoring out the lessons, his eyes watchful beneath a sprinkling of hair that dusts his head like nutmeg. The chalk is in his right hand; his left rests on the desk near a coiled black whip, with which he keeps order among the rougher, older boys in the back.

In the middle row sits her master's son Ben, a skinny slack-jawed boy of eleven. He has his father's round snub-nosed face but lacks his father's grace, and knows it. His mouth is devious and his blue eyes, habitually narrowed, are turned toward the door. Her appearance at school, she knows, arouses in him a glee so keen it nearly makes him salivate; so keen it quickly catches like leaping sparks around the room. She watches him, thinks of his room: the tumble of his sheets, his drawings on the walls, all of flowers—how many mornings she has cleaned there, wondering if he'd ever take to her. Now, at his desk, his eyes are on her. Here with his pals and allies, he relishes his lordliness over her, avenging himself again and again for all the attention she has gotten from his father. His hatred of her, strong and pleasurable, is like a sharp stick in his hand, brandished at her from the middle row and honed with time. He has the power to isolate her from the others, warning her repeatedly, through his teeth and in a voice so terrible as to summon the dead, *"Don't you dast come near my friends."* He has the power to ensure that she has the wrong books and he has the power to make her late, which he has again exercised the morning after the lap supper.

She can see herself now: standing in the schoolhouse doorway, Ben's eyes and the teacher's lighting on her in the same moment. She hesitates there, ashamed of being late, ashamed as always of her poor-farm clothing; ashamed even more deeply of having to sit with the youngest children in the first row. Her scant attendance, governed by her master's moods, has made it impossible for her to keep up with the lessons and she has fallen back as far as she can. From the doorway she sees her empty place. She feels Ben's eyes, pinlike, on her face. She thinks of turning, running back to the house; knows that would be worse. Her troubled state hangs over her like bad air, the events of the previous day whispering in her mind.

Prodded by the teacher's gaze, she moves forward to take her seat, hearing as she does the faint wave of snickering that mostly follows her across this room. Usually in the past, she has swaggered through it, walking with an uppity nose-in-air pose, but today her feeling of worthlessness is too strong. She ducks her head and pushes through the smells of pitch pine and chalk and damp wraps to the front row. Roll call has already begun. She keeps her face turned toward the stove in the corner as another wave of snickering breaks over her head.

"... James Ingraham."

"Sit down please, next?"

"Lawrence Kirkwood."

"Next?"

"Ginny Lockhart."

"Next?"

"Nnhhnn Mssses."

"Can't hear you."

"Annmoses."

"Speak up, child."

"Annie. Moses."

... And behind her she hears the whispers starting, rolling forward, *"Moses Poses, Moses Poses,"* it always starts with that. She fixes her eyes on the row of wet mittens spread on top of the stove, but at her shoulders the whispers hang large, "No one knows where she gets her clothes-es." All through the lessons she hears it, "Moses Poses" through the shriek of chalk on the board, "Got no rag to blow her noses," through the scratch of pens, the flutter of paper, even through that fine smell in the spines of new books, "Moses Poses, Moses Poses." At recess, that dangerous gap in the morning, it is no longer a whisper, it is loud as a cheer, sharp as a whistle, the laughing mouths in a circle, circles of sharp eyes, fingers pointing in time to the rhyming, "Mo-ses Po-ses, *Mo-ses Po-ses*, MOSES POSES"—Ben and his pals, pressing closer around her, fingers reaching out to pinch, and in Ben's eyes she sees the flat gleam of pure disgust, and on his lips she sees the words form clearly: "She kissed my Papa . . . she messed with my Papa . . ." He is miming it, lavishing wet slobbering kisses on the back of his hand, moaning and wiping the slobber off on her cheek, and though she hits out at him, he is too fast for her, *"Messed with my Papa, I saw, I saw."* And now the older boys join in, "Moses Poses is a slut, MOSES *Poses is a* SLUT"—they are pulling at her dress, the faces slanting, sliding toward her; she can't breathe, can't see past them, and she hears as if from a great distance the sound of her skirt ripping in someone's hands. In front of her now Roy is dancing, the oldest boy, the biggest young tough, swaying his hips at her while Ben holds her arms. Roy's huge hamlike face is close to hers, his freckles blurring, his tongue lapping at his thick pink lips, and suddenly as his fingers part his fly, he sings out softly, "Moses licks dicks, Moses licks dicks." Her head is forced down, the chanting louder, and she feels cold sweat drenching her, she feels legs and knees pressing against her, her head pushed lower, down toward his fly, and just then she feels the warm sour surge of vomit in her throat. Gagging, gasping, she is dropped unceremoniously on the ground. The circle pulls back, but for one moment a deep fury powers her up from that pool of puke, her voice raised in an odd tight yell. She punches out at Ben, feeling his nose squash against her fist like some overripe fruit; just as his blood spurts out the schoolmaster reaches them, breathless, on the run, his whip in his hand. He takes it all in quick: blood on the boy from the house up the lane; fist on the girl from the dregs of the poor farm—he cracks his whip once, over her head. *"Troublemaker, bad'un!"* he shouts, his voice quivering with anger and fear, and without waiting another moment, she is running out through the gate and up the lane, running till she reaches the house.

She waits outside a minute, breathing hard, tasting the sour slime still coating her tongue. She cannot stop shaking, she cannot wait longer; carrying her heavy shoes in her hand, she slips inside, unable to keep herself from running up the stairs. No one has seen her; she almost doesn't care. She rushes into her room, coming face to face with herself in the long pier glass: sees herself, framed in slender strips of polished oak, sees herself trembling, cowering, her hair tangled, her dress torn, streaked with dirt and vomit—sees in that shining surface Moses Poses, and she strikes out at herself, raising her shoe at the face in the mirror, and the glass shatters with a great tinkling crash. Immediately there is the sound of rapid footsteps on the stair. The door bangs open and her master is there, her mistress peering over his shoulder—Annie snatches up a piece of glass, darts past them and down the stairs.

She sees the steps rise up, tilting at crazy angles, and he is pounding down the stairs after her, *"Bitch, little bitch."* She is driven into a corner of the hall, wedged behind the horsehair chair, holding her shard of glass swordlike before her. He nears, still cursing her, and slowly the hall seems to fill with the sound of their breathing. "We take you into our

home," his voice punches out, "take you in, what do you do
. . . little bitch, rotten to the core . . . I see what you are now,
I see . . . no wonder your mother sent you away, no wonder—"

Her voice is a scream, "Send me back then," and she
slashes out at the smooth horsehair, "send me back, that's
what you think, send me back!"

"You'd like that, wouldn't you, that would be your triumph—you won't have it," and he lunges at her, twisting her arm until she hears the dim musical clink of the glass
against the floor. He is shaking, she can feel it, struggling for
control, and she is quivering in his hands. "Get the switch,"
he shouts to his wife, and holds Annie facedown; she is
beaded in cold sweat as the swatch of wall and trouser leg
within her sight begins to blur. And then she feels the switch
lay a hot strip of pain across her back, and then another, strip
by strip. She hears his breathing above her, fuzzing the sound
of the howl in her throat; she cannot stop it, each burning
slice of the switch raises another, and a curtain of red pulses
before her eyes. The pain is biting deeper, she will break, she
will die, and beneath her the floorboards are melting; they
slide her into a flowing darkness where there is something
soft beneath her, and when she opens her eyes, the switching
is over.

She is lying facedown on a mattress, her head whirling, a
fiery pain running in ridges across her back. She stays there,
too spent to cry, too pained to move, listening to the sounds
above her on the next floor: scrapings and sweeping and the
sliding of drawers. She turns her head, sees the wall, a strip of
door with a chipped glass knob. She knows where she is now:
not upstairs, not in the beautiful yellow bedroom. She is in
the small chamber behind the kitchen, with the moldy smell
and the old stored bottles; in the dim closetlike space
that has always been called "the hired girl's room."

The door opens. Her clothes are flying through the air: her
shifts and stockings and drawers, her two good dresses, her
nightgown. They float to the floor dreamily, like strange
birds. There is the *clunk-unk* of her shoes, the whisk of her
basket. A sheet is thrown in last, with a pillow and blanket,
and the door clicks shut. Slowly, painfully, she raises up on

her elbows, all the misery in her churning again, darkening the room before her eyes. She buries her face in the nightgown that has fallen nearest her. "Maryjane," she cries, rocking over the soft flannel, *"Maryjane."*

From that night on she lived in the hired girl's room behind the kitchen, half believing even then that she still might be forgiven, drawn once more within the circle of smiles. But she was never again the shining child who had been taken in, brought along; the child who had found fortune at this door. She was never again shown a book or a gown or a clock, she never again rode in the buggy or sat at the table. They knew what she was now. She knew what she was now: hireling, outcast, scapegrace, drudge—Moses Poses. Those hateful words, carried home on Ben's lips, became the family's name for her, half mocking, half serious, from then on.

She wondered at first why she wasn't dismissed, then saw that her master's pride wouldn't allow it; his experiment must seem to go on. She prayed that her mother might fetch her till her master read out a rare letter from home: there was a new baby, the money was needed more than ever. And he, humane man, would keep her on. She carried the letter in her pocket for days, but it was a rustling reminder she had no escape, and after that, "the grayness" came on. It was within her, around her, and through it she moved slowly, as if walking into a constant wet wind; a grayness stitched together from the stuff of her chores in the house, her humiliations at the school, and the punishments which still descended upon her, openly now, at unforeseen intervals.

"I've always called it that, 'the grayness,'" she said slowly. "Never knew how else to describe it, even then. That year, that whole next year it was there, whatever I did. I slept in it.

Woke up in it. I'd go down to that school, you know, whenever they wanted me out of the way—I'd go in the grayness. I'd hear the kids, that chant. And I'd know it was for me, but I didn't fight it anymore. Moses Poses—it got to be my name. Something that went with me, belonged to me. I answered to it. Answered to it, heard it through the grayness.

"Maybe it blunted things a little, Jimmie, I don't know. But the punishments, they didn't seem so bad then. Maybe they didn't surprise me so much anymore. Don't misunderstand—it pained plenty when he'd switch me, but how can I say this . . . I didn't struggle like I had. And Jimmie, the worst of it is . . . at first, when I'd see him coming toward me, that look in his eye, I'd feel . . . I think I'd feel a kind of hope somehow. Because always before, after he'd punish me, he'd be good to me again. And at first, I thought that was how it would be. But it never was. I'd like to tell you I was blameless, innocent all the time—I wasn't. I'd do things . . . burn things on the stove, mostly on purpose—oatmeal, a good copper kettle, once a very choice leg of lamb. He knew it wasn't just carelessness. Things would just find a way of breaking in my hands, nothing big, a pitcher, a glass. . . . Sometimes I'd feel scared of this spitefulness inside me—it made me feel even more of a bad'un—as he'd said, rotten to the core. But sometimes . . . more and more of the time . . . I'd just feel numb, and I'd make mistakes because I didn't really care how I did things anymore.

"Looking back now, I can only think of one or two times the grayness didn't seem to be there. That winter, I remember, one of my chores was to go upstairs after supper with the bedwarmer. It was brass, beautiful, with a design on it in the shape of a little tree. I'd fill it with coals from the stove, shut the lid, and carry it up the stairs—I remember how I'd hold it out ahead of me like a fishing rod. The family would be in the parlor sometimes. And once I remember seeing them all together there—they were clustered around a copper bowl of popcorn, and oh Jimmie, how it hurt my heart, seeing that. Seeing where I could have been. Where I thought I'd be by then. I passed the horsehair chair in the hall, didn't look at it. Didn't let myself. Didn't want to see the scar I'd made on it, it showed where the stitches were. I went on up the stairs to the master bedroom, turning up the lamp on the dresser there, like always. I remember seeing the frost on the windows, feeling that cold night all around the house—but that room was never cold. I stirred the fire, went over to the bed. Turned back the peach-colored spread. Slid the bedwarmer up and down those white sheets. The brass made this soft skidding sound I liked, almost like a sled. And once I'd done with the warming—after I'd listened for any sound in the hall—I did something, did it every time I could, something I couldn't even explain. I lay down in their bed. On those warm sheets. Just for a few seconds, that was all I dared. I would feel perfectly contented in that bed. I would feel . . . blissful. But that wasn't all. Just as strong as that, I'd lie there and I'd get this queer little tingle, all through me, of revenge. I was invading them. I was lying where they lay. Me—Moses Poses, I was pressing myself onto their clean warm sheets. And they never knew it. I remember that feeling, Jimmie . . . it shames me so to tell you . . . the only pleasure I had then, a thing like that . . ."

She drew a shaky breath, then another. "Well . . . of all my chores, that was the only one I enjoyed. And of all the chores I had to do, there was one so hard I could scarcely bear it. It was worse than scouring out the stove, worse than liming the privy. It was cleaning the upstairs bedroom that had been mine. That yellow room. That room where I'd felt raised up out of myself with joy.

"I'd go up there with my bucket. With the mop, the dust-pan. And I'd stand outside that door, and Jimmie, I wouldn't be able to open it. Oh God, I'd just stand there and shake. It got to be opening that door was hard as opening the door to the 'idiot room' back at the Infirmary. And once I'd opened it, that room would just shine out at me—all that yellow, you know, and the sun—and I'd feel this terrible misery come over me, just looking at it. I can still feel it. That longing, that . . . loss. And that feeling of worthlessness, like . . . chills, like waves of sickness.

"That April, one Saturday when I'd been there about a year, I remember being up there, cleaning . . . looking at that dogwood tree in bloom outside the window—so white, it looked like it was just floating there. I'd forgotten about that tree. . . . I went to the window, looked into it. I could see Ben down there on the lawn, running with his friends, shouting, throwing a ball in the air . . . they looked so . . . so free, so careless down there, five or six boys . . . and nearer the house, I saw my master and mistress. I could almost look right down on the top of his head. It shone real blonde in the sun. And his two hands were waving on either side, those big sweeping motions of his, broad strokes, like he was painting on the air. And beside him, my mistress's wide straw hat with a blue ribbon. Her hand, so white, holding this big spray of pink azalea, and that lawn, all sunny. . . . I saw Ben running off with his friends, it got quieter out there. And I could hear them talking, my master's voice . . . 'just might try . . . a simpler lesson . . . once more'. . . . Just for an instant, I felt my heart give a jump. But my mistress's voice was harsh, saying something I couldn't hear—she dropped her flowers flat on the ground and walked off. Even if she hadn't, I knew nothing would come of it. I'd overheard him say that once or twice since my disgrace, his voice with that high fast thrill to it . . . then he'd brood for days, tinkering with his clocks. And that would be the end of it. I remember how I leaned on the window that day, giving the bucket a little kick, and all at once he turned, looked up. His face changed when he saw me, flushing dark. I felt this prickling of fear all over me . . . and still I couldn't move, couldn't break his gaze. I could feel the stiffness in my back from the last switching I'd had. I could see the purple bruise on my knuckles where he'd cracked his knife handle down . . . and Jimmie, I just stood there. Frozen. Staring at him. Him sending me that look, that long killing look—it could just rake me down to nothing. Ever since that night by the stairs, he seemed to hate me so much, I'd see it in his eyes. I'd feel it coming out of him, almost like . . . like heat. And I'd feel hate too. But not for him. For myself. For being hated.

"He turned away then, stomped off across the grass . . . I turned back to the room. I was supposed to take the rug up for cleaning, and there in the dirt underneath it I found a piece of that mirror I'd broken. Just a small piece, long and thin, like a blade of grass. Half a year had gone and there I was, bent over that little sliver, tears on my face all over again. I could still hear that glass shattering. And it seemed to me that at the moment it shattered, I'd become who I was now. Moses Poses. I put the glass in my pocket and took that rug out back and beat the dust out of it—beat it so hard I broke its backing. 'Moses Poses,' I kept thinking, beating harder, harder, '*Moses Poses*' . . ."

Her voice trembled and she paused until she was able to steady it. "I remember it was the day after that, I was hustled off to school again. He was having some men in, county men— 'out of my sight, out of my sight,' till after supper. And that day, when I came—late—into the schoolroom, I knew it would go even worse with me than usual. The teacher, Mr. Lacey, he was out ill and there was a new teacher in his place for the day—a small redheaded lady teacher. Even with her high-collared black dress, her hair on top of her head, I could tell she wasn't much more than a girl. And I wondered how long she'd be able to keep those big boys down. Down and away from me. I stayed inside during recess, hearing the chant start out in the schoolyard—just sat at my desk, fingering that scrap of glass in my pocket, feeling the teacher's eyes on me. I sat hunched there the whole of that day, letting the grayness come down around me. And then, just as I'd feared, the second the teacher dismissed us and left, the taunting began again. And I didn't have the will to struggle, the grayness was too strong. They were backing me across the room, Roy, Ben, the rest. And finally I was against the empty coat cupboard, its door half open—I just let them back me into it, and I sat down inside, letting them shut the door on me. It smelled of mice in there, and mold, but even so it was a relief to be shut away from those faces. Outside I heard laughter, and a strange *whisk-whisk* of a sound: I figured they must have tied the handle shut with twine. Laughter, more laughter. 'Moses Poses Moses Poses.' Then footsteps going out. The door slamming. Then silence. Slowly, I pushed on the door. It budged maybe half an inch. I thought I could work that sliver of glass through the gap, maybe cut the twine with it. But I didn't. I didn't even try.

"I just stood there, leaning on the cupboard wall, watching the light coming in through the cracks in the door. It didn't matter if I came out because I didn't have to make supper. It didn't matter if I came out . . . because it didn't matter was all. I saw the light change, making burnt-looking stripes on my hand. Things came and went in my mind. The dumb-waiter, hiding from Pug. *Think you're so godamighty differ-ent?* I wasn't, I saw that very plain. The grayness, it seemed to open inside me like a well, *rotten to the core*, pulling me down. *No wonder your mother sent you away*. I could see my mother taking my hands off her nightgown, *you see how she is, trouble* . . . the whispers seemed to be in the cupboard with me, whispers, shouts, *troublemaker, bad'un*. I must be, why else had everything come out like it had? I'd gone bad like butter, I'd turned them all against me, my fault . . . and the . . . the loathing I felt for myself there . . . strong, so strong, like a . . . a smell, I wanted to be out of my skin . . . be someone else . . . anyone else . . . even Ellen in her diapers. I was holding that piece of mirror in my hand. Hold-ing it so tight, I felt a sting in my finger . . . then a trickle of blood. It didn't matter. I didn't care. Plainer than ever, I saw what I'd turned into. I *was* Moses Poses.

"After a while I heard footsteps coming back into the schoolhouse. In through the door, crossing the floor. The sound of someone stopping at a desk, the rustle of papers. It startled me so I knocked into the cupboard door, then pulled in tight for fear of whoever was out there. Too late: the footsteps were coming toward the cupboard. There was the rip of a knife through twine, the door came open—and there was the girl teacher, leaning toward me. Behind her the room was full of the twilight, purple shadows on the walls, giving the place this red soft look I'd never seen before. The teacher bent nearer, her face shadowed too, I couldn't see it plain. The last of the sun behind her came through her red hair, lighting it up all around her face. And as I looked at her there, just for an instant I thought I saw my sister. I thought I saw Maryjane.

" 'Come out now?' she said, her voice very kind, I remem-ber it perfectly. 'I was worried about you.' Even so I still couldn't bring myself to move. She crouched down in front of me, the sun still blazing in her hair. . . . the whole school-room was filled with that purple light.

" 'You're the girl from the house up the lane?' she said,

and I nodded. 'You're the girl from the Infirmary?' she said
then, and I hesitated before I nodded again. 'I've been watching you,' she said. And once more I had this odd sense of
Maryjane being near. That voice so like hers, low and firm,
trilling up on the end of a run of words—the hair, the gentle-
ness, the smell of mint. She seemed to shimmer there, reaching out to me, and suddenly I felt tears sliding down my face.
She drew me out of the cupboard, smoothed my hair. I just
put my head down on her shoulder and cried, her rocking me
there until I could stop. Then she smoothed my hair back
again and looked into my face.

" 'I was watching you,' she said, 'because I knew you were
from the Infirmary.' I looked down, shamed, but then she
said, 'You know, I grew up near it, played with those children. I know what it's like.' She saw the blood on my finger,
the glass in my hand. Very gently she took it from me, letting
it drop into fragments on the floor. 'I heard what they were
calling you,' she said. 'But your real name's . . . Ann?' 'Annie,'
I said. 'It's Annie.' 'Annie,' she said, 'that's a good name, a
good name.' She put her hand under my chin, tilting my head
up. 'I don't believe what I've heard about you, Annie,' she
said, and she smiled at me. I remember feeling so relieved, so
fierce-glad somehow, whatever it was she'd heard—and she
didn't say, and I didn't ask.

"She led me over to the teacher's desk then, and I stood
with her, helping to stack some papers she said she'd come
back for. I wondered if she'd really forgotten them, or if
she'd come back on my account. But I didn't say a word, just
watched her hands moving in this steady rhythm, the papers
under them—and once again my sister came into my mind . . .
her hands sewing, smoothing white cloth. And all around us
the light was changing, fading.

"The schoolhouse was almost dark when we left it. She
turned to me on the steps, saying she wouldn't be there tomorrow, Mr. Lacey should be back. I felt this wave of misery
coming over me again. She lifted my face in her hand. 'Even
so,' she said, 'I'll be thinking of you, Annie. Will you remember that? And think of me?' I nodded, speechless. She was
just a silhouette in the dusk by then, but I held how she
looked in my mind, standing there by the door. And she went

on down the road. And I went on up the lane. And I realized I hadn't said anything to her but my name, my real name. I didn't even know hers. But I knew this: when she'd looked into my face, she hadn't seen Moses Poses there. And she would be thinking of me. She would be thinking of me as Annie, she would be holding me in her mind.

"I never saw her again. And after that, nothing really changed for me up at the house. But every night I thought of her. And every night I thought of her thinking of me. I thought of her with the look of my sister about her, my sister who had loved me. And that night after I met her, for the first time since the lap supper, I slept sound."

I‍T was before her next birthday that she stopped going to school. She was still sent there from time to time, but Ben, triumphant, did not report her absences to his father; he seemed only too content to have driven her off his turf at last.

When it was warm she doubled back away from the schoolhouse through the fields, rambling about alone. When it got cold she brought sewing with her and sat in the barn; the needle and thread seemed to steady her. But at night she was too tired to sew; she couldn't turn back to the hall chair for comfort, could not even bear to look at it. And so, for steadiness, for comfort in the nights, she returned to the things she had done so faithfully at the Infirmary.

Every night once again, she would spill open the small cloth sack she wore around her neck, touching the button, the stone; the thimble that had belonged to her sister, the hammer that belonged in the rifle.

Every night once again she brushed her hair fifty strokes.
Every night she washed her face and rinsed it ten times.

Every night after she was in bed she went over in her mind whatever sewing she'd done that day, picturing each stitch, taking pride in their evenness, their span.

Every night she said to herself the names of everyone in her family, living and dead, not the way she said them in her prayers but slowly, imagining each face as best she could, even though the faces were blurring now.

Last of all every night she went over in her mind, very slowly and with care, the exact steps for cleaning, loading, and firing the rifle, to make sure she didn't forget how and even more because of the brief happiness it brought. She drew it out, thinking about the very first time she shot it, and the next, and the next, and she followed each bullet's line till she fell asleep.

She knew now that this litany would not make good things happen but that wasn't why she repeated it. She repeated it simply to hold onto it, to see every night what was still hers, untouched by anything else that had happened, unscathed by where she was.

Sometimes she was permitted to ride an old mare around in the pastureland; it was her only pleasure that next summer and she rode as often as she could. Then, and during her rambles in the fields when she was supposed to be in school, she would imagine that she again held the rifle. She could feel it in her hands, heavy and solid, the butt, the comb, trigger, guard, barrel. She knew exactly where it began and ended in its outlines, cradling it, cocking it; pointing it. She followed birds with her eyes, pleased that even here she could still snap onto crows or quail and sweep with them till they were out of sight. Weeding the garden or laundering the clothes, she would watch for birds; indoors, scraping the plates, she would see their shadows on the kitchen's white wall. Sometimes, to practice snapping the rifle to her shoulder, she used a stick she found in the fields and hid in the barn. On the occasional days when the family went visiting, she thought of taking a gun from the glass case in the back room, but she never did; by that time she no longer wanted to touch anything that was theirs. Even a gun. Especially a gun.

The brick house looked just a bit smaller to her that summer, smaller still that next fall; still solid, not stunted, not shrunken, but from the fence at the property line where she sat alone—yes, smaller. She stood amidst weeds that looked taller than the house did from there, slicing it into jagged sections as the blades blew across her face. In this section sat the father, in this the mother, in this the child: this, the beautiful family.

This was the house the Wolves had built. The Wolves: if they had a name for her, she had a name for them now. Forevermore, this was the house of the Wolves.

This was the house Moses Poses had found, this was where she dwelled. Moses Poses: they would never love her. She knew that now. But she, this girl who stood by the fence watching, where did she live? She did not belong to that house. Not to that house, not anymore.

W HEN she finally decided to run away, she decided out by that fence, her second autumn there.

The family was going away for a day and a night to visit relatives over the Indiana line. That seemed far enough. She was going on eleven now. That seemed old enough. She had been there well over a year. That seemed long enough. Her mother had said the money was needed, but her mother couldn't understand from far away. Surely, surely, if she knew how it was with her, her mother would let her come home. She could sew at home. She could hunt at home. She could earn money there, she would earn it, she would for sure.

She pondered it only in the field by the fence and in the barn, for fear her plans might be read on her face. She was afraid to ask directions of anyone, questions, aid of any kind, even of the traveling peddlers who came to the door. But then just the day before the family's journey, the knife grinder stopped at the gate. She listened to the sizzle of the knives on the whetstone. She drew closer. The knife grinder had gloves that only covered the palms and the backs of his hands, his fingers free and dancing like spider legs. His eyes looked sleepy and scholarly by turns. His face was shaven but his hair was long and he smelled of the swamps. He wasn't the kind of man the Wolves would ever speak to, as far from their world as an itinerant monk.

She stepped up to him.

Where, she asked, would you get the train if, say, you didn't want to walk all the way into Greenville, if, say, you were heading north of Greenville, say up toward Versailles, maybe say out toward Wayne Township, that way?

The knife in his hand spun against the whetstone, scattering blue sparks. He spat brown juice on the ground.

"Jayeville, girlie."

Jayeville. She repeated it to herself. Jayeville, she knew where that was. She could picture the stretch of tracks there unfolding in the sun, and the great black walls of the cars sliding by . . . Jayeville. She could walk there easy, she could do it, it was going to happen, come to be. That night the ring of *Jayeville* in her mind had the ring Cincinnati did later, and later New York, and even Paris, France.

When the family went off the next morning she was at the ironing board and did not allow herself to look up, again for fear it would show on her face. She heard the door click shut behind them, heard the rumble of the buggy on the road, the sound dwindling away. She forced herself to iron the whole basket of laundry, partly in case they forgot something and came back, partly to leave a clean slate. Partly for luck. She folded the sheets, the handkerchiefs, the napkins. She put them away. The stove was cold, the lamps were out; she checked each one. Slowly she moved from room to room, looking at everything one more time. She stood in the parlor, watching the wink and shine of a silver bowl on the table; looking at where she had stood to recite, where the book of poetry sat on its shelf. *She walks in beauty* . . . she climbed the stairs, up through the wary ticking of her master's clocks, their voices lifting around her. The master bedroom: the beds she had made and warmed and lain in; light pirouetting in a powder jar she'd held. The yellow room: the bed, the lamp, the lacelike shadow of the tree on the floor. Standing there she felt a quiver run through her, a weakening in her resolve, but downstairs once more, she let her eyes rest on the stove. Deliberately and in detail, she brought to mind the moment her hand was seared there, and slowly she felt her purpose return.

She took the housekey off the string around her neck, she dropped the key in the cup on the kitchen shelf. The house was quiet but for the clocks; the key chimed in the cup. *Jayeville, girlie.* She would not see these rooms again, or their people; she would not see herself in their eyes. She would pass out of their land, back into her own; she would pass out of their range, and once she was gone they would have no more power over her. She would not be Moses Poses ever again.

In her hand was her bundle. Around her neck, in her cloth sack, were all the coins she had ever been given by her master, small rewards doled out here and there, they would have to pay her fare. She remembered the sight of her hand on the doorknob, the clocks ticking louder, sharper—then she stepped outside, pulled the door shut, and walked down the lane. She walked as if on thawing ice, listening for any sound on the road, jumping at the clang of a rake, the yap of a dog behind a fence. At last she turned to see the house crouching far behind, unable to pull her back now. All she had to do was keep walking and it would disappear forever. All she had to do was keep walking and she would find herself in Jayeville, on the train.

She looked neither right nor left, waiting on the shady dust-streaked platform, counting the splinters in the board at her feet. She glanced neither right nor left as she boarded the car, sliding quickly into the first seat she saw, gripping her bundle and staring fiercely into it until the train, heaving and snorting, lumbered away.

She sat there swaying with the car, wondering at that small hard kernel of bravery within her that had taken her this far. She peered out through the shreds of smoke veiling the window, listening for the call of "Greenville-Green-*ville*," and after she heard it she began to feel safe; after she changed trains at Union City she felt safer. She sat prim and still on the hard yellow lacquered seat, her bundle pressed to her chest, her faded straw hat tilted down over her eyes—pulling in tight to contain the excitement simmering, sizzling within her as the train neared Versailles.

Before it had quite stopped she was leaping from the car, she was across the platform. Her bearings came back. She saw where she was. There was the long meadow. There was the road. She had come about thirty miles—a distance so immense to her as to seem oceanic—so smoothly, so swiftly, it seemed a gleaming good omen. She could already see her mother opening her arms to her, she could picture a homecoming sweet as the winy smell of apples floating toward her on the air. Tears misted her eyes; spills of crimson leaves rippled past her face. There was the stand of maples she remembered. There was that fence where she had set up mason jars to plink at; there was still a faint glint of glass alongside it, after all this time. Nearer, nearer; her blood rushing in her ears, nearer: there was the house, Dan Brumbaugh's slope-shouldered cabin rising over the fields—nearer, nearer, almost there. She glimpsed a flash of white apron through the door, she was running up the path, faster, arms wide, inside now, "Mama, Mama"—and the woman at the stove turned, saw her, screamed. A woman with graying hair and a dusting of freckles; a tall woman, wide-hipped, big-boned. A woman who was not her mother; startled, spilling water down her skirt from the kettle in her hand.

"The jolt of that, oh Jimmie, I felt that clear through me," she said, voice low. "For a second I thought it must be the wrong house somehow. I looked around—it was my stepfather's cabin, no mistaking that. But the furniture was all different, the room wasn't the same. And the woman was talking to me, asking me questions, telling me things—things I seemed to hear through a ringing in my ears, everything blurring around me. My stepfather had died, my mother had moved somewhere up around where we'd lived before with Papa. My wages had been forwarded on to some people named Shaw, they were taking care of my new baby sister while my mother went out on her nursing cases. If I started now, I could reach Shaws' by nightfall, surely they would know how to find my mother: there was nothing else to be done." She sighed, her voice suddenly weary. "I don't remember much else about that day. I had something to eat there, then I was back on the road. Scuffing through the leaves, holding tight to my bundle. Head down, going slow. I'd lost that shine I'd felt on me since morning. And all I could think, over and over, was that my mother had moved and I hadn't known. My mother had moved, months before, and she hadn't even sent me word.

"That was still running and running in my mind when I got to the Shaws' at twilight. My mother wasn't there either—but by then I hadn't expected her to be. I didn't let myself think of running into her arms another time. She was off on one of her nursing cases, no one knew where or for how long; I could stay at Shaws' till she stopped by. And even though I was grateful, even though I was glad to see my new sister, even though old widowed Mr. Shaw seemed kind—I don't know, I guess the grayness had come back over me. All that time longing to get home, and home wasn't even there. I felt sick in my stomach, and so let down, so tired too, I fell asleep right after supper. Next day it was the same, that grayness, that haze all around me—trailing after the Shaw children. I had to go to school with them that day. But as soon as I saw the schoolhouse there at the end of the road, I went cold, knew I couldn't go inside. By the time we got up near it I was starting to shake, so I stayed on the steps while the others went in. And after a while, I remember, leaning against that wall there in the sunshine, I started to feel just a little better. I wasn't home, but I wasn't at the Wolves anymore, wasn't at the Infirmary. It was such a fine day, September, clear, breezy. The wall against my back was so warm, so sunny, smelling just a little of pine sap. I was safe, after all, I was away. I started to drift off into a sleep sitting there, lulled I guess, by those voices behind me, real soft and slow: 'The ma-jor products of Ohio: corn-*and* wheat-*and* . . .' I drifted deeper. 'Hogs-*and* lumber-*and* . . .' No more voices then, I was asleep there in the sun.

"Next thing I was hearing a little *ching* of a noise. It seemed far away. But it was a noise I remembered. A jingle from somewhere. A jingle I knew. There it was again. I sat up, opened my eyes, and oh Jimmie, there it was—the yellow buggy, there on the road by the steps. And there was my master, halfway up the steps, coming toward me. The sight of him there—it slammed into me so hard I jolted half off the step. This was no dream, I knew it, this was really happening —I just screamed 'No!' when he reached for me. His face, the way it was then—so intent, so sure—that's how it looked to me all those years later in that theater in Lima, I'll never forget it. Never.

"He got me into the buggy someway, me kicking, screaming. And at the very last, just as he was driving off down the road, the teacher came out of the schoolhouse and looked after us. But his face was just a blur—I knew he couldn't hear what I yelled, I knew it was too late.

" 'Shut your goddamn mouth,' my master said. He leaned over, slapped my face—when I kept on screaming, he cracked me hard across the shoulders with the handle of his whip. That blow knocked me forward—I felt it all through me, little lights dancing before my eyes. After that I kept silent, hunching over on the farthest end of the seat, shaking, shaking . . . and so stunned, Jimmie, by everything that had happened. How could he have crossed that boundary I'd made up, that line between his land and mine? How could he be that powerful, how could he have found me so easy, so quick? . . . these things kept repeating in my head, I couldn't take them in. I just cowered there, watching him from the side of my eye, afraid he'd hit me again. I saw the veins standing out in his head. I saw his hands tight on the reins, he must have driven off so quick he'd forgotten his gloves. After a while he started to talk, shouting words to me in quick little jabs, glaring straight ahead all the while: 'How dare you . . . little gutter brat, little *nothing* . . . how *dare* you run out on me . . . all those times I should have thrown you out, all those times . . . but did I? Gave you chance after chance . . . greedy, un*grate*ful, typical. . . . You don't leave till *I* say, damn it . . . you were bound over to me, your word is your word, do you hear, *do* you? . . . Goddamn it, you answer me. . . .'

"I muttered something, watching him close all through that long ride, hour after hour . . . the fields going by so sunny, leaves flying all around us—to me it might have been raining. It seemed all wrong for this to be such a fine day. My mind kept coming back to that other day, going to town with him. Full of that poem, that pride, *when Johnny comes marching home again, hurrah, hurrah* . . . and then the horse was clattering over the bridge. There was the mounting stone on the right, passing alongside. And there, up ahead now, I could see the roof of the Infirmary. Beyond the Infirmary, just a mile past it, was the house. The house of the Wolves. I could picture it there, waiting for me. The stove in the kitchen. The chair in the hall. All the clocks on the shelves. I could hear them ticking, ticking forever. I could see myself, Moses Poses, crouching there in a torn dress, with a dirty face, greasy braids . . . a sound was coming from me. I knew I couldn't bear it, knew I couldn't go back.

"Down where the road curved close to the Infirmary's door, I saw two of the Eddington children swinging on the gate. A pink skirt. A yellow one. And Mrs. Eddington's black one, I could hear her calling them to come inside. And suddenly I was calling to them, waving at them, just like everything was fine—my master, I knew, would have to be polite. He had to rein in as they turned to us, turning real slow, it seemed, like in a dream—waving back, coming to cluster around the buggy. I saw this flash of anger on his face, then his smile slid down. And just as he lifted his hat, I threw myself off that buggy, running as soon as I hit the ground. The building was a red blur and I made for it, my feet pounding up the path, my breath coming in gasps. I burst inside, crashing down the hall, past doors, doors, which one, which one—there, at last, over the threshold of Mrs. Eddington's study. I waited, crouching behind the desk. And when she finally came in, alone, breathless herself, I clung to her, the crying flooding out of me, babbling everything out at once. I remember that she smelled of talcum. I remember the wet patch I made on her dress. And I remember how she knelt down, listening to me. Holding my chin in her hand, her eyes very keen behind her spectacles, all the while I rattled on. I was so afraid she wouldn't believe me, I pulled down my dress to show her the welt from that last wallop in the buggy. And when she saw that, I thought something changed in her face. She told me to wait there. And then she left me alone by her big desk, shutting the door behind her.

"I don't know how long I stood like that. Waiting, staring at that door. When I think of it now, it gives me a chill—my word, a child's word, against his, a grown man, a man of his stature. And how many times had she heard a story like mine—she wouldn't believe me, I just knew. He'd tell her what a bad'un I was, what a troublemaking liar, and of course she'd believe him. And make me go back with him. And if that happened . . . Jimmie, if that happened, I thought . . . I knew I would die. My teeth were chattering in that warm room—there was a fire in the grate. I tried to concentrate on the roses in the rug. The green blotter on the desk. The brass inkwell. And still I couldn't stop. I saw Mrs. Eddington's gloves lying on the blotter, cotton gardening gloves, streaks of soil on them, and I picked them up. They smelled of earth, grass. I held them against my mouth until I heard her footsteps coming back, clicking along the hall from the company parlor. She came in smiling at me, her head cocked to one side in that way she had. The door shut behind her again. She stood there just a second, looking at me—me frozen there, her gloves at my mouth. And then she said, very clear, very soothing, that I would be staying there until my mother could come for me, it was all arranged.

"I remember I just stood there another second, taking it in. Listening to the echo of it in the room, just to make sure it was true. And looking at her, there by the door. This little plump woman in her black dress. She looked beautiful to me. She looked like the head of an army, the captain of a ship. Tears stung my eyes. And then I just flew to her.

"I never knew what she said to him, Jimmie, or he to her. I'd doubt she accused him of anything—him a bank trustee, prominent, a powerful friend of the Infirmary's. I'm sure he told her all the bad things I'd done, maybe he said good riddance. But I knew too that her eyes had changed when she'd seen my shoulders. And I knew somehow, standing there in her study, that she cared about me.

"That night, in bed at the Eddingtons' house, the sheets felt cooler, smoother to me than any sheets had ever felt before.

The quilt, lighter, airier. That pillow—I thought it felt soft as a big fresh-baked bun. Next morning, first thing, Mrs. Eddington would write to my mother. Mrs. Eddington knew everything that had happened to me, soon my mother would know. And once she knew, soon, very soon, my mother would be coming to take me home.

Don't think badly of her mother.
She said that and crimped the handkerchief in her lap.
Mustn't think badly of her mother.
She wound the handkerchief around her finger.
Mustn't, really, mustn't judge.
She dropped the handkerchief, watched it fall.
Mother, mustn't, don't, try to understand.
She said that and bent to pick up the handkerchief and looked at me, then away. She glanced around the room, at the headdress on the wall, at the gun rack in the corner, at the door. And back at the hands in her lap. Her lips tightened, her chin trembled. For an instant her face was that of a child who's been told to be brave.
Well then.
Her control was admirable, a professional's control, summoning her voice back, clearing her throat, steadying her hands once again.
Where was she.
Oh yes, yes of course.
She was at the Eddingtons' house two days when Mr. Shaw came. Mr. Shaw, Joseph Shaw, whose family was looking after her baby sister, whose children were in the schoolhouse when she'd been taken away. Kind elderly Mr. Shaw, not her mother, with his gray beard and his dim eyes and her bundle of clothing. He had the softest voice she had ever heard in a man, he had gentle hands with brown spots on them, and polished-looking pink ears. He was a widower, she knew that; did she also know then that he was courting her mother? Maybe she had guessed, maybe she knew that he would soon be her new stepfather. Her little sister had called him Grandpap, he invited her to call him Grandpap, and he seemed to be speaking for her mother.

He sat there with her in the company parlor, looking at his shoes, saying that Mama was busy right now, but she would come sometime and take her home. Sometime soon. Quite soon. Real soon, honey. She must try to be patient, just a little while, just a little longer. She wasn't going to cry now, was she, there's a good girl. He handed over her bundle.

She could tell by the way he said that, did that, it wouldn't be a little while. She wouldn't be going home. She would be staying at the Infirmary, like before. She could tell he didn't know what else to say. She put the hope of home aside then, laying it neatly out of the way with her bundle. She didn't cry; not then, not for a long time to come.

She knew how things stood with her then, she knew and she let them be and without the hope they pained her less. She knew she would go on living here in the Infirmary, here amidst the whitewashed hand-stained walls, here amidst the voices that moaned in the nights "Ahh-ah," and sang, no tune, "Sally go round the mulberry bush." She knew she would be sleeping in the long room with the rows of beds, each bed with its gray blanket, its china night pot. She knew she would be sewing in the basement room, in the high thin light, at the second machine, Clara's pins glinting beside her. She knew she would take her meals at the long tables, and she knew she would not look out the window, and she knew she would empty the chamber pots from the "idiot room." She would never cease to dread that; she didn't know until her first day back at its door how much. She had come up earlier, just as the room's inmates were being led out for the evening, and walking with them, her gray shift soiled, her eyes wide and unlit, was Pug; Pug with her hands tied behind her, her face candled from within by some dimmer light. The sight of her like that frightened Annie even more than her taunting had done: if that could happen to Pug, strong Pug, it could happen to her.

She carried the fear of that with her to bed, to the sewing machine, to meals, but only for a little time; then she let it die like the hope. Untended, it went out like a smoky flame, and she went through her days quietly, trailed by the large gentle shadow of Fannie. A new inmate, her new friend Fannie was heavy, stolid and slow, blue-eyed and oddly beautiful;

a grown woman with lines starting in her forehead, she would be there for always. When Annie was given other chores, checking the springhouse, stocking the storeroom, Fannie would hold a lamp, heft a bucket, and follow her around protectively.

"Annie-roo," she'd say in her soft throaty voice, "me and you." She'd smile out from under her matted length of thick black hair and rock on a stool or a crate. "Me, my husband left me, so I'm here and here and here. You, they left you too, you poor thing. No one want you neither. Don't let it make you sad, Annie-roo, don't let it give you dreams. Don't let you be like me."

Don't let me be like Fannie. Every time she had the dream she would whisper that to herself. She had the dream almost every night the first month or two, the same dream.

In this dream she would see herself standing in the bluish light of early morning, opening the door to her old house, her mother's house. She would see a yellow spill from the lamp as the door opened, and inside she would see, slowed and sodden as if under water, the strange woman turning with the kettle in her hand, her face pinched and startled, the kettle sloshing a dark stain against her skirt. The table would be sliding across the floor, and the chairs, the stools, slithering into new places, and the lamplight would deepen into an acid yellow, and the door would slam shut. She would see herself standing outside again, staring at the buggy, the buggy waiting for her, her master's face looming bright as the moon, eyes fixed on her, and they would be fixed on her still as she struggled to wake up. Sometimes she would be able to wake herself right away, as soon as she saw the house; sometimes the dream would repeat. But whichever way it spun out before her, she knew she would wake in the long room with the rows of beds, and she would watch the early morning light fall across the bedsteads and she would listen to the soft sighing breaths of the girls sleeping next to her.

There was some comfort in knowing this. There was some comfort in knowing how everything would be. She was still in a place for people no one wanted, and she knew now she was one of them; she knew she walked like them, smelled like them, even stole like them now from the pantry. But still, she wasn't at the Wolves. Here there were no shards of mirror under the rug. Here there were no beatings, and with Pug upstairs, no tauntings. No one here seemed to see Moses Poses peering out through her eyes a hundred times a day, wondering if she would be found out, caught, dragged into the light again. No one saw, and no master reappeared to point it out. With Fannie there, she soon stopped fearing he would return to steal her away; she began to think that he too was glad to be rid of her. Even so, even so: it was still hard to keep his house from her mind for long. From the pantry and the orchard she could see the edge of the family's land, fields and pasture, and one of the fenceposts she used to sit on. It was a sight that always made her face change so drastically that Fannie would plant herself stolidly in the way of it, her dark head poking up in front of it wherever it arose—a gesture so touching and so useless it usually fetched a smile.

"Got you smilin' now, Annie-roo, get you laughin' next for sure," Fannie would say, the lines smoothing out in her forehead. She spread her arms out at her sides. "Somethin' good's on the way, I just know."

At Christmas there were gifts from home, handkerchiefs, hair ribbons, a box of hazelnuts, and at New Year's, at long last, there was a visit from her mother.

They sat in the parlor. They were served tea, and milk. They watched her two small sisters play, her brother squirm. She wouldn't be going home with them; her mother thought it best for her to stay and earn money at the machine. It wasn't surprising, not anymore. At the end of the visit she watched Mr. Shaw load them into the wagon, piling them chin-high with so many laprobes they dwindled in her sight even before the wagon rolled away.

"I told everyone my mother was building a brand-new house and when it was ready I'd go home," she said. "I told them all, that's what we were waiting for. Brand-new house with my own room in it. A room done in yellow chintz. And in that room my mama was going to put a sewing machine, just for me. And it would be a brand-new Singer. And next to the machine my mama was going to put a new blue dress. And I would likely get it for my birthday. And they were going to have a party for me. A big party, a lap supper.

Everyone would come. And there would be chicken salad, radish curls. And all kinds of cakes, a great setout of cakes. Devil's food, angel food. Spice. Lemon. Walnut. And in front of everyone, I would stand and recite a poem . . ." Her voice had begun to shake.

"I told everyone those things. Over and over. I bragged. But I didn't believe it, not the way I had before. I just said it. To hear it. I said what a wonderful visit it was. What a wonderful time. How much my mother missed me, so much she could hardly stand it. How she told me every little thing that had happened to her and how I'd told her every little thing that had happened to me and how we'd both cried.

"I told them that and I told myself the same. I always have. That's the way I wanted it to be, that's the way it should have been. All the time I was sitting there with my mother, watching her face, I said to myself, 'Isn't this wonderful.' She was talking about people from home. About her nursing cases. About what had come up in her garden last year, what she'd plant next . . . I didn't even hear. I was so wrapped up in looking at her. It had been three years, I hadn't remembered her like that. Hadn't remembered her hair being that dark. Never noticed the lines at the corners of her eyes before. That way she had of tapping her finger as she pronounced a name, that way she pressed her lips together whenever she stopped talking. How straight she sat in her chair. I'd forgotten she had such a low voice and thick eyelashes. And big hands. And again I wanted to put my hands on her face, touch it very carefully, all over. But I didn't. I watched her talking about her garden, and I said to myself, 'This is wonderful.'

"I wanted to ask her if she'd missed me. I wanted to ask her . . . to just *ask* . . . why didn't she ever come to see me . . . just once, once. I knew she was busy, but I knew she traveled all over the county. One time, just one, I couldn't see why she never . . . it wasn't that far. . . . And she was talking about her garden, her nursing cases. . . . And I felt it was bad of me but I couldn't help it, I wanted to burst out asking, How was it she had time to visit all these people, and I . . . but I just . . . I wouldn't let myself say that.

"I said to myself, 'This is the most wonderful day in three

years.' I said to her, 'This is the parlor right over the sewing room, would you like to see it?' Had she always had that crease between her eyebrows? I'd remembered her skin so smooth, her hair so shining. I remembered her sitting on her bed that night before I went away, braiding her hair, and I wanted to ask . . . but that would have spoiled the day. I couldn't ask why she'd sent me off. Why for so long. Why so far. . . . It would have been all right if only she'd come to see me. I wanted to say that. I wanted to ask, Hadn't she wanted to see me an inch taller? Hadn't she wanted to see with her own eyes how I was? Did she wonder, did she worry, did she love me?—my God how I wanted to say it, scream it, *Mama, don't you love me?—Mama, Mama, what's so bad in me?*— but the day would have been spoiled, I couldn't spoil the day. She never said what she felt, she'd be sorry she came if I asked. And all I said was, 'This is the machine I work on,' and I told myself, 'Isn't this wonderful, seeing her hand touch the wheel I touch every day.'

"And then she went away and I hadn't asked her anything, she hadn't told me anything. If I'd paid attention I would have known what she meant to put in her garden for spring. I would have known who'd had the typhoid. But I didn't know what I longed to know, what mattered to me most.

"And I've never known, never asked her, Jimmie, not to this day. I've never known how she felt, me away all those years—not like my sisters, nearby. I've never known what she thought when she heard about the Wolves. Maybe I was afraid to hear what she really thought. Or that she hadn't thought much about me at all.

"All those years, performing, later—I never asked her why she didn't come see me in the show for so long, I couldn't ask that either. I don't guess I ever will. It's too late now. But I can tell you this, Jimmie. No matter how I've tried to explain it to myself, over the years, I've never been able to understand why she didn't visit me back then. Didn't check on me. Three years. And no matter what I've told myself . . . no matter how much royalty I've played for, I've never been able to forget that." Her voice trembled. "I've never been quite able to put it from my mind that maybe I did something. Maybe . . . there was some bad'un thing in me. Something so

. . . so Moses Poses about me she . . . just couldn't love somehow. And the thought of that . . . whenever it's come back . . .
it fills me with such shame, such shame . . ." Her voice had
sunk to a whisper. For some time she sat leaning on my
shoulder, her face wet with tears.

SHE was at the Infirmary a year after she ran away from
the Wolves, not knowing how long it would be, not
knowing if it would be months or seasons or years. She
didn't watch the calendar anymore, didn't cross off any more
days. She didn't cry. She felt something shift inside her,
something change. Something grew over and around her
spirit, as smooth and encircling as the skin of a pear.

She brushed her hair.

She rinsed her face.

She went over each day's sewing in her mind.

She went over the names, the faces, even the ones blurred
beyond recognition; she added new faces, the schoolteacher,
Mrs. Eddington, Fannie.

And she went over, even more slowly and with even more
care, the handling, the loading, the shooting of the muzzle-
loader, and the tracery of the bullet lines arcing, sweeping,
crossing, till the air over her head seemed stitched with the
webbing of them, and studded with the points where they
touched the targets.

Tree frogs were targets, and twigs, and leaves; she was
seeing targets everywhere, the world around her bloomed
with them: dangling walnuts, dropping fruit, clothes blowing
off the line, the pendulum swinging on a clock. When she'd
been shooting at home it had been that way, things that
swung and spun had pulled her sight, daring her to catch
them. She remembered whirling with the rifle in a windy

sweep of autumn leaves; she remembered watching with temptation the weathervane on a neighbor's barn. Back then she'd had to lug the rifle around, loading it with her arms up over her head; now she'd be able to run with it, now she'd be able to get birds. Now she listened to the gunfire in the fields and followed Henry, the hulking groundsman, whenever he had his muzzle-loader in his hands. She would trail behind him as he walked the land, a cigar in his mouth, his jug-eared head tilted down toward her—showing her how he measured his loads, telling her how he hunted deer and lived alone and missed his wife; answering all her questions, his eyes amused, his voice reedy and patient.

In the meantime, between stints at the machine, she roamed the Infirmary's barley field with the feel of a rifle on her arm, alone or under Fannie's alert and amiable gaze. Between the sewing room and the springhouse, she tested her timing and trained her sight on squirrels, rabbits. The barley field was best for birds, best for running and spinning, best for a place to feel fine all around—except that it gave the most direct view of the Wolves' property, a view so expansive it could not be blocked out.

She learned how to make it go out of focus. The barley field was too good to spoil; she learned to keep her sight fixed there, in it, above it. She taught herself to blur those faroff fenceposts out. And when they hove back into her vision, suddenly, sending a spearshaped chip of pain into her chest, looming fit to tip the earth and send the tall brick house and the schoolroom and those two years hurtling toward her— when that happened, she trained herself to stop it, she knew what to think.

That was the fence the Wolves had built.

That was the place of the Wolves.

Beyond that place they could not come, she would not let them, not anymore. She could corner them, conjure them to stay where they were; she had escaped them before.

That was the place Moses Poses had been.

That was the place she had lived.

But this girl, this girl who stood here watching, she had never been a part of that place. She hadn't belonged to it, this girl who came out to this field with her friend and her milk-pail and her rifle thin as air. This girl who brushed her hair a certain way, who rinsed her face a certain way, who remembered the names and checked the stitches, this girl never lived in that house. She never lived here either, here in this place with the whitewashed walls, in the room with the long rows of beds. She didn't even sleep here. Every night, all night long, she rambled the fields miles away, and the grasses rose silvery around her and the long gun gleamed in the starlight, and with the gun she walked the ground like a well-witcher and in her hands it dipped like a dousing wand, but skyward, skyward, and for her it called down the birds.

You have to take care cleaning a muzzle-loader.
The Lord is my shepherd, I shall not want.
You have to make sure no bits of rag stick in the barrel.
The safest pattern is a Godey's Lady's Book Pattern.
You're not careful, bits smolder in there, go off next load.
The best way is often the longest, haste makes waste.
You measure each load according to what you aim at.
The best way to hemstitch is always by hand.
You take out the cap when you ride in a wagon.
Yea though I walk through the valley of the shadow.
You wash it with soap and water, it lasts you for years.
She learned certain things at the Infirmary, certain sayings and guidelines that became a part of her, and when she left the Infirmary that September, she took them home with her. It was suggested that she come home unexpectedly: her mother had wed Joseph Shaw and times were not quite so hard; her sister Lydia was marrying and moving away, there would be a place for her now. She remembers standing before Mrs. Eddington's desk, hearing this news, watching the roses on the carpet suddenly swim before her eyes; she walked

from the room, good wishes in her ears, wondering why all she felt was dazed. She had waited so long to hear those words, *going home*, *going home*, they didn't seem to touch her anymore; they hadn't come when she'd needed them most.

She went home with certain words in her ears, certain firm decisions in her mind packed up tightly like a set of tools carried with her. There were certain things she knew. She knew she would not go back to school again. She would not go on that road south of Greenville. She would never go into town on Wednesdays, the day the yellow buggy sat outside the bank. And she would never speak of where she had been. These were her decisions, her rules, inflexible, inviolable, carried with her that bright fall day as the Infirmary's wagon brought her home.

"I didn't go home in the dress I came in," she said. "I went home in a dress handed down to me from a new girl, she'd come the day I went off—a half-witted girl not likely to leave, she took my place upstairs. I remember that dress so clear, a brown-and-white-checked gingham with a white collar and a daisy embroidered on the pocket, two sizes too big. It smelled a little . . . not fresh, there hadn't been time to launder it. All the way home in the wagon I could smell it, I couldn't quite forget I had it on.

"I came home the day of Lydia's wedding. Henry from the Infirmary had some errands up over to Frenchtown so he drove me, left me off at the crossroads near North Star. I walked from there, up that road with my bundle again—I can't say exactly what I was thinking. Or expecting. Maybe that everything would be gone again, everyone moved away. I know I walked slow, steeling myself for that. And then I began to hear the music of a fiddle, faint at first, *turkey in the straw*, *turkey in the straw*, getting louder, leading me on. I remember coming around that bend in the road there, seeing Mr. Shaw's house and the wedding party spread out across the grass in front of it—all those skirts swirling, blue, yellow, pink. And the tables set out with those checked cloths, the fiddler on a tree-stump, I remember that very plain. And there was Lydia, a wreath of flowers in her hair, hers the only white dress—she looked so fancy in it, so happy, dancing—this sister, I suddenly realized, whose face I'd completely forgotten. I didn't know her anymore. I looked around at my other sisters . . . my brother, my mother . . . all of them clapping hands, watching Lydia and Joe dance a reel alone— I hardly recognized any of them. I'd thought of them all so much younger . . . and that's when it started to come to me, you know, how much time had passed, how long I'd been away . . .

"I remember how I just stood there in the road, in that Infirmary dress. Watching everyone. Feeling so apart from them. These people I didn't seem to know. This house I didn't know. Everything so different. I stood there a little longer, smelling that dress around me. Then I made myself walk forward, walking like a stranger into my sister's wedding. Lydia was hugging me then, and my other sisters, Johnny, my mother—but over their shoulders, the whole time, I could feel the neighbors staring. I could just hear them thinking, 'That's the one been off in the nuthouse.' Lydia was bringing me over to Joe, Joe was twirling me around to the music, and I could still feel those eyes, 'That's the one was sent away.' I stood there feeling strange all the while Lydia tossed those little tin charms in Joe's hat, passing it around to us girls. All those charms glittering in the sun there—the one you drew meant something about your next beau, the girls were all laughing over them. And someone got a clover for luck, someone got a ring for marriage. I drew the last one in the hat, a tiny cup like a goblet. That meant joy, Lydia said, a full cup of joy, 'a fine beau for Annie.' I held that charm tight in my hand, didn't put it away till Lydia and Joe were driving off in the wagon—off in a big cloud of rice to catch the train for Cincinnati. I saw how she looked, Lydia, flushed, rice in her hair—I saw how Joe kissed her. And suddenly I was thinking of Maryjane kneeling by that wedding dress she'd made that time, it seemed so long ago. And I wished so much that she was there, wished she was welcoming me home. I wished for her, thought of her, the whole time we were sweeping up the rice, putting things away.

"My mother was talking to me. Talking to me in a matter-of-fact voice, just as if we'd never been apart for a day: 'Hand me that bowl, Phoebe Ann, the blue one. . . . Lydia's

bed's made up for you, that little shelf she had's cleared out.
. . . The potato salad, just cover it, we'll have it for supper. . . .
Acourse we still need you helping out, I'll bring in sewing
next week. . . . No no, don't pour that out, it's perfectly good
lemonade, don't be wasteful, Phoebe Ann . . .'

"Just as if I'd never gone. As if I hadn't just come back
from years away, as if that never happened. I guess I'd been
hoping . . . I don't know what I'd been hoping. Some word,
something, I. . . . But all I could feel from her was this . . .
this coldness. This uneasiness. As if she was afraid I'd ask her
something. Or say something. Something she didn't want to
hear. And so I didn't say anything. I finished sweeping the
rice off the steps. I went upstairs to change my dress. I kept
thinking that's all was wrong with me, it was that dress. All I
needed was to put on one of mine, one of the old ones I'd left
at home, and I'd feel fine again.

"Upstairs I found my old trunk—I was so glad to see it
again. I hurried to open it, lifting out one dress, and another,
another. I dropped the brown-and-white gingham on the floor,
pulled my favorite calico over my head. It came as far as
my shoulders, it wouldn't pull down any farther than that. I
don't know how long I was there, struggling with that dress
before I'd believe it: it didn't fit me anymore. Of course it
didn't. None of them would. I stood there, up under the eaves
by that trunk of old clothes, stood there angry, so angry—
then the tears came into my eyes. And it hit me then, hit me
hard: I couldn't pick up where I left off. Oh Jimmie, maybe it
was foolish—I guess I'd thought, still thought somehow I
could. But I knew then, standing there with that dress: that
time, those years, they were gone. I couldn't get them back,
make up for them. It wasn't just that I'd come home older,
bigger, I knew that then too. I'd come home changed. Where
I'd been, what had happened, it had changed me. There were
places in me, things I kept seeing, no one here knew about. I
was different now. And I knew I'd always feel different after
that.

"Downstairs I could hear my mother's voice, cool, even,
talking to my brother. I stopped hearing the words. Her voice
seemed so far away. The voices that seemed near to me sang
'Sally go round the mulberry bush,' called me Annie-roo—

called me Moses Poses. I shook my head. I wouldn't think of that anymore. Would not. I thought of how I'd learned not to see the Wolves' land from the Infirmary's barley field, how I'd learned to blot it from my mind. I thought of myself running in that field with Fannie, with that invisible rifle. And all at once I knew what I wanted to do.

"I pulled the Infirmary dress back on and went downstairs to look for the muzzle-loader. I felt this little prickle of fear, you know, seeing it wasn't up over the hearth anymore. And it wasn't in the lean-to, it wasn't in the cupboards. Finally I went out to the barn, looking through the rakes, the hoes and shovels, scrabbling through them in the shadows there, and at last, in a corner, I found it. I took it outside into the light and looked at it, and then I just kept walking, carrying it out with me into the fields. When I was far enough away, I sat down in the midst of the grasses and I looked at it again. I'd seen it over and over, so many times in the nights. And now it was here, whole and straight across my knee. I ran my hands over it. Everything else was changed, but this was the same. It still felt fine in my hands, it still fit me—fit me better than before. I was big enough to swing with it now, to reach with it, reach the birds. For a second, just a second, I could feel Maryjane peering over my shoulder, *Well, try it again, jam it real tight into your shoulder.* And I lifted it. And I jammed it real tight into my shoulder. I swung with it, felt how it balanced in my hands. Then I sat down again. I laid it back across my knees, pushed the hair out of my eyes. I ran my hands over the rifle. It would need cleaning, sanding, it would need oil and tools, but I could do that later, that could wait. I took the little sack from around my neck and spilled it in my hand. There was the button like a ruby, the stone like a half-moon. There was Maryjane's thimble, the tiny cup. And there, in the center of my palm, was the hammer I'd kept all this time. I reached out and I pressed it back into the rifle. And for the first time that day, I felt a kind of warmth come through me. For the first time I felt something like the way I'd thought I would feel, coming home."

* * *

Within three months she had set herself up as a market-hunter, not a seamstress, her rifle in order, supplies laid in. Within three months she was out in the fields all day every day but the Sabbath, rain or fair, shooting rabbits and ruffed grouse but mostly quail; quail she would draw and gut and wrap in swamp grass, selling them in town for ten cents a bird, twenty-five cents a brace, to Katzenburger Brothers and to Frenchy LaMott who sent them on to Cincinnati.

It wasn't proper, her mother said.

She could not in good conscience say yes to the hunting.

She could not in good conscience say no to the money.

After all, it was better money than sewing fetched. After all, the mortgage on the new house had to be paid, and Johnny was too young to hunt, Mr. Shaw's eyes were too weak. After all meat and money could not be nay-sayed, and so Annie went on into her fourteenth and fifteenth years as a market-hunter out in the fields; that second year Lydia invited her to Cincinnati but she hesitated, not wanting to leave what she'd found there quite yet.

If I had come upcountry in those years, and if I had gone up above Greenville, up around a village called North Star, I would have seen her, from a distance at first, a tawny speck dodging in and out of the far corn rows; moving nearer then, a fine-boned figure with a long rifle and a wide-brimmed hat, skirted in brown woolens, vested in a burlap sack marked TRIPLE H FLOUR or GRADE A OATS or LEFRANC COFFEE. I would have seen her there, nose taut with sunburn, her mouth flickering into a smile at a good hit—the Cincinnati restaurants paid more for birds shot through the head. If she wasn't careful I would have heard her coming, clanking and glittering in the sun like a peddler woman, rods and pouches and flasks hanging off her, the gamebag slung over her shoulder. I might have seen her sitting against a fence, the shine of small treasures in her hand, her lips purpled by the blackberries like a cache of jet beads in her hat. I might have seen her whirling in the weeds with her rifle, glorying in her mastery, her domain—here where the fields carried her on their tides, spreading around her the color of sea water, here where they rocked her under the wide-smiling sky, and smelled of

214

safety, of earth and grass, and tossed the birds into the air for her every new day. From here, her mother looked small, inconsequential, down by the clothesline and the voices of the past seemed far away. But if I stayed longer I would have seen her tense, freezing still and tight at the jingle of a buggy on the road or the shouted taunts of children on the way back from school. I would have seen her stride break and change as she emerged from that wash of fields, scuffing between the pump and the house; the house where the dresses didn't fit, where the bed wasn't hers, where her mother's face was a constant reminder of where she had been, and the old grayness came over her again.

Every week or so she would tramp up the road away from town to the graveyard. She didn't think about why. She went, that was all. Mostly she went in her burlap sack from the fields. Mostly she still carried her rifle, and flowers, whatever was growing by the side of the road: daisies, day lilies, in winter a spray of evergreen. And mostly she would meander for a while inside the wormwood fence, never going directly to the grave she visited, but sidling up on it slowly, eyes elsewhere, often approaching it from the back. MOSES, the stone read above the flowers she laid down. R.I.P. MOSES. And if she wasn't careful, if she didn't come up on it just right, that name would slap her in the face, it would slam her in the chest, and she would hear it coming back again, the chant of the schoolyard, the call of that house, the name of that time, that self she had been then.

It was important not to feel that way at this grave. She needed to feel peaceful here, to set her back against the sunwarmed stone and feel close to that tall syrup-flinging father, faceless now in her mind, and to that redheaded streak of a sister; clearer, but not so clear as before. If anyone must move within her, singing, whispering, making candy, it should be they, and so it was important to come at the stone just right: to miss the name, and to remember that its brand no longer followed her into town, where the French traders pronounced her name *Mozee*. *Mozee*: she would hang onto that when the old times flooded through her mind, swamping her in their midst. *Mozee, Annie Mozee*: she would say it to

215

herself, but even that wasn't enough. Anywhere but the fields she wasn't safe. Anywhere but the fields the old things could come back, claiming her, undimmed by passing time, unfolding over and over again like a long stained cloth before her eyes. And finally she couldn't bear it anymore.

"How do you unlive something—how do you do that?" She pressed her fingers to her eyes. "I had to know—had to, that day in the graveyard. That day I came on the headstone straight on, first time in a long time. MOSES—the name jumped out. And, oh God, I just turned and ran. Knees shaking, back out through the gate. Back to the road, my flowers falling, I was running, running. It was happening the way it always did—I was back in the nightmare again, the road wasn't the road. The air, oh God, even the air was changed, green, smelling of spring medicine. I was running down the hall of the Infirmary. I was running down the stairs from the Wolves. I was different, dirty—I was someone who smashed mirrors, slashed chairs, a bad'un—I was running scared, running stupid, a slut, a bitch. Running from the schoolhouse, from my master—from me, from *me*, Moses Poses Moses Poses. And I fell in the road, face down. Giving up. Just lay there. I don't know how long. After a while a wagon went rumbling by, close, close—this voice called down 'Look out, gal.' I looked up then. Felt something wrong. Realized in that scramble, that run, I'd dropped my rifle. Dropped what was most precious to me in the whole world, right there in the road. I could see it gleaming there a ways down. Oh Jimmie, I crouched there, sobbing, still hearing it, *Moses Poses Moses Poses*—and I saw myself, as if from far off somehow: Cringing there in the dust. All over dirt. My rifle dropped, my flowers dropped. My knees scraped, and my hands. Cowering, shivering like some animal. I saw myself like that, and this rage ran through me. Rage like a knife. Like a flame.

"I picked up my rifle, started to run again. Back up the road. Back to that graveyard. In through the fence, over the grass. No one there—couldn't have stopped if someone was. That headstone, came at it face to face. MOSES, it jumped out at me again, hit me like a punch, MOSES MOSES, oh God.

Seemed like I could hear it. Shouting it, everything was, *Moses Poses*, the stone, *Moses Poses*, even the fields. I saw a shovel by the fence. And I picked it up. Grabbed it up. I swung it at that stone—again, again. Harder. As hard as I could—harder, *again*. The blows jarred through me, rattling my teeth. *Again*, the stone coming up at me, earth tilting, *again*, stone swerving, again *again*. The shovel clanging out, loud so loud, sparks flying off it, harder *harder*. Swinging, swinging, sobbing, no more—*again*—no more Moses Poses, no more ever again. And when I stopped—worn out, panting —there was that gravestone, just looking up at me. *No* harm done. *No* change. That name still there. *Still* shouting up at me—cut into that stone for all time."

Her fists pounded the bed, her face wet with tears, and when at last her hands went still they clenched the edge of the quilt, knuckles white, and still her face streamed. She took a breath and through the tears her voice came strong.

"And so. I decided. I decided there, and I'm telling you this so you'll understand, I decided I would be free of this once and for all. I would not let this mark me anymore. Not me, not my family. Not anyone I cared about, anything I might have. I would change that name for all time, in places where names last. There on the stone in the graveyard. In the Bible records. Wherever I found it. However I could. I would wipe that name off the earth, off me. And off my father, and Maryjane. So no one could come to this place and say, There lies the father of the hired girl. There lies the sister of the hired girl. That girl Annie Moses, Moses Poses, everyone called her that, remember her? The girl who was sent away. Who was in an institution. Who couldn't improve herself nohow, ruined her chances. Remember her, that bad'un, that slut with the dirty face? The one with the family all broken up. The one *nobody wanted*."

Her fists clenched tighter; her voice rose louder, stronger still.

"No. I would not let them say that. I would not let myself think it, hearing it day after day. I couldn't hide in the fields, not for always. I had to finish this, as best I knew how. And I stood there and I swore I would not let that name, that time—everything it meant—I would not let it follow me another step. As soon as I got enough money I would change that gravestone. Set a new one in its place. As soon as I got home I'd change the names in the Bible, and everywhere else. But right then—right there—I was not Annie Moses anymore. I would never be again. I was Annie Mozee, market-hunter. That's who I was in the fields, in town. That's who I'd made myself, who I'd become. That's who I would be, from that time on. And once I decided that in my mind, I felt something lift. I felt the distance coming up between me and that name on the stone. Between me and that time. And I knew I had already started. I had already started to go on."

Her voice lingered on the air of the room. In the faint beginnings of gray morning light, I saw the tears in her lashes, the wet tracery on her cheeks. She looked at me, eyes red-rimmed, lips trembling; her hand made a small hesitant flutter on the air. I took her hand, drew her close. How long she leaned there, weeping softly into my shoulder, I don't know. How tight I held her, my own eyes full, I couldn't say.

Gradually the room brightened around us. Sounds quickened in the street below. And still we sat, still we rocked there. I wished with all the strength and will within me that I could have saved her from those years. I thought of her moving through them, and of myself moving through them not far away; not near enough. I thought of her standing in that graveyard, stepping alone across that jagged scarred place in her life. And I thought of how, when she had made her decisions and when she had gathered her strength, Annie Mozee, market-hunter, left the place of Moses Poses and came to Cincinnati, to the city where I waited.

She did keep her word, her promises to herself. As far as I know, she never used that old name again. She changed the Bible, the records; she changed the gravestone, paying for it as she could by mail. And she did outrun that time. She did put it behind her. Except for those brief intervals when it bled through the new healed skin of her self, she did triumph over it at last.

May Hearst and his men not waken it anymore. And if they do, damn them for devils. To have this dragged through the papers, to have that old name stitched to this life—that would be unbearable. For her. And for me.

Let the past sleep now, I think, smoothing her hair back. It will always be here with us, a little, but now I know what it is. And I know her again; I understand. Her face, spent, softens, drowsing now. She stirs in my arms. Hsht, Missie. Let the past sleep. And let us.

NEWARK, NEW JERSEY
JANUARY 19, 1906

As always when I place a story in the newspapers, I've come down to the hotel lobby to wait for the boys to bring in the first editions. I stand and pace and jingle the change in my pocket while Annie stays upstairs, packing; waiting too.

The paper comes: I scan it fast, checking to see the story's in, looks all right—no names misspelled, nothing misquoted. Pleased, I carry it back upstairs. She's there at the door in her green dressing gown; I can see the glint of her earrings, the white of her smile down the hall. I wave the paper at her, my step lightening. Now it feels truly finished, this Chicago business; seeing it in print puts the crown on.

The last of the trunks is packed, standing open in the sitting room. Behind her on the bed, laid out in her usual orderly way, are the dress and petticoat she'll wear today on the train; it's nearly time to leave. We spread the story out on the desk, clipping it first as we always do. Her sewing scissors streak around its edges, and with a lilt of relief in her voice, she reads it aloud for both of us:

" *'Annie Oakley, famed lady shot, emerges from retirement this week after winning a protracted lawsuit against publisher William Randolph Hearst. Miss Oakley was awarded upwards of $25,000 in Chicago for a damaging report on her in Hearst papers over two years ago, which caused the suspension of her career.*

'According to Frank E. Butler, Miss Oakley's husband and manager, Hearst's agents attempted to further impugn the sharpshooter's name. All attempts failed, and Miss Oakley is triumphantly resuming her performing schedule.

' "It's been an ordeal, but it's over, that's the main thing,"

says Little Sure Shot, as she is known to millions around the world. She goes on the road this week with appearances slated throughout the Northeast and Midwest . . .'"

She lays it in the scrapbook and as the paste dries it to the page, I turn back to the desk. This great stack of paper, this counterstory I've written these past months, is still on the blotter. I lift it, weigh it in my hands a moment; then I truss it up firmly with twine. Her arm comes around me as I lay it away, with those poems I'll never send to *The Atlantic Monthly*, in my strongbox firmly marked *Do Not Open Until After My Death*. Praise the end of it.

Historical Afterword

Annie Oakley won at least $27,500 in the settlement of her suits against various newspapers, newspaper chains, and news services. The suits centered on a newspaper story run nation-wide in August, 1903, which stated that Annie Oakley had been arrested for stealing in order to purchase morphine; actually arrested was a drug-addicted impostor named Maude Fontenella. Oakley's most crucial suit against the Hearst chain was particularly bitter and did in fact involve detectives investigating her past. This suit was settled in Oakley's favor on January 17, 1906, after which she resumed her full performing schedule.

Between 1906 and 1910 Annie Oakley shot in matches and gave exhibitions, many for charity. During this time Frank Butler represented the Union Metallic Cartridge Company and Annie Oakley lent her name to at least one of its advertisements. In 1906 she and her husband became close friends of Fred Stone, the scarecrow in the original *Wizard of Oz*, and stayed with the Stones for a summer at Amityville, Long Island, where Oakley gave shooting lessons.

In 1911 Annie Oakley and Frank Butler joined the young Buffalo Wild West show and toured with it for two seasons. This show was not owned or managed by the original Buffalo Bill's Wild West, which was sold at auction in Denver, Colorado, in 1913. In that year the Butlers built a house in Cambridge, Maryland, on the Choptank River. The house became their home base for the next few years. The Butlers' previous house in Nutley, New Jersey, built in 1893, had been rented out after only two or three years' residence and was sold in 1904.

Between 1910 and 1912 they began spending time at the

Lakeview Hotel in Leesburg, Florida, where they enjoyed quail-hunting. About this time they also began spending some of the winter months in Pinehurst, North Carolina, at the Carolina Hotel. They became popular members of the staff there, Oakley giving shooting lessons and Butler supervising the skeet range.

In 1918, a year after Bill Cody's death in Denver, they began giving benefit performances at army camps across the country. Their setter Dave performed with them and became well known as "the Red Cross Dog."

In November, 1922, Annie Oakley and Frank Butler were injured in an automobile accident on the way to the Lakeview Hotel in Leesburg, Florida. Butler recovered well enough to resume hunting but Oakley was permanently lamed; a fractured hip and ankle required her to walk with a brace from then on. She did not shoot in public again, and in 1923 she had all the medals in her possession melted down, the proceeds going to charity.

Annie Oakley and Frank Butler moved to Dayton, Ohio, in the spring of 1926, where they stayed with her sister Emily Brumbaugh Patterson at 706 Lexington Avenue. They were visited there by their friend Will Rogers, who wrote a tribute to Annie Oakley in his newspaper column. That summer they stayed with her niece and nephew Bonnie and Rush Blakely in Ansonia, Ohio. In early autumn Annie Oakley, suffering from pernicious anemia, was too weak to travel to Florida with her husband. She took up residence at the Broderick-Zemer boarding house at 227 North Third Street in Greenville, Ohio, and lived there as an invalid. Frank Butler was taken seriously ill on the way to Florida and was cared for in Royal Oak, Michigan, by Oakley's niece Fern Campbell Swartwout.

Annie Oakley died in Greenville on November 3, 1926. A public funeral was held in Cincinnati; Frank Butler was too ill to attend. According to Oakley's wishes, her ashes reposed in a silver loving cup awarded her in France, unburied until Frank Butler died eighteen days later. On Thanksgiving Day, 1926, a private funeral was held for them and they were buried together in Brock, Ohio, a few miles north of Greenville.

Every year in Greenville, Ohio, July 25 is set aside to commemorate Annie Oakley's performance there in 1900. In 1981 a special marker was dedicated at Annie Oakley's birthplace near what is now Willowdell, Ohio, in Darke County.

Acknowledgments

I am very grateful to the Darke County Historical Society, and to Toni T. Seiler, Director of the Garst Museum in Greenville, Ohio, for her generosity of time and spirit. Mrs. Seiler provided me with valuable information and materials and, just as important, refrained from attempting to influence my interpretation of them or the shape of the novel around them.

Special thanks also to John Steinle, Curator of Manuscripts at the Cincinnati Historical Society; Roy A. Jordan, Social Sciences Division Chairman at Northwest Community College in Powell, Wyoming; the Buffalo Bill Historical Center in Cody, Wyoming; Ann Eustace of the Nutley Public Library in Nutley, New Jersey; John Murphy and Arthur Jones of Cambridge, Maryland; Robert Reece of the Fairfax Rod & Gun Club, Fairfax, Virginia; sharpshooter Walter Walsh, U.S.M.C. (Col., Ret.); Alan Gallay; and Irene Maxwell Black and the late Rush Blakely, Annie Oakley's niece and nephew. I am also grateful to Joanna Hanley for her help in preparing the manuscript, and to my friends Susan L. Hartt, Karen Lubieniecki, Pamela Marchiolo, and Lynne Olson.

Most of all, affectionate thanks to my agent Jacques de Spoelberch, my friend Kathleen Currie, and my husband, Jim, whose faith, contributions, and support were sustaining.

A complete bibliography cannot be included here, but I wish to acknowledge the following works: *Buffalo Bill: The Noblest Whiteskin*, by John Burke; *The Life of Dave, as Told by Himself*, by Frank E. Butler; *The Story of Annie Oakley*, by Edmund Collier; *Annie Oakley: Woman at Arms*, by Courtney Riley Cooper; *The London Nobody Knows*, by Geoffrey Fletcher; "Annie Oakley in the South," by Claude

R. Flory, *The North Carolina Historical Review; Annie Oakley of the Wild West*, by Walter Havighurst; *The Golden Age of Shotgunning*, by Bob Hinman; *Acts Between Acts*, by A. L. Kaser; *Illustrated Cincinnati: 1875*, by Daniel J. Kenney; "Annie Oakley's Untold Love Story," by Bonnie Kreps, *Ms. Magazine; American Vaudeville*, by Joe Laurie; *The Complete Book of Trick and Fancy Shooting*, by Ernie Lind; "Powders I have Known/Used," by Annie Oakley, E. I. du Pont Nemours Powder Company; untitled autobiographical reminiscences by Annie Oakley serialized in the Dayton, Ohio, newspapers, 1926; *The Old West: The End and the Myth*, Time-Life Books, text by Paul O'Neill; *Vas You Ever In Zinzinnati*, by Dick Perry; *The Wild West*, by Don Russell; *Annie Oakley and Buffalo Bill's Wild West*, by Isabelle S. Sayers; "How To Hunt Quail," by H. B. Stowers in *The NRA Guidebook for Hunters; Missie: The Life and Times of Annie Oakley*, by Annie Fern Swartwout; *Americans and Their Guns*, compiled by James B. Trefethen, edited by James E. Stevens; and the original source material in the form of letters, news stories, interviews, press releases, programs, posters, and advertisements in the collections of the Garst Museum in Greenville, Ohio; the Buffalo Bill Historical Center in Cody, Wyoming; the Cincinnati Historical Society; the Nutley Public Library; and the Library of Congress.

Author's Note

It is important to emphasize that this is a work of fiction, not biography, although the story is based on events in the life of Annie Oakley between 1866 and 1906. The novel's perspective is grounded in fact: neither the newspaper case nor the misery of Oakley's childhood is fictive. A major source for the latter was *Missie: The Life and Times of Annie Oakley*, by Annie Fern Swartwout. Swartwout, Oakley's niece, was close to her aunt and uncle in their later years, and although her book must be considered reminiscence and not documented biography, it does cast a personal light on the subject not found elsewhere. Swartwout's book discusses the name change, the adjustment of the gravestone and the Bible records, and the rhyme "Moses Poses," as well as the impression childhood events made on Oakley's later life. In her own autobiographical sketches, written during her last two years, Oakley refers to "the Wolves" with emotion, but never by name. She kept much of her childhood private throughout her life.

Due to the tireless efforts of the press agents, there are several conflicting versions of many events in Annie Oakley's life. In some cases differing versions of events were reported by Oakley and Butler themselves. This situation makes it impossible in several cases to state absolute facts, but does give the novelist room for interpretation and invention.

Annie Oakley was born on August 13, 1860, in what was then Woodland, Ohio, north of Greenville, in Darke County. She was the fifth of seven children born to Susan Wise and Jacob Moses (another sister, Emily, was born of Susan's second marriage, to Daniel Brumbaugh). Although Oakley's parents were of Quaker heritage, their children seem

230

to have been raised in a broader Protestant tradition. All sources agree that Annie Oakley began shooting at a very early age. However, the actual circumstances of her start as a hunter are unclear. It has been suggested that her father or her brother taught her to shoot, but both explanations seem unlikely. Oakley was not yet six years old when her father died and her brother was two years her junior. Oakley's autobiography seems to conform to a press agent's version of the event: that at the age of eight she decided to hunt for the family, taught herself to shoot, and on the very first try hit a rabbit. However she learned to shoot, she did indeed hunt for the family and became a market-hunter in her early teens. Oakley herself was guarded about her time at the Darke County Infirmary and "the Wolves." Understandably, she tried to put a better face on that time for the newspapers, but although she ascribes her Infirmary stay to Mrs. Eddington's fondness for her, the evidence shows she was placed in the institution. It is impossible to determine precisely when she changed the family gravestone or the Bible records; it seems probable that it was during her vaudeville period, when she would have had enough money. At first she spelled her new name "Mosey," which is how it appears on the grave, but by the time she was giving newspaper interviews she spelled it "Mozee," continuing to give that as her maiden name for the rest of her life, and in her will.

There are several different versions of the Butler-Oakley match in 1875, though all agree that Oakley was the victor by the last point. I have used the most plausible and traditional setting, in Cincinnati at Schuetzenbuckle, Shooter's Hill in the Fairmont area. Although many sources state the targets were clay pigeons, Ligowski did not invent these artificial targets for nearly another decade. It seems more probable that the targets were live birds rather than glass balls. In any event, Oakley did win the match and catch Frank Butler's eye. They were married in 1876 and again in 1882, although there are two different months given for the first wedding. The Darke County Historical Society uses June 22, 1876. The happiness of the Butler-Oakley marriage is not invention; there is ample evidence for it, in Butler's and Oakley's writings, as well as the observations of others. There is no evidence of any competition between the two at any time. There is also no reason to suppose Oakley did not travel with her husband in the early years of her marriage, aside from brief visits elsewhere. It is usually assumed that Oakley replaced her husband's partner Graham almost immediately after she and Butler were married, but the original sources indicate this was not the case. It is also not clear when Oakley took her professional name: certainly by 1884, when it appears in the Sells Brothers Circus advertisements. As usual, there are several versions of how she happened to choose Oakley. I can find nothing to support the hypothesis that it was a name in her mother's family. Other sources ascribe its origin to place names in Cincinnati and Chicago; of the two, Cincinnati seemed the more plausible. There are also differing explanations for the nicknames "Missie" and "Jimmie"; the one selected best serves the story.

The first date of Oakley's meeting with Sitting Bull is another matter that remains unclear. The press agents said that the two first met in St. Paul in 1883, but it seems unlikely. I have used the more traditional view, that they met in Buffalo Bill's Wild West.

Some sources dispute the existence of a written contract when Oakley and Butler joined Buffalo Bill's Wild West in 1885, but it is true that the long association between them began with a tryout period. The split between Oakley and the Wild West did occur after the first season abroad, in 1887, but the exact circumstances surrounding it have been obscured. This is another matter Oakley did not choose to discuss in her autobiographical sketches, but the most common explanation for the rupture is professional rivalry and jealousy.*

Oakley's long and successful career with the Wild West was a favorite topic for the press and press agents of her day. The flamboyance of the press agents has in some quarters cast doubt on Oakley's actual prowess. It is true that the press agents routinely minimized her age and maximized her image as a demure little girl; in addition, she was billed as "The

* The section here dealing with the performance at Windsor Castle telescopes certain events for the sake of clarity.

Maid of the Western Plains," which she was only within the show itself. But her prowess as a markswoman is not the product of public relations. Her match scores and shooting records prove beyond doubt that she was an excellent shot and one of the best in her time.

The location of the wreck of the Wild West show train in 1901 has been disputed, but contemporary newspaper accounts place it near Linwood, North Carolina, between a stand in Charlotte, North Carolina, and Danville, Virginia. This accident, which injured Oakley and whitened her hair, did not cause any paralysis or crippling, even temporarily, as some sources report. Within a few months, Oakley was shooting in matches and exhibitions again and continued to perform free-lance, with Frank Butler as her manager, until the newspaper scandal of 1903, which caused a temporary hiatus in her long and illustrious career.

℗

Quality PLUME Paperbacks for Your Bookshelf